For Ryan:

May His will
be yours!

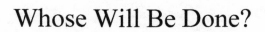

Whose Will Be Done?

Whose Will Be Done?

Essays on Sovereignty and Religion

John H. A. Dyck, Paul S. Rowe, and
Jens Zimmermann
Foreword by Eric Elshtain

LEXINGTON BOOKS
Lanham • Boulder • New York • London

Published by Lexington Books
An imprint of The Rowman & Littlefield Publishing Group, Inc.
4501 Forbes Boulevard, Suite 200, Lanham, Maryland 20706
www.rowman.com

Unit A, Whitacre Mews, 26-34 Stannary Street, London SE11 4AB

British Library Cataloguing in Publication Information Available

Library of Congress Cataloging-in-Publication Data Available

Includes bibliographical references and index.
ISBN 978-0-7391-9963-3 (cloth : alk. paper)
ISBN 978-0-7391-9964-0 (electronic)

∞™ The paper used in this publication meets the minimum requirements of American
National Standard for Information Sciences Permanence of Paper for Printed Library
Materials, ANSI/NISO Z39.48-1992.

Printed in the United States of America

Contents

Foreword

Eric Elshtain

In 1983, my mother made what must have been a daunting decision: inviting her sixteen-year-old son on a trip to Soviet-controlled Poland to see Pope John Paul II on his second pilgrimage to his home country. The trip was a long one, and its final leg was a flight on Lot (the Polish airline) from Milan to Warsaw; my mother spent the entire bump-ridden flight rummaging through her purse, just keeping her head down and mind occupied to keep her anxieties at bay. I heard her whisper something that she later told me was "My God, what have I done?" The plane seemed to be made of matchsticks, pushed and tugged by high winds. The wooden, fold-down seats added to the impression of danger and antiquity.

But we made it safe and sound, picked up at the airport by our host, Zbigniew, with whom my mother had struck up a conversation some years before while queued up to see Lenin's Tomb. They continued a correspondence until Zbigniew said to her "If you are interested in politics, Poland, right now, is the one place to be in the world." She took him at his word and took me along.

We had just settled in, sitting down at the family table, and before we knew it "Mama" was setting a copious amount of food in front of us, including several sausages. Even though my father had coached me to accept whatever food I was offered despite by vegetarianism, my mother caught my look of disappointment. Before I could say anything, she quite literally gave me a swift kick in the shin, saying, in effect, you will eat what our hosts feed you. And I did, later understanding how difficult it must have been for this family to get their hands on the food they were feeding us, given the rationing and the expense.

Looking back, though, I see in that moment a perfect encapsulation of my mother's private and public concerns: a deep respect for humanity and a consistent bristling at any form of tyranny or totalism, be it the terrible machine of the old Soviet Union, the vile mistreatment of women in certain societies, or my preempted attempt to impose my vegetarianism in the face of an incredible gesture of generosity on the part of our Polish hosts.[1] To my mother's great credit, and probably great regret, this acceptance of our hosts' magnanimity included my not having to "say no" to the vodka that was poured for us quite liberally throughout our stay. The family saying in chorus "Eric, you are man, you must eat, you must drink!" later became part of the lore of that trip.

I will also never forget my mother thrusting herself between me and a flint-eyed, armed militia man as we marched arm in arm across Poniatowski Bridge under Solidarnosc banners. At the time, of course, I was embarrassed; as a father I now understand that fierce instinct. My mother was tough, to say the least, and did not shy away from tough questions or difficult topics (she, in fact, once had a regular column in the *New Republic* titled "The Hard Questions," in which she tackled a wide range of topics from radical feminism, to cloning, to rights talk). She did not seek these difficult situations out, however; she was not a provocateur for the sake of stirring up trouble. It seems that her form of "radical Centrism," a political position she once half-jokingly applied to herself, sometimes rubbed those on all sides of the political spectrum the wrong way. She would find herself deemed too liberal *and* too conservative based on a single position she had taken in print or during an interview. She was, maybe even aspired in some ways to be a "solitaire independent of parties" as one of her great intellectual heroes, Albert Camus, is described, one who was also decried as a reactionary by those on the Left and too much of a Leftist by the reactionaries.

The quote and description of Camus is from a longer passage in Herbert Lottman's biography of Albert Camus that is one of four quotes my mother had typed onto 4" by 6" index cards and taped onto the wall above her desk (these index cards now hang in my house). Along with the quote about Camus, two are the last paragraphs of pieces of cherished literature, the James Joyce short story "The Dead" and Fitzgerald's *The Great Gatsby*. The fourth is a quote from Walter Benjamin's *Illuminations*. Benjamin describes the angel of history facing the catastrophes of the past and wishing to "awaken the dead, and make whole what has been smashed. But a storm is blowing from Paradise," Benjamin continues, a storm that pushes the angel "into the future to which his back is turned. . . . This storm is what we call progress." This relationship between past and future is echoed in Gatsby's belief "in the green light." Nick Carroway reflects, "brooding on the old, unknown world," and considers Gatsby's belief in an "orgiastic future" and how we all "beat on, boats against the current, borne back ceaselessly into the past." At the end of "The Dead," the character Gabriel is ready to set out "westward," the snow falling on "the living and the dead," the dead that includes Michael

Fury, a symbol of past and lost love. Gabriel looks both backwards and forwards to discern the needs of the present.

All of the quotes regard the difficult position we as humans try to make for ourselves between the tug of the past and the push towards the future, and my mother worked to help us wrestle with those historical and hopeful angels, even while that work placed her at odds with some powers that be. Above all, though, my mother loved to debate with those who disagreed with her and those with whom she disagreed. She always disliked when people used "argument enders," as she called them—categories, appellations that fenced positions off from the possibility of debate and compromise. For example, once you call someone a "fascist," there is really nothing else to say. It is easier in some ways to try and just end the argument, as any responsibility for one's own position ends as well. My mother took the tougher path, I think, never wanting to end an argument, always wanting the conversation to continue. Personally, a year out from my mother's death, I still want to hear what she has to say, about so many things: the Islamic State, Pope Francis, executive actions, Robert Redford's last film, my daughter.

Through volumes like this one, thank God, conversations with my mother and her work can continue.

NOTE

1. Flashing forward to the summer of 2014, my seven-year-old daughter Christie had just finished reciting the quote etched in a circle beneath the dome of the Jefferson memorial, "I have sworn upon the altar of god eternal hostility against every form of tyranny over the mind of man," before remarking "Grandma would have loved that." Well, she did and she does. . . .

I

Understanding Sovereignty

Chapter One

Introduction

John H. A. Dyck, Paul S. Rowe, and Jens Zimmermann

This book is a tribute to the work of the late Jean Bethke Elshtain, partly because her outstanding scholarship deserves recognition, and partly because her interest in politics, religion, and culture aligns itself naturally with the vision of our own Religion, Culture, and Conflict Research Group (RCCRG). We founded the RCCRG in 2005 at Trinity Western University (TWU) to explore intellectual and practical ways for addressing the contemporary debates concerning politics, religion, and culture. Much like Elshtain herself, we were dissatisfied with the dominant polarizations in this debate.

On the one hand, the hardened secularist approach to this topic, epitomized by the strident rhetoric of the new atheists such as Sam Harris or Christopher Hitchens, regards religion as an irrational force, prone to violence, and motivated politically by a desperate attempt to reestablish its lost former power and significance in the contemporary world.[1] Religion, in this view, is atavistic, primitive, and unreasonable. Religious leaders who point out the religious roots of democratic values of human dignity, equality, and freedom, such as Pope Benedict XVI, for example, are all too easily lumped in with every other religious fundamentalist seeking to recover some theocratic form of government.

On the other hand, an approach more friendly to religion recognizes the abiding social relevance of religion but, fearing religious dominance may pose a threat to secular democracy, still insists that religion conform to the dictates of reason. The German philosopher and public intellectual Jürgen Habermas, for example, argues for the essential role religion plays for secular, pluralistic societies. For one, religions are part of our cultural DNA. Religious concepts and their secularization have shaped our modern modes of thought. Religions are part of "the history of reason itself."[2] Even more positively, religions have the important political role of supplying moral insights to curb the excesses of scientism and naturalism. At the same time, these truths must be translated into secular reasoning and secular language. [3] On the one hand, demanding this kind of translation from the "religious citizen" makes sense, since neither religious experience nor religious language is immediately accessible to non-religious folk. Moreover, Habermas's assertion that secular reasoning should be agnostic and refrain from the rationalist demand to decide beforehand "what in religious teachings is rational and what is irrational."[4]

On the other hand, one wonders about the implicit hermeneutic framework for interpreting the universal truth content of religions. Given that Kant's moral philosophy is one of Habermas's favorite examples for such translation, one wonders whether we have really gotten much beyond the implicit logic of this approach which goes back to the comparative religion paradigm that arose with the Enlightenment: once we eliminate all dogmatic particularities from religious belief, we will see that religions pursue at bottom the same goal of inner spiritual well-being and peaceful coexistence. In this view, religious differences are minimized to find a fictitious common denominator that exists only within the framework of secular rationalism itself. The proponents of this view seek to eliminate both inter-religious conflict, and any societal frictions between secular authorities and religious bodies in one fell swoop: if only religions would realize that their particular beliefs can be resolved into general, rational moral categories, all conflict would be at an end. In so doing, they rob religion of its particularity: the very thing that defines and differentiates one religious tradition from another.

Our group seeks to go beyond both approaches by acknowledging religious differences and their effects on cultural formation. We do not seek a solution to conflict among religious traditions by eliminating faith from the public sphere or by watering down religious belief to some artificially constructed Enlightenment paradigm of human reasoning. In the contested marketplace of the modern, secular public square, religion is not only undeniably present, but it also has an important positive role to play in addressing the needs associated with the human condition and therefore contributes essentially to human flourishing in healthy societies. Neither do we uncritically embrace all religions in the qualities that seem superficially to unite them. We are interested in exploring the various ways in which religious traditions and doctrines relate to cultural practices and ways of thinking, and in turn how both religion and culture relate to fostering or ameliorating conflict. We seek to take religion seriously in all its forms. We are convinced that in taking religion and religious differences seriously there is no inevitability of clash. Rather, we seek a forum in which people who take religion seriously may discuss their religious differences and use reason to unpack the wealth of insight that derives from their traditions.

Since there is no religion without culture, and, as Habermas had indicated, no culture without religion, the only way forward beyond simplistic secular-sacred oppositions or compromises is clarity about the religious roots of each society's own culture. Anything else will only lead to some form of secular or religious fundamentalism, or what Olivier Roy has called "holy ignorance."[5] We are convinced that a better grasp of one's own religious tradition will also enable a better understanding of other religiously based cultures. The challenge to compare the religious traditions of East and West must be done carefully and without Orientalist superiority. At the same time it makes sense to contrast the varying ways in which religion and culture intersect in the world's societies. Simplistic application of religious fundamentalist and revisionist approaches to our cultural history neglect the fullness of our religious traditions. By approaching these traditions with respect and interest one might avoid the simple conflation of faith and culture that radicals use to short circuit religion.

Allowing religious traditions their own voice instead of imposing foreign rationalist categories on them will in turn enrich contemporary philosophical and political discourse. Religion has long had an important role to play in inspiring and paralleling the development of all philosophic traditions. Important ancient, medieval and modern philosophers or theorists of the past such as cannot be divorced from the religious tradition of which they were a part, and many of our basic Western liberal values stem at least in part from philosophers who had specific religious convictions or loyalties. Indeed, important religious concepts continue to exert influence in present theoretical and political discussions. Important ideas of this sort come from Hinduism and Jainism—*himsa* and *ahimsa* (violence and non-violence), *dharma* (duty), and *satyagraha* ("truth-seeking," the Gandhian form of non-violent resistance); from Islam—*umma* (nation or community), *shura* (consultation), *ijtihad* (independent reasoning), and *ijma* (consensus); from Judaism—*mishpat* (justice), *tsedaqah* (righteousness), and *hesed* ("loving kindness"); from Christianity—forgiveness, submission, the separation of church and state, sovereignty, just to name a few.[6] These categories only scratch the surface of important public and social values that work in conversation within and between the major religious traditions.

Religious ideals about human nature and society spring essentially from our understanding who God is, something that Toft, Philpott, and Shah refer to as a political theology that motivates action.[7] Put differently, theological anthropology, the question of who we are in relation to God, has profoundly shaped political theories in the past. Therefore, recovering understanding of these developments and applying these insights to contemporary political problems is a necessary scholarly task, one that Jean Bethke Elshtain (1941–2013) thoroughly understood and pursued with all her considerable energy and courage. In her last major work, *Sovereignty: God, State, and*

Self, she sought to provide an integrated critique of religion as it conceived of sovereignty. Some religious polities conflated literal assumptions about religious authority with the authority of the state and the self. So did many avowedly secular ones. It is to her work and effort that we have dedicated this essay collection.

In this book, *Whose Will be Done? Essays on Sovereignty and Religion* the contributors explore and test the cogency of one of the most basic and essentially contested concepts in politics: sovereignty. Sovereignty in this context has to do with the definitions and limits of power in human societies—something that deeply concerned Elshtain. In order to frame the investigation in manageable terms, the editors had invited Jean to give two lectures at Trinity Western University in the fall of 2009 in which she would further address the concept of sovereignty which she had first systematically developed in in her Gifford Lectures (2005–2006) and then published as *Sovereignty: God, State, and Self* (2008). Elshtain had worked for many years to lay the groundwork for *Sovereignty*. In this book, we add the work of several scholars to extend her legacy and her reflections on the topic. These papers are united by their interest in the intersection between faith and authority: the limitations of authority articulated by religion, the religious context in which sovereignty is understood, and questions that religion raises for the untrammeled use of state power and individualism, of state and of self.

For Elshtain, speaking publicly about her research was an opportunity to appear in the public square. As a widely published political theorist, ethicist and public intellectual, she argued that the academy owed citizens the insights and conclusions of their research. Her accepted role as a public intellectual in the United States allowed her to speak frequently to universities, policy makers, and the general public about the moral malaise she believed the Western Judaeo-Christian world suffered from. Decrying the self-imposed reluctance of many contemporary academic scholars to draw moral conclusions from political action, Elshtain constantly drew attention to political trends, or fashions she thought undermined the vibrant civic political culture that was the lifeblood of modern pluralist democracies. She was convinced that all political arguments were also moral arguments. She spoke and wrote on a myriad of contemporary issues, drawing on her Christian reading of classical political texts to warn of beguiling temptations to self-aggrandizement. She cajoled, and encouraged her contemporaries to embrace the human frailty inherent in the human condition and live the spirit of incarnational love and respect for others.

The accepted divorce between science and religion, between fact and value, was challenged repeatedly in her writings and public addresses. Sometimes consciously, other times unconsciously Elshtain infused her writings with "religious (specifically Christian in origin) ideas and commitments I scarcely knew I held at the time. I refer to such weighty matters as ontological presuppositions, anthropological considerations, ideas of human purpose and dignity, birth and death, the moral development of the child, and the 'ethical polity,' as I called it." This unapologetic stance on questions of right or wrong, truth, and moral responsibility is further demonstrated in the lectures she gave at Trinity Western University.

Following a brief bibliographic essay, the text of those two lectures, "The Myth of the Sovereign Self" and "Religion, Enlightenment, and the Common Good" appear in the first section of this book under the rubric of "Understanding Sovereignty," together with a paper on Dietrich Bonhoeffer that she delivered late in her life which illustrates some of the ways she understood religion to inform the political. Elshtain graciously agreed to a long interview with the editors while she was at TWU and this appears in edited form in the book as well.

In her first chapter, "The Myth of the Sovereign Self," Elshtain presents a hopeful theme: the truly free responsible self accepts limits. Her discussion of the "sovereign self" in *Sovereignty: God, State, and Self*, centered on the danger of self-aggrandizement, the modern self's usurpation of sovereign claims over nature, commensurate with its new status as an autonomous free agent. In this essay Elshtain looks to a number of her favorite authors for hopeful portrayals of the indomitable spirit of the non-sovereign self, conscious of its fragility and need for others. Elshtain follows up her message about the hope for humanity that is promised with each lived experience in her first essay with a sober examination of the alternative monism of scientific liberalism in the second essay. Contrasting the stark, religion-less rational self-created world forecast by Huxley with the humane, emotionally embedded life and teaching of Pope John Paul II, Elshtain paints a menacing picture of a utilitarian instrumentalist world in which the value of each human life is calculated for worthiness. Rejecting the bleak determinist outlook of atomistic monism, Elshtain reminds the reader that each person has to choose between a model of being-in-this-world based on excarnation (an autonomous, sovereign self) and a model based on incarnation (a social self aware of its inherited traditions and responsibilities). Extending the scope of her analysis from the self to the impact of globalization and democratization in the contemporary world, she attests to shameful actions and attitudes of imperfect states which frequently betray both their espoused values and their people, not to mention their neighbors.

Even as atrocities are committed against humans or self-interested foreign policies of neglect condemn peoples to deprivation and starvation, Elshtain draws on the ideals claimed in the various Declarations of Human Rights accepted by the United Nations. Elshtain accepts the limits the United Nations places on state sovereignty, including the right to intervention in cases of extreme injustice or terror. She writes: "To the extent that an international common good—under the equal regard/justice model I have noted—is realizable, it may well demand and require disproportionate sacrifices from some in the interest of the many." Elshtain concludes her essay with a warning and an exhortation: "The democracy movements now active in our international life will either take a culturally specific monistic or plural form, with the monistic form one that may well, either immediately or over the long run, put negative pressure on the ideals of democratic decency and human dignity that animated freedom protestors in the first instance, or embrace and work to sustain a plural framework."

Elshtain takes aim at a particular case study in the interplay of religion and sovereignty in her chapter "Bonhoeffer for Political Thought." Elshtain sees in Dietrich Bonhoeffer (1906–1945), the German theologian and Nazi resister, a theological exemplar for taking up civic responsibility even to the point of political activism despite his pacifist convictions. She seeks to introduce Bonhoeffer's thinking to the realm of political philosophy by illustrating how his understanding of the limitations of sovereign power was marshaled to challenge the overweening power of the Nazi state. Such limits constrained the power of governments, for "government must never aspire to totality, for then it becomes murderous." But how does the individual justify the attempted murder of a sitting head of state? Does not such an act strain the limits of self-sovereignty? Indeed it does, if it is mere assassination. But this is "why the distinction between assassination and tyrannicide is so important." The assassin seeks a private good, while tyrannicide is to seek a public good. To understand Bonhoeffer's act is to understand it as "the action of a particular 'we' on behalf of the wider community." It is an act of wider communal sovereignty, and not the actions of a singular ego.

In part two, "Sovereignty through the Ages," our contributors deal with Dr. Elshtain's work in different historical and political contexts. Marc LiVecche, in his essay "Mars Bound: Limited War and Human Flourishing," juxtaposes two concepts that occupy a prominent place in J. B. Elshtain's extensive writings: "limited war" and "human flourishing." He intends thereby to find a way to rescue war from its inhumanity. A former student of Elshtain's, Marc LiVecche captures the essence of the interplay and interdependence between "limited war" (or just war) and "human flourishing" in his commentary on the Renaissance painting by Sandro Botticelli *Venus and Mars*. LiVecche observes: "Venus and Mars—love and war—embrace and reform one another in mutual self-giving without either annihilating the other." In this image, LiVecche sees the vindication of Elshtain's claim that tough love includes discipline, punishment, even limited war. For Elshtain, the primary purpose of the state was to protect its citizens in order to allow them to flourish and realize their potential. LiVecche posits that:

> The just war, too, perceives the human soul as a work to be realized. In the face of evil, it captures our moral repugnance and strikes the tinder of our

resolve to rise against the injustice and it cultivates the chivalric capacity for meekness—not the invertebrate meekness of the milquetoast but the Aristotelian conception of power under restraint. Elshtain understood this to be crucial for our times.

In his essay on Elshtain, "Incarnational Selfhood: Dietrich Bonhoeffer as Guide to the Political Ethics of Jean Bethke Elshtain" Jens Zimmerman offers a comparative analysis of Dietrich Bonhoeffer's and Elshtain's social and political ethics by, first, outlining the basic incarnational features of Bonhoeffer's social ethics and his religious grounding of the political, to show, second, how his theology models and serves as inspiration for Elshtain's incarnational vision of humanity and politics. Zimmermann shows that Bonhoeffer expresses theologically the same convictions Elsthain articulates in terms of political philosophy: a healthy, democratic society depends on certain anthropological beliefs in the social and transcendent qualities of human beings.

In her essay, "Sovereignty and Chastened Liberalism" M. Christian Green examines the origins, nature, and implications of "chastened liberalism" in the political theologies of Georgia Harkness and Jean Bethke Elshtain in connection with states and selves. While recognizing that Elshtain makes no reference to Georgia Harkness in any of her writings, Green identifies the concept of "Chastened liberalism" as a term that defines much of the work of both scholars. Green concludes: "Both Georgia Harkness and Jean Bethke Elshtain had lasting significance in the development of Christian political theology. As Christian ethicists, they were both committed not only to theory, but to the practice of public scholarship and public engagement of religion with the political realm and the public square. Their writings and work demonstrated deep engagement with the great theological and political issues of their day."

John H. A. Dyck in "Sovereign Selves: 'We Have Met the Enemy and He/She is Us!'" examines one of the key malaises that figure prominently in the work of Charles Taylor and Jean Bethke Elshtain. In their analyses of modernity, both Taylor and Elshtain recognize the importance of the emancipation of the individual self through the rise of Protestantism and the Enlightenment. An old order of class rigidity with freedom for only a few was gradually replaced by open democratic societies which reward individual initiative and promise equality and human flourishing. In many parts of the world ordinary people can now choose where and how they wish to live, have the right to vote for their political representatives, exercise their right to religious freedom and speak and act on their convictions. Our liberal democratic societies are built on the premise that a strong civil society (composed of diverse communities that interact and work together for the public good through voluntary associations) provides the necessary foundation for human flourishing.

At the same time as we have developed institutions and practices that constitute the *sine qua non* of a healthy civil society, other, more pernicious features of the modern self are also coming into prominence. Lonely individuals exist in a crowd of humanity, there are self-absorbed individuals who primarily regard others as means to their ends, and we have all become a greedy consumer who wants it all even if others are to do without. Civil society is fracturing as new technologies decrease our dependency on others and we lose our sense of belonging together. Atomism, narcissism, self-indulgence and other distortions of the true self have manifested themselves in a modern consumer driven world which is focused on self-gratification. This essay focuses on Taylor's and Elshtain's diagnosis of the "the punctual self," the "buffered self," the "disengaged" agent that no longer recognizes its being in community. What is lost when citizens no longer live in solidarity with each other, willing to sacrifice themselves for the good of others? If the individual is disengaged, where is sovereign authority recognized and authority located: in God? In the State? Or in the Self? Through exercises of historical retrieval, Taylor and Elshtain outline avenues of recovery for the original true self in its proper sphere of accountability

In section 3, "Sovereignty in Context", three authors seek to relocate the notion of sovereignty: to Latin America, to the Islamic world, and to the global system. One finds limitations in the way that Elshtain's work travels to the global South; the second sees in Elshtain a means of interpreting key developments in the history of political Islam; the third brings Elshtain into conversation with theorists of international relations theory in order to illuminate key ways in which religion should inform that field. In his essay, "God and Power in the West and Latin America," Andrés Pérez-Baltodano asks why Latin America territorial states have not adopted the "same sense of order and collective self-identity" as the Western societies even as they claim the same political-theological tradition. His answer is that "the cultural conditions of Latin America were . . . incongruent with the idea of the modern state." He charges Elshtain with presenting a one-dimensional narrative in *Sovereignty: God, State, Self* while ignoring the "particular cultural and material conditions" in which ideas of sovereignty are articulated and implemented in Latin America. He contends that her primarily text-based analysis projects a common "transfer of authority from God to the State" within the Christian tradition in Western Europe but this "never took place in Latin America." He argues instead that "ideas of sovereignty become constitutive forces of history only when they enter into a relation of "elective affinity" with a dominant or potentially dominant historical tendency operating in the context within which they emerge."

In his essay, "No god but God? Nominalism and Political Islam" Paul S. Rowe applies Elshtain's developmental narrative of the sovereign self to Islamic thought. He addresses the way in which nominalism crept into Islamist thinking during the early years of its development and deepened in the hearts of many activists in the post-caliphal age. Today's Islamist theoreticians struggle with what Jean Bethke Elshtain would have called a self-sovereign nominalism that arose among the post-caliphal scholars. Arrogating to the Islamist movement the place of divine judgment, Islamist radicals commonly subordinate the traditional Islamic constraints on authority such as *shura, ijtihad,* and *fiqh*, even as they pay lip service to these concepts as a means of justifying their uncompromising use of authority. While many mainstream Islamic scholars work to develop the critical modes of inquiry encouraged by the early pioneers of Islam, they must frequently contend with nominalist champions of a more radical form of political Islam.

Robert J. Joustra puts forward the thesis in his essay "'Revolutions' in Political Theology: Protestantism and the International State System," that there is a similarity between Elshtain's focus in her book *Sovereignty* and his own essay for this book. Elshtain establishes that within the western tradition, the trajectory of sovereignty begins with a triune God who, through creation, establishes an ordered universe in which the pinnacle of creation—humans—is created in God's self-image. Joustra suggests that both he and Elshtain posit similar questions regarding sovereignty. Elshtain states in her opening chapter: "The central question and puzzlement is this: If God's power is absolute and immutable, is God in any way bound, or is, instead, God free to undo what he has already done? Her answer to this question that she traced for those Gifford Lectures is not altogether different than the one Joustra proposes in this essay, namely: "do such *theological* understandings make possible and indeed underlie the modern, ostensibly secular, concept of sovereignty, and—therefore secondly—does this not throw the whole claim of secularity and 'sovereignty' into disarray, if so?"

We embarked on this project to honor the scholarship and intellectual achievement of Professor Elshtain. Our high estimation of her scholarly legacy does not mean that we agree with every one of her theses, but that we pay tribute to her fearless curiosity and the humanity with which she approached every topic. We can testify from personal experience during the few days we spent together, that her acute, open, and ever curious mind together with her firm but humble personality, embodied the non-sovereign, incarnational philosophy that Jean Elshtain regarded as the basis of healthy democratic societies. We hope that this collection extends her efforts to a new generation of theorists considering the relationship of sovereignty and religion.

NOTES

1. Sam Harris, *The End of Faith* (New York: W.W. Norton, 2004); Christopher Hitchens, *God is not Great* (New York: Twelve, 2007).

2. Jürgen Habermas, *Zwischen Naturalismus und Religion*, Philosophische Aufsätze (Frankfurt: Suhrkamp, 2005), 13.

3. Habermas, "Religion in the Öffentlichkeit," *Zwischen Naturalismus und Religion*, 137–38.

4. Habermas, "Religion," 149.

5. Olivier Roy, *Holy Ignorance: When Religion and Culture Part Ways* (New York: Columbia University Press, 2010).

6. Harold Coward and Gordon S. Smith, eds., *Religion and Peacebuilding* (New York: SUNY Press, 2004), 297–301.

7. Monica Duffy Toft, Daniel Philpott, and Timothy Shah, *God's Century* (New York: W.W. Norton, 2011).

Chapter Two

Jean Bethke Elshtain: a Retrospective, 1941–2013

Paul S. Rowe

Dr. Jean Bethke Elshtain was born in Timnath, then a farming community outside the town of Fort Collins, Colorado, on 6 January 1941. She was the eldest child of Paul and Helen Bethke, the descendants of German immigrants from Russia. Her father was a school teacher, principal, and superintendent of education.[1] At the age of ten, Jean Bethke contracted polio, an illness that left her with mobility challenges for the rest of her life. The effect of her post-polio symptoms gave her a clear notion of the need for society to care for and protect its most vulnerable citizens. This vision of a caring and civilized society was a defining part of her defense of traditional values and the received wisdom of the past. Jean's trust in the social and intellectual traditions of Western societies as a means of defending civility, cultivated in small-town Colorado, would guide her work throughout her life.

Jean grew up in Fort Collins and attended Colorado State University, from which she graduated in 1963 with a BA in History. She later studied History at both the University of Wisconsin and the University of Colorado before beginning studies at Brandeis University in Waltham, Massachusetts. It was there that Elshtain applied her deep knowledge of history to the study of normative political thinking, completing her PhD in politics. Her dissertation was entitled *Women and Politics: a Theoretical Analysis* and it set her apart as one of the early political theorists reading political philosophy through the eyes of the feminine. Though she brought insights to political theory and philosophy uniquely informed by her gender, Elshtain was always interested in the wide application of normative political theory.

Soon afterward, Elshtain took up her teaching career at the University of Massachusetts in Amherst, where she taught from 1976 to 1982. It was her publication of *Public Man, Private Woman: Women in Social and Political Thought* in 1981 that brought her wider fame. In the book, Elshtain demonstrated her varied breadth and understanding of the classical roots of modern liberalism. She took various philosophic streams of feminism to task for their tendency to relativize both the intellectual tradition and the practice of democracy. She argues that they oversimplify the distinction between the private and public as a means of limiting the influence of women in political thinking. Her work demanded instead that feminists seek a more discursive and contingent approach to women's liberation. Elshtain sought a political discourse that included women but not at the cost of all that has been gained over the centuries by the great classics of philosophy and literature. Reviewing *Public Man, Private Woman* in 1983, Nancy Lipton Rosenblum wrote that "Elshtain's ethical polity plainly aims at a rich, diverse, *complex* life, with nothing lost."[2] As an early critic of feminism, Elshtain was ahead of her time. Asked whether or not she was a feminist toward the end of her life in an interview for this book, Elshtain replied that while she was wary of labels, she felt that "to the extent that feminism has to do with the status and dignity of women, I would say, 'Yes, I am.' "

In 1988, Elshtain arrived at Vanderbilt University, where she was to spend the next seven years of her life and set down roots in Nashville, Tennessee. Upon her appointment, she became the first woman to hold an endowed professorship at Vanderbilt. Her years at Vanderbilt allowed Elshtain to develop her reputation as both a feminist critic and a broader social ethicist. Her 1987 book *Women and War* sought to demystify the role of women in war. It was described as "an ambitious attempt to come to terms with the fascination and popularity of war and the cultural stereotypes that link women with pacifism and men with fighting."[3] The common perception of man as belligerent and women as passive agents is undermined by the complexity of women and men in the real world. The truth is that women also support war and make possible the jingoism and gendering that popularize the idea of war. While we have been raised to think of women as "Beautiful souls" who stand in contradistinction to the male as Warrior, Elshtain sought to understand the more complicated relationship between men, women, and war.

The end of the Cold War in 1991 introduced a new era of politics in the West. The demolition of the Berlin Wall and the collapse of worldwide Communism ushered in talk of a peace dividend and the triumph of democracy worldwide. In the early 1990s Elshtain turned her eye to the health of democracy when she was invited to deliver the 1993 Massey Lectures by the Canadian Broadcasting Corporation. The lectures were collected together and published in *Democracy on Trial* that same year. In her lectures Elshtain argued that far from being triumphant, democracy was in danger of declining amid anomie and disinterest. The declining bonds of family and community threatened the health of civil society, the essential foundation of democracy. Civic spaces had been evacuated, creating an emptiness, a void of meaning that left citizens detached from one another and their governments.[4] The renewal of a notion of civility and the social good, fostered in the community, was as important to the proper functioning of democracy as the respect for individualism and civil liberties. "Political power . . . comes into being when men and women acting in common as citizens, get together and find a way to express their collective hopes and possibilities."[5]

The lectures that became *Democracy on Trial* provided recognition of the growing importance of Elshtain's work to the North American and global audience. One reviewer pronounced her "an American Jeremiah," whose "often elegant writing carries an important message: the necessity for a sense of narrative and continuity."[6] By the mid-1990s Dr. Elshtain had solidified her reputation as a public intellectual and was increasingly called upon to travel and speak on applied ethics, justice, politics, and feminist themes. In 1995 she was invited to take up a position as Laura Spelman Rockefeller Professor of Social and Political Ethics at the University of Chicago. For Elshtain, this meant the commitment to a peripatetic lifestyle as she maintained a home in Tennessee while teaching in Chicago and traveling to speaking engagements throughout the world on a regular basis.

The search for a common notion of citizenship led Elshtain to begin a search for a way to understand a moderate path between collectivist tyranny and a deracinated, individualistic culture. In *Who Are We?*, published in 2000, she developed her critique of both the detached self and the tyrannical state. On one hand rabid individualism denies the natural desire to defend the good amid a demand to serve selfish desires. On the other, dominant states seek ultimate power to supersede the familial and social ties that grant meaning to the self. The preservation of "selves-in-relation" against the self and the state was Elshtain's answer to keep the self and the state at bay.[7]

In the mid-1990s, Elshtain had embarked upon deeper reading of Augustine, publishing *Augustine and the Limits of Politics* in 1995. Her understanding of Augustine was framed by her essential understanding of liberal moderation—Augustine's moral certitude was expressed through neither the drive to dominate nor the need to satiate selfish desires. Her understanding of Augustine made the idea of a just war that much more palatable and laid the groundwork for her defense of U.S. foreign policy in the following decade. In the early 2000s she embarked upon a study of the public intellectual in the person of Jane Addams, the Chicago-based social activist and Nobel laureate of the 1920s and 1930s. The outcome was *Jane Addams and the Dream of American Democracy*, published in 2002. Elshtain's interest in the role of the public intellectual was obviously personal, and it was a role that she would take up in a new way in the first decade of the twenty-first century.

In the September 11, 2001 terror attacks on the World Trade Center and the Pentagon, Elshtain saw a direct attack on the civilized values of the West. Her interpretation of the motives of the hijackers became one of the most common apologies for the American administration's initial response to the attacks: "[t]hey loathe us because of who we are and what our society represents," she wrote in *Just War against Terror*.[8] Elshtain saw the al Qaeda movement as the spearhead of a society of norms that defended theocratic tyranny, oppression, and *purdah*. Terrorists by definition did not abide by the just war tradition, instead targeting and killing civilians without regret. They contrasted deeply with a society that obeyed the rules of civilized combat, one that sought to better the lives of people in foreign countries. Employing the just war criteria she defended the decision of the Bush administration to go to war in Afghanistan.

Of all of Elshtain's work, it was her defense of the war on terror that was most controversial. Defense of a just war against terror seemed very clearheaded in the wake of the 9/11 attacks, but as U.S. conduct of the war on terror spread to include the invasion of Iraq, the detention of enemy combatants in Guantanamo Bay, and extraordinary rendition of suspects to interrogation rooms in allied states, it became mired in controversy. There is no doubt that her position in favor of the war on terror increased the number of her critics, but even the fiercest of these saw her justification of the war in the context of her larger understanding of the civil society of which she was a part.

For the last few years of her life as Leavey Chair in the Foundations of American Freedom at Georgetown University in addition to her work at the University of Chicago, Elshtain worked toward a fusion of her work on feminism, civil society, tyranny, and moral authority. She was invited to deliver the 2008 Gifford Lectures at the University of Edinburgh, in which she developed these themes under the rubric of Sovereignty. These lectures were published that year as her final *magnum opus* entitled *Sovereignty: God, State, and Self.* In *Sovereignty*, Elshtain provided a synthesis of her work from *Democracy on Trial* and *Who are We?* This book summarized much of what had gone before in *Augustine and the Limits of Politics* and *Who are We?* In it, she developed an intellectual history of the Western tradition through varying conceptions of sovereignty—the overweening demand that the state assume the position of God on earth and the parallel assertion that human beings themselves had this right were both contrasted with a more limited sovereignty rooted in the assumption that "[h]uman finiteness is the grounding of any form of human life, including political life."[9] Her work gained her both admiration and criticism. Reviewing her work in *Slate*, Alan Wolfe wrote that "No one can read this book and not come away impressed by the compassion Elshtain shows toward society's most vulnerable human beings," even as he concluded that Elshtain's derision of self-sovereignty throws out the very thing that had created the search for modern human rights and freedoms.[10] Others argued that she had synthesized a brilliant intellectual history of the past several centuries of human sovereignty, "one that holds up a mirror to who we are, or think we are, and shows us that we are still very much creatures of an idea resilient, imposing, and finally rather inhuman."[11]

Dr. Elshtain was still traveling and speaking on the themes developed in *Sovereignty* when she suffered increasingly declining health in 2013. She passed away on 11 August 2013 at the age of 72. Jean Bethke Elshtain was the author of over a dozen books and almost five hundred articles and essays. She was a public intellectual who traveled extensively throughout her academic career, attending dozens of conferences and other public events. In spite of the limitations on her mobility, she was a tireless speaker and a person of endless curiosity. She valued invitations to speak to both small and large audiences. She was deeply committed to the life of the university, in particular the need to raise up a new generation of scholars: when she spoke, she insisted on prioritizing student questions over those of academic colleagues as a means of ensuring the accessibility of her presentations. Many spoke of the way that she spoke directly to her interlocutors, always engaged in the conversation of the moment.

Readers of Elshtain's work will gain an appreciation of her wide knowledge of political philosophy, literature, theology, and intellectual history. Among her influences, she often mentioned religious figures such as St. Augustine, Martin Luther, Dietrich Bonhoeffer, and Pope John Paul II alongside atheists and agnostics such as Albert Camus and Hannah Arendt. Literature, both classical and popular, was a constant influence on her mind, and she declared her love of both American and English authors from Nathaniel Hawthorne to Willa Cather and mystery writers such as P. D. James, Ian Rankin, and Michael Connelly.

Though Elshtain did not usually speak directly on religion *per se*, the idea of faith ran throughout her work. The penultimate authority of the state derived from her deep belief in the ultimacy of divine justice, a justice that shared her concern for the weak and the vulnerable. Elshtain saw God in the limitations of human beings. She believed deeply in the basic good that guides human activity, against which selfish humanity contends for the right to define our own destiny. At her core, Elshtain was a classical liberal seeking a moderate vision of a truly civil society that defends the weak against the tyranny of the state and the individual. She had a strong faith in the power of social convention to prevent such tyranny, seeking out the basic norms of civility that defined Middle America.

NOTES

1. Paul Vitello, "Jean Bethke Elshtain, a Guiding Light for Policy Makers After 9/11, Dies at 72," *The New York Times* 15 August 2013.

2. Nancy Lipton Rosenblum, Review of *Public Man, Private Woman*, in *Journal of Politics* 45, no. 1 (February 1983), 244.

3. Christine L. Williams, Review of *Women and War* and *Gender and the Two World Wars*, in *Gender and Society* 3, no. 1 (March 1989), 127.

4. Jean Bethke Elshtain, *Democracy on Trial* (New York: Basic Books, 1995), 5.

5. Elshtain, *Democracy on Trial*, 123–24.

6. Harry C. Boyte, Review of *Democracy on Trial*, in *Journal of Politics*, 58, no. 1 (February 1996), 263.

7. Jean Bethke Elshtain, *Who are We?* (Grand Rapids, MI: Eerdmans, 2000), 144

8. Jean Bethke Elshtain, *Just War against Terror* (New York: Basic Books, 2003), 3.

9. Jean Bethke Elshtain, *Sovereignty: God, State, and Self* (New York: Basic Books, 2008), 5.

10. Alan Wolfe, "Why Me? The case against the sovereign self," *Slate* 9 June 2008.

11. Collin May, Review of *Sovereignty: God, State, and Self*, in *Society* 46, no. 4 (2009), 386.

Chapter Three

The Myth of the Sovereign Self

Jean Bethke Elshtain

In my most recent book, *Sovereignty: God, State, and Self,* my Gifford Lectures, I entertain a sustained examination, critique, and interpretation of understandings of the sovereignty of God, states, and selves. As I neared the conclusion of that endeavor, I recognized that it does not suffice simply to deconstruct, to leave behind the rubble of what one has discarded. One must also fashion alternatives. The question to be posed to the sovereign self, deeded to us by our complex history, is to ask whether it is possible to tame such selves?

Why should that be necessary? A problem we face today is an attitude that sees in the past only ruin, ignorance, and error. If the past is jettisoned entirely we can never rebuild—unless we fantastically claim that it is possible to create a new world, a new self de novo. Not only is such a stance astonishingly arrogant, it is flat-out wrong about selves and societies. We are indebted, for good or ill, to what has gone before. In seeking a non-triumphalist self—for the sovereign self is nothing if not prideful, characterized by an excess of superbia—we must rely on insights, moments, and accomplishments from the past, on what has gone before.

The irony that prompts my reflections is this: the notion of the sovereign self undermines the dignity of the human person. How so? The answer lies in the fact that in divinizing human will and choice, in making an idol of the self alone, we sometimes subtly and sometimes egregiously assault the delicate tendrils of relationship that alone lift up and display our humanity.

If we are not fully masters in our own house, what, then, are we? If we are not perfectly autonomous are we autonomous in any way? What sort of achievement might chastened autonomy be? If we are not at one with ourselves after the Fall, if we are estranged necessarily, how, then, do we fashion a self? If radical, limitless freedom, driven by will, is a destructive dead-end what does freedom with limits offer? And what limits might those be?

The great writer, Albert Camus, is surely right: one who denies every-thing and assumes absolute authority lays "claim to nothing short of total freedom and the unlimited display of human pride. Nihilism confounds crea-tor and created in the same blind fury. Suppressing every principle of hope, it rejects the idea of any limit."[1] For Camus, this is the dark night of nihilism and his reference is to twentiethth century totalitarian ideologies but his words apply to any notion of total freedom which implies, of course, the freedom to kill without limit in order to achieve one's ends.

Let me recast this in order to underscore certain salient points: personal autonomy, rightly understood, is a great achievement. Persons are not born as mature members of society but they can grow to become such. Until they reach maturity, there are defensible reasons for treating them as immature beings in need of protection. Being a mature member of society does not entail complete independence from everybody else but, instead, requires a willingness and ability to build and to sustain rich relationships with other people. Given the historic achievements of self-sovereignty as well as its dangerous excesses—when man decides he is utterly autonomous, indeed, god-like—we need other sorts of selves to forestall the worst. Contra Thomas Hobbes and Immanuel Kant, in their own distinctive ways, the subject is intrinsically relational.

Indeed, the person before me sets a limit to my own projects. The respon-sible self acknowledges the one before her and lives in the dialogic space thus created. Camus reminds us that the will to dominate and the will to submit are part and parcel of the same triumph of the will and certainly not the stuff out of which grows the responsible life. As well, the self cannot be what St. Augustine calls the proud "selfsame," a point of reference unto itself.[2] In strong versions of sovereignty, the self soldiers on alone as the self is entirely volitional and grounds all reality, whether in the form of the self-maximizer of homo economicus, the biologically reductionist self of genetic engineering fantasies, and other candidates for contemporary sovereign selves.

By contrast, the self I have in mind seeks meaning and dignity and finds a measure of both not in total liberation from nature or total domination over nature nor, alternatively, in some utopian attunement and at one-ness with nature but, rather, in growing to become a person according to our human natures. Because that nature is intrinsically social, we must refrain from doing everything of which we are capable. If we refuse to observe a limit, we become destroyers. Camus describes the process of becoming a self as a much harder birth than one's first: "to be born as a child and then to be born in harder childbirth, which consists of being born in relation to others."[3] These are words St. Augustine would understand, as he would appreciate

Camus's insistence that we are born to and for joy and gratitude. In his posthumously published novel, *The First Man*, the young boy Camus describes in this eloquent semi-autobiography "felt tears coming to his eyes along with a great cry of joy and gratitude for this wonderful life."[4]

Above all, we are created to love and to be loved. Think of the human beings we downgrade or, in our benighted twentieth century past, that National Socialism or communism aimed to destroy, including persons with mental capacities who cannot reason ("idiots and imbeciles and morons" in the gentle language of the time), all those who are infirm, dependent. What such selves have in common is that they cannot be sovereign in the manner extolled and assumed by self-sovereignty. They become a problem at present to and for liberal societies that presuppose that selves are free-standing and completely autonomous.

In our society at this moment and in Western democracies in general, we are pursuing a paradoxical project: we are more aware of those with physical and mental disabilities; we want to provide them access. Yet at the same time, many of our most enthused-about projects aim at creating a world with no such persons in it. We will genetically engineer them away and, until that time, we can eliminate them through selective abortion—the fate of around 87 percent of Down Syndrome pregnancies in the United States. And all of this with no apparent regard for how persons with disabilities might come to the conclusion, indeed, they have, that so called "right to die" statutes are a way to say "right to eliminate non-sovereign selves" and this just might threaten them. When we read that there have been at least two hundred cases of euthanizing Spina Bifida infants in the Netherlands, it gives concrete evidence that such fears are not misplaced.

So where do we turn for alternatives?

I have suggested that we look at moral fables in order to fight contemporary excarnation—a term used by the philosopher, Charles Taylor. Such fables warn us of hubristic overreach, of superbia, human pride; of run amuck curiositas, a curiosity turned deadly as it recognizes no limit, no constraint. Writes literary critic, Roger Shattuck, concerning Mary Shelley, the author of the famous story of Dr. Frankenstein, "Her judgment of the presumptions and self actions of Frankenstein in creating and then abandoning a new form of life"[5] is instructive. Apparently "it required a woman to inventory the destruction caused by the quest for knowledge and glory carried to excess, and to invent the counter power to Faust."[6] Well, it doesn't really require a woman as we find a similar motif and warning in the moral fable of Jekyll and Hyde by Robert Louis Stevenson.

The point is: we experiment with our natures at our peril. By "experiment with our natures," I do not, of course, mean "attempt to forestall terrible illness," say, or healing injury. The reductionistic argument often thrown in the face of one calling for limits is ridiculous, to wit: "I see, well, because it means messing with our natures, I guess you would never have wanted pneumonia to be treated or a polio vaccine developed." One sees how beside the point is such a rejoinder. By assisting us in being whole in body and spirit, as whole as we can be given what was given us at birth, we help to complete our natures, not to alter them radically. So we return to classic moral fables to instruct us on the excesses of sovereign selves.

One feature of celebrations of, and arguments for, self-sovereignty is a strange abstractedness, a refusal to keep one's feet on terra firma, perhaps because that reminds us "from dust to dust," that we are earthy and earth-bound creatures. We can soar only if we are disembodied: the phenomenon Taylor calls modern excarnation. This invites a hyper-exaggerated notion of what can be achieved through various philosophical modalities: we create systems, we live in our own heads, we expect selves and society to conform and then we shall have established sovereign control.

But if we lose our embodied, relational selves, which should make us less all-knowing, less harsh, we lose dialogue, we lose a sense of what is appropriate to, and achievable by, creatures like ourselves. We also lose history—the living incarnational realities of human life in common. As Pope Benedict XVI argues: without embodied history, political theory becomes an entirely Gnostic enterprise—all words, no flesh; all spirit, no body.

To truly fight excarnation requires that certain possibilities have not been smashed altogether. Here there is reason to be hopeful, not optimistic, but hopeful. Consider the horrific world limned by Primo Levi in his classic, *Survival in Auschwitz.* It is impossible to imagine a world more cruelly designed to defeat the human person than that demonic social experiment, the death camp. Levi alerts us, yet again, to the fact that the camps flowed directly from a process of reason, a terrible rationalism played out to the bitter end. Nazism was not a vast irrationalism at all. There is a major premise; a syllogism; and the end of the chain is the death camp. If indeed there are "lives unworthy of life" it follows inexorably that those who are "worthy of life"—sovereign selves—must remove those "unworthy of life" who have already been defined out of the human universe in any case.

Levi characterizes life in the camp as a "journey toward nothingness."[7] But then he says something remarkable. "Yet no world of perfect unhappiness can exist. Our human condition is opposed to everything infinite. There is a limit on every joy and on every grief."[8] In the camps, human beings were reduced to phantoms, their bodies disappearing. The demolition of man, Levi calls this.[9] Your life was reduced to the lowest level. You were a "man who is no longer a man."[10] First, Levi tells us, they annihilate you as a person and then they kill you. It isn't enough just to kill you. They must kill the human spirit first and our spirits are fragile. And yet . . . and yet. . . . The conviction that "life has a purpose is rooted in every fiber of man"[11] and for some inmates of the camps surviving the "insane dream of grandeur of their masters"[12] kept them going.

Levi keeps his own sense of purpose alive by attempting to recall "The Canto of Ulysses" from Dante's *Divine Comedy*: there was beauty and form and sense in the world; there might be again. Levi concludes his haunting memoir, a moral fable of the twentieth century, the most horrible of all centuries, in this way: "No human experience is without meaning or unworthy of analysis."[13] In the camps thousands of human beings who differed in "just about every way people can differ," were "thrown into a vast social experiment."[14] And out of this he learns that human beings are not "fundamentally brutal at base."[15] It is "far more complicated."[16] Many social habits can be "silenced, quashed."[17] But they cannot be destroyed utterly.

If Primo Levi can redeem this much from the demonic horrors of the death camps, surely we can find resources to draw upon as we look to common sense, decency, dignity, to our sense of shame, our capacity for joy, our ability to recognize when our dignity is affronted, our ability to love, not just to use, others. The non-sovereign self has readier access to all of this precisely because he or she finds intimations and realizations of such a self all around, sees beauty, sadness, hope, mystery, truths to be found and discerned, as part of the very fabric of the universe.

Several other writers come to mind to help us combat modern excarnality, to tame self sovereignty. The great poet, Czeslaw Milosz, and the novelist, Marilynne Robinson, understand that persons, by contrast to isolated individuals, are unique and unrepeatable. They cannot simply be replaced by a new recruit. Each understands that pure thought is not greater than love. The Nobel laureate, Milosz, is also the author of one of the great books essaying the nature of the totalitarian, *The Captive Mind*. This great work was derided by many when it was first published in the early 1950s, attacked by those still enamored of the world-historical project of Marxism. Indeed, Milosz told me over the course of a dinner conversation that he had been informed by a member of his tenure review committee at the University of California, Berkeley, that he received tenure in spite of the fact that he had written such a politically incorrect book.

If we take a look at *The Captive Mind,* we enter a world of incarnationality and leave behind a world of lifeless ratiocination. Here I have in mind Milosz's determination to be fleshly, concrete and particular. An incarnational text is a world of concrete presences: it derives from an impulse to make real that which is symbolized or represented. A symbol, a metaphor, a figure does not stand apart from but participates in "the thing itself," so to speak. The writer aims neither for a pure realm nor an ideal form but for a way to express reverence for that which simply is, most importantly the flesh and blood human beings around us.

I think, for example, of my favorite passage from *The Captive Mind* in which Milosz describes walking through a train station in Ukraine in the desperately disordered time of the beginning of World War II. He is caught up short by the following scene:

> A peasant family—husband and wife and two children—had settled down by the wall. They were sitting on baskets and bundles. The wife was feeding the younger child; the husband who had a dark, wrinkled face and a black, drooping mustache was pouring tea out of a kettle into a cup for the older boy. They were whispering to each other in Polish. I gazed at them until I felt moved to the point of tears. What had stopped my steps so suddenly and touched me so profoundly was their *difference*. This was a human group, an island in a crowd that lacked something proper to humble, ordinary human life. The gesture of a hand pouring tea, the careful, delicate handing of the cup to the child, the worried words I guessed from the movement of their lips, their isolation, the privacy in the midst of the crowd—that is what moved me. For a moment, then, I understand something that quickly slipped from my grasp. [18]

Perhaps, one might suggest, something about the fragility and miracle of the quotidian. Milosz is rightly celebrated for capturing such moments in his poetry, moments that quickly slip or threaten to slip from our grasp. His poems, he tells us, are encounters with the peculiar circumstances of time and space. The portrait of that forlorn bit of humanity, huddled together, uprooted, yet making and pouring tea—this says something about the quotidian. For Milosz, the touchstone for twentieth-century politics was terror and the immediacy of stark, physical pain—a phenomenon that self-encloses us, cuts us off. And yet . . . those cries can still be heard if our thinking is not excarnated and remote. We can still acknowledge the delicate ritual of the family making tea.

The twentieth-century mind was susceptible to seduction by socio-political doctrines that abstractly dealt out death. The twenty-first century has already treated us to examples of the same. Milosz puts on display the impoverished, one-dimensional, flattened out view of human beings that a totalizing ideology of politics and self-sovereignty requires and feeds on. He indicts the "vulgarized" knowledge that voices birth to the feeling that everything is controllable, for example, "the young cannibals who, in the name of inflexible principles, butchered the population of Cambodia" and "who had graduated from the Sorbonne and were simply trying to implement the philosophic ideas they had learned." [19]

In her award-winning novel, *Gilead*, the novelist Marilynne Robinson, opens up a world of simple and complex beauties and often unremarked goodness. "Any human face is a claim on you," her protagonist, the dying pastor, John Ames, writes, "because you can't help but understand the singularity of it, the courage and loneliness of it." [20] In her incarnational writing, she highlights the "body blessed and broken" in Christian theology and in everyday life. Pastor Ames talks about the gift of "physical particularity and how blessing and sacrament are mediated through it."[21] It follows that God's love and mortal love are not so separate. There is a splendor "revealed" in a child's face.[22] Robinson's protagonist also reminds us that the great Hebrew prophets of Scripture chastised and loved a concrete people, something too many moderns who don the mantle of prophecy seem to have abandoned as they despise those they criticize and the country that is their home.

We also have theologians to turn to, those who insist on the concrete living realities of communities and the relational dimensions of all human propensities and projects. What theologian Alasdair McFayden in *Bound to Sin* alerts us to is the harm—the "deeply distorting, distorted and damaging relationship"—that results when some human beings are systematically harmed by others, calling this recognition a "relational ecology."[23] This reminds us that every human being enters the world under a burden of history and that history teaches us—or should—to beware "highly optimistic assessment of the possibilities of reason."[24] Even the architects of Nazi genocide found it difficult to kill face to face, or to witness such killing, or to view the aftermath of it. In implementing their plans for mass murder, they required a distance that eliminated the moral space of the "in-between" myself and another.[25]

Narrow rationalism tethered to boundless will generated a tyrannical nightmare. What is the upshot for McFayden? We must reject certain dichotomies: it is neither autonomy, nor abject surrender. God is neither utterly transcendent—so removed there is no coherent analogy relating God to ourselves—but nor is God so entirely immanent that we are simply subsumed into this god-substance and become indistinguishable from it. This ecology of relationship doesn't treat human beings as agglomerates delimited by race or sex or class or some other category made absolute; no, the dignity of the human person is irreducible and cannot be wholly subsumed into these abstract categories.

Anti-Nazi theologian, Dietrich Bonheoffer, reminds us throughout his work that "bodilyness and human life belong inseparably together" and this has "very far-reaching consequences" for our understanding of every aspect of human life, for we can use our bodies and that of the others well or ill.[26] The right to live is, for Bonheoffer, of the "very essence"; indeed, even the most "wretched life" is "worth living before God."[27] What should ongoingly amaze us is that many of the lives we imagine are utterly wretched are, in fact, not: people find purpose and even joy in the midst of extraordinary difficulty and suffering. This is not all they find, of course, but we can see redemptive moments where we might least expect them.

"Freedom is not a quality of man, nor is it an ability—it is not a possession, a presence, an object, nor is it a form of existence—but a relationship and nothing else. In truth, freedom is a relationship between two persons. Being free means 'being free for the other,' because the other has bound me to him. In relationship with the other I am free."[28]

These are strong words that bespeak incarnational realities. Human life is always lived in concrete communities, not in no-where. Even as God is dialogic and related and gives of Himself, so are we called to be likewise. In a society such as ours, with our history, these recognitions can be ongoingly rekindled and no doubt resources from other faiths offer similar possibilities of renewal. Over simply, we are never in a zero-sum game in this life of ours, never in a situation where the exact sum I "give" is something taken away from me absolutely and appropriated by someone else: that is Sartre's "hell is other people," a desolate, dead, and lonely world.[29] It is not the world of people who embrace the quotidian rather than despise it; who find joy in simply things; who find dignity in a decent job well done. Our bodies define a limit, yes, but also a possibility as we enter into community, for we can "be" by virtue of others.

Augustine's fear was that as we gave up on God's sovereignty, then other forms of human sovereignty, not of the chastened or limited sort, would drive to become superordinate and destructive in the ways I have assayed. Augustine was keenly aware of the fact that any human institution can be turned into an idolatry, whether of family or state, or anything else. The altar at which we worship nowadays is the sovereign self whose key terms are control, doing your own thing, choice as a kind of willfulness rather than as the sometimes tragic weighing of options where there is no knock-down good or bad on either side. The Augustinian pilgrim is one who can challenge the idolatries of his or her age without opting out, as if one could, or fleeing into a realm at least theoretically removed from the vortex of social and political life.

I turn now to some concluding thoughts from Albert Camus, a thinker who lived through and was defined by our culture of self-criticism so characteristic of the West. He was an unbeliever, not an atheist, he said, one who lived in an ongoing dialogue with Christians. He understood our indebtedness to those who had gone before, who had crafted the possibilities for such a culture, for Europe at her best. Exploring a world of moral relativism and absolute nihilism, Camus indicts philosophies that are used as goads or alibis for abstract mass murder, indicts those who take refuge in ideologies and erect slave camps under the flag of freedom. In his great essay, *The Rebel*, he writes:

> If we believe in nothing, if nothing has any meaning and we can affirm no values whatsoever, then everything is possible and nothing has an importance. There is no pro or con: the murderer is neither right nor wrong. We are free to stoke the crematory fires or to devote ourselves to the care of lepers . . . . Since

nothing is either true or false, good or bad, our guiding principle will be to demonstrate that we are the most efficient, in other words, the strongest. That is the only measure of success.[30]

Camus here sketches a world of the will-to-power triumphant, a world of "executioners and victims," as he put it.[31] And how does one tell the story of this triumph? It is nothing less than "the history of European pride."[32] In rebelling against a world that is cruel or murderous or systematically unjust, the authentic rebel observes a limit. He affirms the "existence of a border-line . . . that there are limits and also that he respects—and wishes to preserve—the existence of certain things on this side of the borderline."[33] When a person rebels, he identifies himself with others, according to Camus, rather than repudiating them utterly. He eschews resentment, a corrosive envy of what one does not have. The authentic rebel wishes to defend what he or she in fact is: a human being, a person. And in rebellion he finds not isolation, but solidarity. So strong is Camus's claim in this regard that he declares that anyone who "claims the right to destroy this solidarity loses the right to be called rebellion and becomes instead acquiescent in murder."[34] For rebellion "must respect the limit it discovers in itself—a limit where minds meet and, in meeting, begin to exist. I rebel, therefore we exist."[35]

The alternative is unlimited freedom, the "negation of others and the suppression of pity."[36] What is a totalitarian society but a story of unbridled freedom to kill? The nihilist would become god-like, a rival of the Creator, perpetually demanding some sort of unity (of victim and victimizer) with hatred of the creator transmogrified into hatred of creation. Augustine and Camus would come together in an answer to what happens to people who live without grace and without justice. Nihilism supplies the answer. A frenzied will to power triumphs. Finally, one must insist, Camus tells us, on the fact that there is a human nature that resists all attempts to turn it into the rubble of historic forces.

> Absolute revolution presupposes the absolute malleability of human nature and its possible reduction to the condition of a historical force. But rebellion, in man, is the refusal to be treated as an object and to be reduced to simple historical terms. It is the affirmation of a nature common to all men, which eludes the world of power.[37]

These are words the totalitarian would scoff at and the radical post-modern could never speak. But speak such words we must and Camus reminds us that the fruit of Western culture requires that we remember both Jerusalem and Athens, belief and unbelief, skepticism and faith. And, for Camus, the beauty of this world and our ability to respond to it is one possible source for regeneration of our culture which recalls "the common dignity of man and the world he lives in and which we must now define in the face of a world that insults it."[38]

In his novel, *The Plague*, Camus's narrator, Dr. Rieux, "bears witness" to the sufferings of innocent people laid low by the terror of the plague.[39] After the plague is gone and people greet one another in open plazas and laugh and drink and eat, Rieux warns that we should never be complacent, never smug:

> Nonetheless, Rieux knew that the tale he had to tell could not be one of final victory. It could be only the record of what had had to be done, and what assuredly would have to be done again in the never ending fight against terror and its relentless onslaughts, despite their personal afflictions, by all who, unable to be saints but refusing to bow down to pestilences, strive their utmost to be healers.
>
> And, indeed, as he listened to the cries of joy rising from the town, Rieux remembered that such joy is always imperiled. He knew what those jubilant crowds did not know but could have learned from books: that the plague bacillus never dies or disappears for good; that it can lie dormant for years and years in furniture and linen-chests; that it bides its time in bedrooms, cellars, trunks, and bookshelves; and that perhaps the day would come when, for the bane and the enlightening of men, it would rouse up its rats again and send them forth to die in a happy city.[40]

Selves that are less-than-sovereign understand this moral allegory and live with this mordant recognition. Far easier to be comfortably sovereign and "in control." But then one lives in a kind of dream world that will fade or crash to bits as all dreams of incandescent glory can and must. Selves immersed in a world with and among their fellow human beings, that relational ecology we have noted, affirm, respect, and find joy in life's everydayness and its simple joys and pleasures.

NOTES

1. Albert Camus, *The Rebel* (New York: Vintage Books, 1958), 282.

2. "Now, whatever is out of [God], must necessarily be of the self-same nature as Himself, and therefore immutable: but the soul (as all allow) is mutable. Therefore it is not out of Him, because it is not immutable, as He is." Augustine, *Anti-Pelagian Writings: Nicene Fathers of the Christian Church, Part 5,* ed. Philip Schaff, trans. Peter Holmes and Robert Wallis (Whitefish, MT :Kessinger, 2004), 316–17.

3. Albert Camus, *The First Man* (New York: Alfred A. Knopf, 1995), 195.

4. Ibid., 195.

5. Roger Shattuck, *Forbidden Knowledge* (Orlando: Harcourt Brace, 1997), 98.

6. Ibid., 98.

7. Primo Levi, *Survival in Auschwitz* (New York: Touchstone, 1996) 17.

8. ". . . perfect happiness is equally unattainable. The obstacles preventing the realization of both these extreme states are of the same nature: they derive from our human condition which is opposed to everything infinite. Our ever-insufficient knowledge of the future opposes it: and this is called, in the one instance, hope, and in the other, uncertainty of the following

day. The certainty of death opposes it: for it places a limit on every joy, but also on every grief." Ibid., 17.

9. Ibid., 26.

10. Ibid., 171.

11. Ibid., 71.

12. Ibid., 73.

13. Ibid., 87.

14. "We would also like to consider that the Lager was pre-eminently a gigantic biological and social experiment. Thousands of individuals, differing in age, condition, origin, language, culture and customs, are enclosed within barbed wire: there they live a regular, controlled life which is identical for all and inadequate to all needs." Ibid., 87.

15. "We do not believe in the most obvious and facile deduction: that man in fundamentally brutal, egotistic and stupid." Ibid., 87.

16. Ibid., 87.

17. ". . . the only conclusion to be drawn is that in the face of driving necessity and physical disabilities many social habits and instincts are reduced to silence." Ibid., 87.

18. Czeslaw Milosz, *The Captive Mind* (New York: Vintage, 1990), 248–49.

19. Czeslaw Milosz, *The Witness of Poetry* (Cambridge, MA: Harvard University, 1983), 9, 42.

20. Marilynne Robinson, *Gilsead* (New York: Picador, 2004), 66.

21. Ibid., 64.

22. "I could never thank God sufficiently for the splendor he has hidden from the world—your mother excepted, of course—and revealed to me in your sweetly ordinary face." Ibid., 237.

23. Alistair McFayden, *Bound to Sin: Abuse, Holocaust and the Christian Doctrine of Sin* (Cambridge, UK: Cambridge University, 2000), 61, 78.

24. Ibid., 83.

25. Ibid., 97.

26. Dietrich Bonhoeffer, *Ethics* (New York: Touchstone, 1995), 155.

27. "The right to live is the matter of the essence and not of any values. In the sight of God there is no life that is not worth living; for life itself is valued by God. The fact that God is the Creator, Preserver and Redeemer of life makes even the most wretched life worth living before God." Ibid., 162.

28. Dietrich Bonhoeffer, *Witness to Jesus Christ: Making of Modern Theology*, ed. John de Gruchy (Minneapolis: Augsburg Fortress, 1991), 112.

29. Jean-Paul Sartre, *No Exit and Three Other Plays* (New York: Vintage, 1989), 45.

30. Camus, *Rebel*, 5.

31. Ibid., 16.

32. Ibid., 11.

33. Ibid., 13.

34. Ibid., 22.

35. Ibid., 22.

36. Ibid., 42.

37. Ibid., 250.

38. Ibid., 277.

39. ". . . Dr. Rieux resolved to compile this chronicle, so that he should not be one of those who hold their peace but should bear witness in favor of those plague-stricken people; so that some memorial of the injustice and outrage done them might endure." Albert Camus, *The Plague* (New York: Vintage, 1991), 308.

40. Ibid., 308.

Chapter Four

Religion, Enlightenment, and a Common Good

Jean Bethke Elshtain

When I was an undergraduate—over forty years ago now—I attended (with all the eagerness of one keen to hear traditional "anything" take a critical beating) a lecture by Sir Julian Huxley, scion of the Enlightenment and distinguished branch off the tree Huxley. He was formidable in his demeanor and his absolute certainty. Without any qualification or hesitation he pronounced a prediction, nay, a certainty for the future of the West: By the year 2000 religion would have disappeared, having been supplanted by the total victory of scientific rationality. Nationalism would have disappeared, having been supplanted by the total victory of internationalism and some sort of world order. The view of the human person celebrated by Huxley was very much that of the sovereign *individual*, ruler of his own domain, master of all he surveys, bringer of control and "reason" to what would otherwise be the messy chaos of life. [1]

But a few short weeks ago—I write in May, 2005—a beloved Holy Father, Pope John Paul II, lay in repose in Rome. As his body was carried out into St. Peter's, the pallbearers made a circle through the crowd of millions, and then took solemnly into the basilica itself as crowds wept and applauded, there was another reality, another future, even another international order here embodied. In addition to the chanting, the cries, and the applause of millions, this great man's body was accompanied to its final resting place by the litany of the saints with its beautiful, haunting chant that tells us we are not alone; that when the believer makes his or her way to eternity, he or she is accompanied by the saints departed to join them in the other life. The view of the human person celebrated in the litany of the saints and honored by the overwhelming spectacle of the millions who poured into Rome to peacefully celebrate and mourn one of the greatest lives of the twentieth century was very much that of the ensouled body, a life that is intrinsically social and whose meaning, being, and purpose is defined, not by the relentlessly immanent but by the gloriously transcendent. And all this very much in harmony with St. Augustine's wonderful insistence that God has made us to Himself and "our hearts are restless 'til they rest in Thee."[2]

Which represents the West? The view of such "liberal monists" as Huxley or the "sign of contradiction" embodied in the life and death of John Paul the Great? There could scarcely be a more stark contrast between frameworks of meaning, existential attitudes, understandings of a, or the, good. There could scarcely be a wider gap to breach than between a view that sees human life as encompassed entirely by birth, ending definitively with death, and with that birth and death coming more and more under rationalistic and scientific control and, by contrast, a view of human life as a gift and a blessing, one unearned by us, open to grace, and given meaning because we understand that our good is not ours alone but belongs to a wider communion of saints (in the first instance) but a good that links us, at least tacitly, to a world of others who are, in some deep and abiding sense, our brothers and sisters although they may be foreign and strange and even hostile.

That we should wind up poised between two such powerful and contrasting worlds as embodied in Sir Julian Huxley's speech and John Paul II's funeral results from no "incoherence," as some moral philosophers claim, but, rather, from the intrinsic telos embedded in each alternative understanding of human persons and life deeded to us by our shared history. We see clearly that we have a choice—although that choice is often presented to us in mendacious and startlingly inaccurate ways. By that I mean we are told we have to choose between "Science" or "faith" as if the two are irredeemably driven to collide. This, of course, usually comes from the side of "science" trying to discredit and discount "faith." On the other hand, one sometimes sees, from the side of "faith," views of the self that may well surrender too much of our capacity to choose certain goods to forces outside ourselves—as if faith is a leap into the dark, a fideistic certainty rather than a more complex contextual engagement over time.

I shall try to avoid the pitfalls of presenting our situation as starker and utterly contrasting than it already is. The best way to do this, at least for the purpose of this paper, is to examine the fate of "religion" in the Western "settlement" or regime of tolerance; to go on to look at the ways alternative pictures of reality tacitly, if not explicitly, rely on a particular philosophical or theological anthropology; and, finally, to examine what any of this has to do with the internationalization of human rights and the powerful drive toward democracy, on the popular level as well as the level of international "encouragement" under the auspices of such powerful entities as the United States of America.

TWO VIEWS OF LIBERAL MONISM AND A CRITIQUE

In an essay of a few years back arguing against what I called "liberal monism," I noted that one dominant strand in legal and philosophical argumentation pushes toward a monistic logic.[3] This monistic drive assumes that we are to speak civically in a language carefully vetted in order to remove the taint of religious belief and conviction that may cling to it. Now I appreciate that the late John Rawls, from whom much of this argument is traced, modified his views somewhat. But the modification was rather grudging and the monistic drive remained, unsurprisingly given Rawls's neo-Kantianism. The argument assumes tacitly that a strictly secular idiom, carefully pruned, *must* be the language for political deliberation. We must clean up our speech.

Rather than free institutions of civil society or religious belief giving us languages of civic engagement, these forces, from the point of view of monism, are distorted by particularisms and unacceptable because they—especially the views drawing upon religious belief—allegedly view themselves as critically unassailable and, indeed, incorrigible in the philosophic sense. One might think of the monistic demand concerning civic speech as analogous to the constitutional position in American jurisprudence of strict separationism. Strict separationism I take to be a position that would strip all of public life of religious symbols, signs, markers, and speech; those who seek a thoroughly secularized society in which religion is invisible to public life, religion having long ago been relegated to the subjectivities of multiple individual consciences.

For strong separationists in the monistic tradition hold that religion is by definition private. The idea of a "public religion" is a threat to civic life, aiming, inevitably, to sacralize it. Note here that the claim that religion pushes in a monistic direction comes from those who are themselves the carriers of a monistic drive—only they see it as simply the way of the world. Any notion of "two"—of different forms of governance, reference, and meaning internal to a single society—is so troubling that it can only be read as a drive towards theocracy. In an effort to forestall this possibility, it follows that all institutions internal to a democratic society must conform to a single authority principle; a single standard of what counts as reason and deliberation; a single vocabulary of political discussion. This is the logical end-point of the so-called "secularization" hypothesis, now discarded by most explicitly but assumed by many implicitly. Having become dogma, one need only assume it rather than argue on behalf of it.

What is the backdrop to liberal monism? Within political theory there are (at least) two strands that I shall call the Lockean and the Rousseauian. John Locke was in some respects at least the unwitting prophet of liberal monism given the terms under which he declared that religious tolerance must proceed. Many of you are no doubt familiar with his justly famous *Letter on*

Toleration in which Locke draws up a map separating soul craft, the world of religion, from statecraft, the realm of government. One could be a citizen of each only so long as religion meant freedom of conscience rather than strong institutional loyalty to an autonomous religious body that engaged society in all its aspects and was itself a particular form of governance. Locke argued that his separation of statecraft and soul craft created terms that would serve toleration for all religions—save atheism and Roman Catholicism, neither of which was to be tolerated.[4]

Atheists could not be tolerated as they refused to take an oath on the Bible, hence were untrustworthy. Catholics did not fit within the terms of tolerance because they exhibited a dangerous double loyalty: they were loyal to church as well as to polity. Only so long as soul craft did not meddle with statecraft, it was fine. A strong public presence, voice, and action from the side of religion—no, that presented a danger. So private freedom of conscience fits liberal monism but any strong expression of public religion does not. This Lockean formula finessed as many problems as it attempted to solve. For it is not at all clear that human beings can seal themselves off into compartments and be believers one moment, good subjects or citizens the next. Instead, and necessarily, the categories bleed into one another—they do not remain in their "proper spheres." The only sure guarantee against conflict is to render religion utterly private and publicly irrelevant. Now Locke didn't teach this explicitly but his writings helped to pave the way.

Here Jean-Jacques Rousseau enters as a kind of shadow around the liberal monist-disestablishmentarian project. Rousseau, in fact, understood that you couldn't demarcate spheres so tidily. His solution was not pluralism but another "cleaning-up" that requires of religion that it be public but only in a certain way. The drive within his account is monistic as well. It works like this: societies require a civil religion that buttresses the legitimacy and authority of the civic republic. Civil religion welds together different parts of the polity and demands that citizens, through a form of civic membership within which religion is subordinated to the good of the polity, make ongoing manifest their singular devotion to their polity. Any person divided in his loyalty and allegiance can never be a full-fledged participant in a well-ordered republic—and might even pose a treasonous threat.

In his *Social Contract*, Rousseau commends the "wise system of Muhammad," wise because Muhammad fused the "two heads of the eagle" by contrast to Christianity, especially Catholic Christianity, which separated them.[5] Christianity, Rousseau opined, is a lousy civic religion and Catholicism is the worst of all because it divides a person's loyalties and puts him at odds with himself.[6] He becomes schizophrenic. One must heal this division. It follows that the system invented by Muhammad is to be preferred to the schism Christianity introduced in the world when, as Rousseau asserts: "Jesus came to establish on earth a spiritual kingdom. By separating the theological system from the political system he brought it about that the States ceased to be one, and caused internal divisions which have never ceased to agitate Christian peoples."[7]

Rousseau would heal this division by instituting a stern civic religion in which the "patria" substitutes for God as the singular object of devotion and loyalty.[8] A citizen must gaze upon the patria lovingly from the moment he draws first breath. It must be ever in his heart, ever in his thoughts. If temporal and spiritual government are separated, men "see double"—a phrase from Thomas Hobbes who fretted about the same thing.[9] So—in their own ways—both Locke, at least tacitly, and Rousseau explicitly, created a monistic system: one must triumph. (The astute reader will notice the form this argument takes—one must triumph—as in later debates the insistence that "science" must trump "faith" and so on. The point I am making here is that the monistic drive infects all areas of endeavor in modernity.)

The American Jesuit scholar, John Courtney Murray, took on this command to an undivided loyalty to the earthly sovereign, or state, or constitution. He reminds us that there was an alternative "take" on things created rather early on in the Latin Church, the so-called Gelasian doctrine associated with Pope Gelasius I and his "two swords" metaphor.[10] There are two swords—the secular and the spiritual. The spiritual possesses a superior dignity. But the secular (as we would now say) has its own purposes and is authorized by God. Of course, for medieval popes, the spiritual sword trumped in any case of conflict. We need not take this historical issue up here but simply note that there is a huge difference between the view—there must be "one"—and the view—there are in fact "two." The latter invites over time a robust understanding of pluralism and institutional diversity; the former moves to streamline matters and to eliminate any tensions and conflicts by definitional fiat.

Murray reminds us that vital to the Gelasian doctrine was the liberty of the Church. This "freedom of the Church as the spiritual authority served as the limiting principle of the power of government. . . . To put it briefly, the Church stood . . . between the body politic and the public power, not only limiting the reach of the power over the people but also mobilizing the moral consensus of the people and bringing it to bear upon power, thus to insure that the king, in the fine phrase of John of Salisbury, would 'fight for justice and for the freedom of the people.'"[11] In a sense, the creation of what Murray calls "free political institutions" follows from a model of the institutional freedom of the church—and this became absolutely vital for the bulwark provided by the institutional (non-state) church could no longer be assumed as Christendom itself was fragmented, first at Augsburg and, then, at Westphalia with its enshrining of the principle of state sovereignty, the supremacy of states, and the recognition of rulers as arbiters of the religious faith of a people.[12] This led over time to a triumph for internal monism—taking the form, remember, of either an excess of privatization of religion or, contrastingly, an official state religion that defanged Christianity in its dealing with political power.

There is a longer argument that one could mount here about the relative weakness of multiple individual consciences by contrast to the hard work once done by *libertas ecclesia*—but I cannot go down this particular path here. Let me wind this section down by putting the question: Is there a drive in modernity to drive out "the two"? If Murray is correct that the very dignity of the human person demands a different sort of governance than that presented by monism, this is a serious matter indeed. I shall turn to it next.

ANTHROPOLOGIES AND POLITICS

Murray touches on the anthropological question when he suggests that any notion of the absoluteness of *will*, whether that of a sovereign monarch or a sovereign people, creates hideous mutations of the sort that devastated the twentieth century. [13] He touches on a vital matter—what sort of selves are we anyway? What sort of self is assumed by the monistic position and the sovereign mastery of the individual articulated by Sir Julian Huxley? By contrast, what sort of self is suggested at least implicitly if not explicitly by the notion of "the two," of a world of plural sites of power, authority, loyalty, and identity? What sorts of selves committed themselves to hours and hours on their feet, little sleep, little food, for perhaps the most fleeting of glimpses of the body of John Paul II lying in repose in St. Peter's Basilica? Something tells me that the dominant econometric model of our time—human beings as calculators of their own marginal utilities—cannot quite capture that!

There are multiple ways to be a sovereign self. I noted one in brief—modern *homo economicus*. Monism assumes that the self must be internally monistic in order that it participate properly in the project of monism externally. The self cannot handle complexity or plurality. The self should never be put in a position to assess the worthy from the unworthy; indeed, the self is, in a very real sense, brought into being by society itself. In Locke's world we were at least social in some ways before we became political. Human beings did possess rudimentary social forms—but life was full of confusion and inconvenience. (He is silent on whether people pre-civic life had religion or not.) Only the constitution creates clarity and it does this by spreading the writ of the sovereign over all areas of life, although that hand rests gently in some respects. Religion, as I have already noted, can be "left alone" so long as it is a religion of private piety and conscience. So there is a social self—an individual—who can multiply his "goods" by acting with others but who is interested primarily in protecting his goods, his property, including a property interest in the self.

Rousseau's monism is more sinister by far. In Rousseau's world, we were rather stupid wandering isolates, slaking our thirst at streams, eating berries, coming together during mating season but not forming social units. His long story of our evolution—really a devolution away from our original isolated sturdiness—need not concern us here. Suffice to say, we were isolates and we remain such *unless* we are forged together into a "general will" by our initiation into a polity. Rousseau speaks of this initiation in religious terms. We put off "instinct" and put on "justice."[14] We are utterly transformed; utterly in debt to the social power; we cannot dissent from the general will at any moment or in any particular or we, in effect, dissent from the whole, we become traitors to that which gave us our identities. We are outlaws at that moment and must be expunged. The Jacobins had read their Rousseau.

Various permutations of these and other strands, including those represented by Huxley's celebration of "Enlightened reason" by contrast to the old superstitions, including faith, have culminated in our own time in the articulation of strong sovereign selves. Sartrian existentialism would be one example of this. Some version—only some—of American jurisprudence would be another. Some—only some—variants on American radical feminism also underscore a relentless vision of self-sovereignty. We are ourselves only when we are in control. We refuse to recognize intrinsic limits—to our own projects. This notion of freedom extends not only to the world of money, property, possession, and commerce but to all areas of human existence. Indeed, we have arrived at the point where everything is in principle commodifiable and nothing is valued for its own sake. There are so many variants on this theme but one might just point to the selling of sperm and eggs, even the open advocacy of baby-selling by entirely respectable, and respected, academics and jurists, as a potent example. Anything that expands choice, enhances control, and extends the freedom we associate with these, anything that diminishes the sphere of the "unchosen," we celebrate. It follows that anything that smacks of limiting choice, or acknowledging our inability to control all outcomes, or insisting that many of our obligations and, indeed, our blessings are "unchosen," must perforce be excoriated as belonging to the backwardness we have allegedly moved out of. Philosopher Charles Taylor calls this entire cluster of commitments a position of "excarnation"—the self is steadily disembodied, disassembled into its component parts, all driven by will and a self-sovereignty that can assemble or alienate its own parts at will.[15]

What contrast does the world of "two," of many, of pilgrimages, say about the self by contrast? A world of incarnation by contrast to excarnation? In one of my books I spoke of "incarnational being-in-the-world" as a task involving displaying the fullness, the dignity, and the wonder of creation—the horror, then, at its wanton destruction.[16] Modern "deadness" is all around us—the conviction that the world is so much matter to manipulate. Within the vision of the pilgrimage self, we are not so much individuals whose sociality is the result of voluntaristic motion but persons whose sociality is given. As humans moved into modernity, the transcendent dimension of this complex concept of person that fused together dignity, intimacy, relationality, interiority, and other features of persons began to fade. Unsurprisingly, by the seventeenth century, the dominant metaphor for political organization had shifted from anything suggestive of the corporate to everything generated by contract. The presupposition underlying social contractarianism—whether of Locke's or Rousseau's varieties—is founded on a kind of deficient sociality. The contract metaphor implicates us in a contraction of personhood. Our excised sociality follows us about as a kind of phantom yearning to be manifest.

Pope John Paul II captured this bleeding away of incarnational being and ongoingly lifted up the powerful alternative—his favorite mantra—the "dignity of the human person."[17] This is no mere slogan but a potent idea. For John Paul II, as for Augustine before him, human beings are the only creatures "God desired for himself."[18] It was this unique status he defended throughout his life whenever and wherever human dignity was threatened. Our "being" is not reducible to psychological, biological, sociological, or economic predicates.

Let's take a closer look as John Paul's theological anthropology. In his 1981 encyclical, *Laborem Exercens*, John Paul links a proper understanding of work to human dignity. Scorning all materialistic and economistic thought that reverses the right order of things by ignoring the meaning of work for the human subject, John Paul insists that all human beings, including those with disabilities, should have a place at the great "workbench of life."[19] All systems of forced labor; all systems that turn work "into a means for oppressing man and exploiting human labor," must be repudiated because they do damage "to the dignity and subjectivity that are proper to him."[20]

Further, this dignity of the human person, male and female, is inseparable from a view of human freedom worthy of endorsement. This vision of freedom is dramatically at odds with culturally prominent pronouncements that proclaim us sovereigns of ourselves, wholly self-possessing. In *Evangelium Vitae*, John Paul writes that, "if the promotion of the self is understood in terms of absolute autonomy, people inevitably reach the point of rejecting one another. Everyone else is considered an enemy from whom one has to defend oneself."[21] The implications for society are dire, he continues, for "society becomes a mass of individuals placed side by side, but without any mutual bonds."[22] In his argument against abstract notions of absolute human freedom and self-possession, John Paul criticizes all those who worship at the idol of the self. True human freedom is attained only in and through incarnated realities—relationships with others and between Creator and creature. One of the tragedies in late modernity is that, when we flatten the moral horizon and make our own projects absolute, we treat our bodies and those of others as means alone.

In *Veritatis Splendor*, John Paul insists that truth and freedom belong together.[23] This encyclical (1993) focuses on "anthropological and ethical presuppositions" that detach human freedom from truth.[24] Each of these, in severing freedom from considerations of truth, affronts human dignity. In chapter 2, "Do Not Be Conformed to This World," John Paul insists that, while the church's magisterium "does not intend to impose upon the faithful any particular theological system, still less a philosophical one," it is the Church's responsibility to expound the word of God and to "state some trends of theological thinking and certain philosophical affirmations" that are, in fact, "incompatible with revealed truth."[25] Some of these trends include exalting freedom into "an absolute" with man as the only source of values and meaning.[26] This invites both "subjectivism and individualism" of a sort that undermine the moral evaluation of human acts and weaken our commitment to the dignity of ourselves and others.[27] Certain physicalist and naturalistic epistemologies and philosophies reduce the human being to a physical or biological datum. It follows that human nature, "understood in this way, could be reduced to and treated as readily available biological or social material."[28] Such approaches cannot begin to appreciate the nature of freedom.

Cultural determinists—and this would surely include the political views of social contractarians for whom society creates the person in some basic way—come in for criticism, too. It goes without saying, John Paul insists, that human beings always exist in particular cultures and exhibit in many ways the signs of that culture—through language, gestures, aesthetic sensibilities, historic understanding, and so on. The problem is that the cultural determinist is one who, by definition, believes that man is "exhaustively defined" by culture.[29] How can this be, asks the pontiff? If this were indeed the case, there would never be anything in human beings "which transcends those cultures."[30] That something lies in our very natures and the yearnings deep in the human soul for freedom and for truth, yearnings that direct our aspirations in ways consonant with our God-given dignity.

In his extraordinary follow-up to *Veritatis Splendor*, "Evangelium Vitae," (1995), already cited, John Paul evaluates entire cultures according to whether or not they honor the value and inviolability of human life. The heart of the matter is the "incomparable worth of the human person."[31] John Paul sees human dignity threatened in many ways—in "murder, genocide, abortion, euthanasia or willful self-destruction" in "mutilation, torments inflicted on body or mind, attempts to coerce the will itself; whatever insults human dignity."[32] As if this weren't bad enough, John Paul notes expanding threats to human dignity in the "new prospects opened up by scientific and technological progress"—the very process celebrated and sanctified by the version of Enlightenment and the secularization hypothesis articulated by Mr. Huxley.[33] All of these developments come to us in the guise of perfecting our biology or easing human suffering. All assume human beings are raw material to manipulate. John Paul notes a terrible paradox at the heart of late modernity. On the one hand, we solemnly affirm human rights. And, on the other, we deny those rights in practice given a "notion of freedom which exalts the isolated individual in an absolute way and gives no place to solidarity, to openness to others and service to them. While it is true that the taking of life not yet born or in its final stages is sometimes marked by a mistaken sense of altruism and human compassion, it cannot be denied that such a culture of death, taken as a whole, betrays a completely individualistic concept of freedom, which ends up by becoming the freedom of 'the strong' against the weak who have no choice but to submit." Such a view of freedom can only lead to a "serious distortion of life in society."[34]

When we pose "serious distortion" over again a vision of the triumph of individuality, what we see is not, I submit, modernity vs. anti-modernity, or religion vs. enlightenment, or faith vs. reason, but one vision, and version, of modernity by contrast to another, quite different, one.[35]

Which one plays itself out in contemporary political projects that claim, and aim, for an international common good? Are anthropologies in play at all? Does this angle of vision give us any critical leverage? It is to this topic, one that may seem but thinly connected to what has thus far been said, but, upon closer examination, can be seen to be intrinsically connected to it, that I now turn.

FREEDOM, DEMOCRACY, AND AN INTERNATIONAL COMMON GOOD

There are forces unleashed in our world that seem difficult to harness or to tame. One is globalization. A second is democratization. And yet we are all deeply implicated, and our lives will be touched one way or another, by which version of these powerful currents prevails. One cannot separate any consideration of the great forces of freedom and democracy apart from thinking of justice. Since the ancient Greeks, justice—concerns to whom it is owed as well as in what it consists—have preoccupied political thinkers and moral philosophers. Over the centuries there were challenges to the sharp "us" (citizens) vs. "them" (foreigners, barbarians) of the Greek polis. One of these challenges was embodied in Christian teaching. Christianity put pressure on the notion that good or ill treatment should be meted out differently depending on whether or not a human being was or was not a member of one's own particular tribe or polity. Instead, hospitality extended to all without exception. One of the most famous of the parables of Jesus of Nazareth illustrating this claim is the story of the Good Samaritan. If a Samaritan, with whom the Jews of Jesus's day had only hostile relations, could treat a beaten and robbed Jew with tenderness and mercy, was it not possible for a Samaritan to be good and for the normative presuppositions to be reversed? Hospitality—*caritas*—obliged believers, whether the one to whom aid was proffered or from whom aid was received was a family or tribal member or a stranger.

The ancient distinction between justice (between citizens) and force (against strangers) of the Greek world never disappeared, of course. It made a powerful comeback in the writings of Machiavelli, Rousseau, and other so-called civic republicans. It was re-encoded by the Peace of Augsburg (1555) and the Treaty of Westphalia (1648). With Westphalia, the norm of justice as pertaining to members of a particular territorial entity was given official sanction in its recognizably modern form, marking the beginning of the international state system. At the same time, Christian universalism remained alive not only in theological and moral argument, but present as well in several traditions of theologically grounded political practice. Where the matter of international justice is concerned the most important of these was the just or justified war tradition—a theory of comparative justice applied to considerations of war and intervention. Among other things, this means that the post-World War II universalization of human rights, itself flowing from powerful developments in the West (Christianity, natural law, natural rights, etc.) enhanced the importance and reach of the just war perspective rather than running counter to it. Just war argument and universal human rights not only are not incompatible; they can and should be placed within the same frame.

This is not the time or the place to take up just war in detail. Suffice to say that, within this mode of argument, no unbridgeable conceptual and political divide is opened up between domestic and international politics. Just war politics insists that a war of all against all does not, in fact, kick in once one leaves the hearth, the neighborhood, or the borders of one's country. There is, instead, a presumption of neighbor-regard that may well yield certain obligations. This principle of equal regard flows directly from anthropological presuppositions of inviolable human dignity. Let's take a brief look at universal human rights and contemporary forces of democratization with the anthropological presupposition I have just articulated in mind, bearing in mind as we do so that the other powerful "self," the "sovereign" one, generated by forces that ushered in modernity, must be lurking somewhere nearby.

I think it fair to say that the first table (so to speak) of the Universal Declaration of Human Rights, those rights that speak most directly to intrinsic human dignity, are tethered explicitly to the anthropology I have noted and fleshed out in the work of John Paul II. Governments are not permitted to "disappear," arbitrarily arrest, systematically torture, and murder people.

Governments cannot violate freedom of worship—and so on. The second "table" of human rights speaks to what is sometimes called "positive freedom" or rights, namely, what governments are obliged to do for me. Health care, education, the list is rather robust. I suspect that a combination of the embodied social self and the sovereign self lie at the root of this articulation of positive rights or entitlements. Certainly a vision of human flourishing is here announced. If one accepts the universal declaration as foundational to any international justice or common good, it surely follows that societies that egregiously, systematically, and ongoingly violate these rights—especially those that touch most deeply on human dignity in its rock-bottom aspects of bodily integrity—must and should be stopped. It follows further, I believe, that if various modes of diplomacy and sanction do not suffice, armed intervention remains an ever-present possibility. For armed intervention can serve a common good—and not just a common good of particular polities but an international common good.

I have heard many objections against the universality of human rights and the vision of human dignity and human freedom attached to it as I go around speaking on many of America's college campuses. What I find most extraordinary is when young women, no doubt under heavy tutelage by unthinking celebrants of "diversity," opine that it violates "diversity" to protect and promote human rights—and this in the context of the many horrors visited upon women within the world of Islamist fundamentalism and extremism. Purdah—a difference? Being shot in the back of the head for alleged adultery as form of "diversity"? Being murdered by one's own father or brother for "dishonoring" the family just "their" way of doing things? When confronted with this sort of moral defeatism, I tell the questioners that an Iranian woman friend of mine once said, in response to a similar question: "No woman wants to be beaten 70 times for accidentally displaying a bit of ankle." Surely not! And in making this statement, my friend tapped, at least tacitly, an anthropology of human dignity. If one's vision of human freedom is tied to this understanding of human rights—as I believe is President George W. Bush's in his several speeches on liberty as "God's gift to humankind" and a "yearning" in all human hearts—it makes direct contact not only with an anthropology of intrinsic human dignity but, at the same time, with the world of "two," of plural forms of life deeded to us from the Latin West.[36] But to trash this "Western imperialism" demeans persons and deflects the central issues.

We hear a great deal about the dangers of universalizing a particular political form—democracy. We are told that particular cultures are not suited to it. (I remember this sort of argument as a colonialist hang-over in the days of decolonization when I was an undergraduate. No one called the view that Africans were unsuited to political freedom a "progressive" or "radical" view then. It was clearly reactionary. How the political worm turns!) We are told that open advocacy of it is itself a form of Western imperialism. Yet somehow the people of Iran when they voted, the people in Ukraine and Lebanon when they took peacefully to the streets, seem to believe that freedom and democracy applies to them, too. Are we going to tell them they are mistaken about their own understanding of their dignity and the politics consistent with it? Who, save those for whom multiculturalism has turned into a rigid ideological dogma, will dare say any such demeaning thing?

At the same time, we—Western scholars and intellectuals—do right to express concerns that democracy not become an ideology but remain at the level of an ideal, one way we "name" human dignity in modernity. Democracy is not a total catechism and it must not be sacralized. But even John Paul II, in his encyclical *Centesimus Annus*, defended the position that democracy, rightly understood, is the political form that the dignity of human persons takes in our time.[37] And at this point the challenges really begin. Remember my comments about the possibility of armed intervention in behalf of human dignity and conducted under the presuppositions of the just war tradition. Suppose we are confronted with a justice claim that takes a direct political form: people should not be treated in certain ways and when they are something should be done about it. We are not permitted to stand by as people are being rounded up and slaughtered. Everything in a universal commitment to universal human rights tells us this. This makes the insistence that there are grievances and horrors to which "we" must respond provided "we" can do so in a way that avoids, to the extent that this is humanly possible, either deepening the injustice already present or creating new instances of injustice, doubly difficult to sort out.

Nevertheless, one needs to draw out an implication for an international common good that flows from the presumption of equal moral regard, namely, the right to have force deployed in your behalf if you are the victim of egregious, systematic, and continuing violence and no other means have proved adequate to stop this violence. Genocide is the most obvious case in point, of course, but there are many others.

Here it is worth noting, once again, that the obligations of *caritas* in Christian theology are themselves constituent features of the just war tradition. The secularization of just war thinking and its insertion within a Westphalian model diminished the neighbor-regard features of the just war tradition but did not entirely obliterate those features. Too, if one scratches the post-World War II universalization of human rights that serves as a background to the neighbor-regard issue, albeit in non-theological terms, one finds lurking underneath the anthropological commitments of which I speak. Approaching the many horrors of our international world in this way is better than the strategies of evasion and denial of the sort visible in the 1994 slaughter by Rwandan Hutus of Rwandan Tutsis. Exculpatory strategies at the time included claiming that the full extent of the slaughter was unknown. Or that, as bad as the slaughter was, it wasn't as bad as other cases of genocide, and so on. In this and other well-known cases, one was confronted with the spectacle of officials speaking boldly about universal human rights but going on to revert to a narrow doctrine of national self-interest, and self-sovereignty, in order to evade the implications of embracing these rights. This tension is lodged in the heart of the United Nations itself—a universal body whose members are sovereign states, hence the final judges of their own interest.

The state's primary task is maintaining civic peace. Constitutive of that civic peace is justice. None of the other goods human beings cherish can flourish if one lives in a world in which, in St. Augustine's mordant phrase, people are "devoured like fishes."[38] The equal regard doctrine, as I have here articulated it, is an elementary requirement of international justice, one consistent with both the anthropologies of sovereign and of intrinsically dignified selves—pending further unpacking. That is, one cannot say at the outset what version of anthropology an analyst embraces when he or she speaks of international justice and democracy. More unpacking, as I indicated, is required. Minimally, however, an implication shared in either case is that persons are not to be slaughtered with impunity. What follows further is that we—the more powerful—respond to attacks against persons who cannot defend themselves because they, like us, are human beings, hence equal in regard to us, and because they, like us, are members of nations, states, or would-be states whose primary obligation is to protect, not to ravish, the lives of those who inhabit their polities. Thus, all states or would-be states have a stake in building up an international civic culture in which fewer horrors such as Rwanda or Kosovo or Saddam Hussein's "republic of fear" take place and in which those that do take place trigger a level of concern that warrants the use of armed intervention, unless grave and compelling reasons preclude such intervention.

People should not be slaughtered because powerful nations are dithering, hoping the whole thing will be over soon, or using domestic political considerations as a trump card in refusing to do the right thing. Doing the right thing is frequently, if not uniformly, consistent with the interest all states have in preventing the emergence of deadly cycles of violence. As Samantha Power notes: "People victimized by genocide or abandoned by the international community do not make good neighbors, as their thirst for vengeance, their irredentism, and their acceptance of violence as a means of generating change can turn them into future threats."[39] An equal regard standard is central to a well functioning international system composed of decent, if not perfect, states. These states may or may not be democratic in our—America's—constitutional and representational sense. But some form of what is usually called "democracy" is essential in the sense that avenues for public involvement and engagement in the life of a polity as a dignified human subject, must be available. This is no "imposition" of some alien "Western" ideal. As I already indicated, the discourse of human rights and democracy is now world-wide. At the same time, it is extraordinarily difficult—many would say dangerous—to articulate a strong universal justice claim and to assign to particular states a disproportionate burden of enforcement. But I believe that is our current situation. To the extent that an international common good—under the equal regard/justice model I have noted—is realizable, it may well demand and require disproportionate sacrifices from some in the interest of the many.

We seem to have strayed some distance from the discussions in the first two sections concerning monism, pluralism, and theological anthropology. But I think not. The democracy movements now active in our international life will either take a culturally specific monistic or plural form, with the monistic form one that may well, either immediately or over the long run, put negative pressure on the ideals of democratic decency and human dignity that animated freedom protestors in the first instance, or embrace and work to sustain a plural framework. And it must inevitably be the case that these new democracies, as they emerge out of the incubus of the old, will work to honor, or contrive to dishonor, human dignity. I have insisted that the surest guarantee of that dignity is the theological anthropology of intrinsic dignity and respect for persons. Other versions of anthropology, I fear, either celebrate us as too sovereign or—in a stance I have not, in fact, discussed—as so thoroughly submerged within a social totality we have no identifiable "self" at all, where self-loss is the order of the day. But this latter is another discussion and what I have thus far put on the table is surely sufficient for the time being.

NOTES

1. Julian Huxley, "The Coming New Religion of Humanism," *The Humanist* 22, (1962).
2. Augustine, *Confessions*, ed. Michael P. Foley, trans. F. J. Sheed (Indianapolis: Hackett Publishing, 2006), 3.
3. Jean Behtke Elshtain, "Against Liberal Monism," *Daedalus* 132, no. 3 (2003): 78–79.
4. John Locke, "A Letter Concerning Toleration," in *Two Treatises of Government and A Letter Concerning Toleration,* edited by Ian Shapiro (Binghamton, NY: Yale University, 2003), 230–31.
5. "Mahomet held very sane views, and linked his political system well together; and, as long as the form of his government continued under the caliphs who succeeded him, that government was indeed one, and so far good. . . . Of all Christian writers, the philosopher Hobbes alone has seen the evil and how to remedy it, and has dared to propose the reunion of the two heads of the eagle, and the restoration throughout of political unity, without which no State or government will ever be rightly constituted." Jean-Jacques Rousseau, *On the Social Contract*, ed. Paul Negri and Drew Silver, trans. G. D. H. Cole (Mineota, NY: Dover Publishing, 2003), 91–92.
6. Ibid., 93.
7. Ibid., 91.
8. Ibid., 96.

9. Thomas Hobbes, *Leviathan: With Selected Variants from the Latin Edition of 1668* (Indianapolis: Hackett Publishing, 1994), 316.

10. John Courtney Murray, "The Governmental Repression of Heresy," Catholic Theological Society of America, (1948): 39–87.

11. John Courtney Murray, *We Hold These Truths: Catholic Reflections on the American Proposition* (New York: Sheed & Ward, 1960), 204–5.

12. "It was this political faith that compelled early American agreement to the institutions of a free speech and a free press," Ibid., 34.

13. John Courtney Murray, "Leo XII and Pius XII: Government and the Order of Religion," in *Religious Liberty: Catholic Struggles with Pluralism,* edited by J. Leon Hooper (Louisville, KY: Westminister/John Knox, 1955), 51–52.

14. Rousseau, *Contract,* 12.

15. Charles Taylor, *A Secular Age* (Cambrisge, MA: Harvard University Press, 2007), 741.

16. Jean Bethke Elshtain, "When Faith Meets Politics," in *Faith, Freedom, and the Future: Religion in American Political Culture*, edited by Charles W. Dunn (Lanham, MD: Rowman & Littlefield, 2003) 74.

17. John Paul II, On Human Work: Encyclical *Laborem Exercens* (Washington, DC: United States Catholic Conference, 1982), 52.

18. "The Council points out this very fact when, speaking of that likeness, it recalls that 'man is the only creature on earth that God willed for itself.'" John Paul II, Encyclical *Redemptor Hominis* (London: Catholic Truth Society, 1978), 42.

19. "The disabled person is one of us and participates fully in the same humanity that we possess. It would be radically unworthy of man, and a denial of our common humanity, to admit to the life of the community, and thus admit to work, only those who are fully functional." Paul II, Human, 50.

20. Ibid., 21.

21. John Paul II, Encyclical Letter: The Gospel of Life, *Evangelium Vitae,* trans. Vatican (Boston, MA: Pauline Books & Media, 1995), 37.

22. Ibid., 37–38.

23. John Paul II, *Veritatis Splendor*, in The Encyclicals of John Paul II, edited by C.S.C. & J. Michael Miller (Huntington, IN: Our Sunday Visitor, 2001), 602.

24. Ibid., 586.

25. Ibid., 603–4.

26. Ibid., 568.

27. Ibid., 607.

28. Ibid., 615.

29. Ibid., 619.

30. Ibid., 619.

31. Paul II, Gospel, 14.

32. Ibid., 14.

33. Ibid., 15.

34. Ibid., 37.

35. Ibid., 37.

36. George W. Bush, "Remarks," National Religious Broadcasters Convention (Speech, Gaylord Opryland Resort and Convention Center, Nashville, Tennessee, March 11, 2008).

37. John Paul II, *Centesimus Annus*, in The Encyclicals of John Paul II, edited by C.S.C. & J. Michael Miller (Huntington, IN: Our Sunday Visitor, 2001), 550.

38. "For the sea in a figure is used of this world, bitter through brackishness, turbulent through storms, when men through their perverse and depraved desires, are become like the fish, devouring one another." Augustine, *The Confessions of S. Augustine,* trans. E. B. Pusey (Oxford: John Henry Parker, 1840), 290.

39. Samantha Power, *A Problem from Hell* (New York: Harper Collins, 2002), 513.

Chapter Five

Bonhoeffer for Political Thought

Jean Bethke Elshtain

May I begin with a story? This took place many years ago now in the 1970s, if memory serves, in the township where I was then teaching at a large state university. A local church had advertised a program on Dietrich Bonhoeffer—the screening of a documentary followed by discussion. I was then an informal student of Bonhoeffer, having never read or studied him in any course, and I was eager to discuss his life and thought with other interested persons. As a student of politics, and in light of the strict academic divide between disciplines, Bonhoeffer had never crossed the divide into the realm of political thought. Certainly Bonhoeffer would not pass muster as an advocate and example of the so-called "scientific study of politics," the ideal to which we were then called to aspire.

Let me say a few words about this urgency to study politics scientifically, because it helps us to understand why Bonhoeffer wouldn't pass the test as a thinker worth considering if you were a student of politics. The study of politics in that era was dominated by a strict positivism that yielded a view of politics as a contestation between preferences and interests. Practitioners of this version of political science presumed their own commitment to neutral, scientific objectivity. To this end, they expunged moral norms as a central feature of political study. Political science, in other words, was a value-free enterprise.

Within the epistemological presuppositions of behaviorist political science, to describe and to evaluate were entirely separable activities, and those who mixed the two were considered fuzzy-minded and incapable of rigorous analysis. One could come up with the bare bones of description and then append "values, biases, attitudes, and emotional preferences." This appending was always a second order activity, and those values and "biases" were construed as irrational or arational by definition. The ideal, then, was neutral description to which everyone could subscribe and then later add on whatever "biases" he or she wished.

Ramifications of the behaviorist presumptions seeped into political theory and political philosophy as well. A link between political inquiry and moral imperatives was presumed explicitly by nearly all classical theorists in the history of political thought. Despite this backdrop, contemporary political science severed politics from moral consideration on the view that it was possible to describe human events in an entirely neutral language. Those committed to the view that moral notions and beliefs could be stated apart from description, that such notions were indefensible rationally, and that they could be bracketed perforce tacitly adopted a theory of morality known as emotivism. Terms of moral evaluation were purely emotive; that is, they simply reflected the arational emotional commitments of the speaker.

To insist that political science—or any legitimate study of politics—had to do solely with closed definitions, limited meanings, passive human actors, functions and interests, inputs, outputs, managerial techniques, and game theory scenarios meant forsaking the authentic heart and soul of politics and political contexts as couched in our resonant conceptual language—the language of justice, freedom, liberty, peace, equality, community, the legitimate use of force, and so on. So the entire thrust of the study of politics militated against "normative theory." That was one issue. A second was that chasm—that huge gulf—between political science and other disciplines, most especially an enterprise like religion or theology. What had this to do with politics? The answer was: "nothing, nothing whatsoever."

So this was the context that pertained as I entered the church that evening for the screening of the documentary. The gulf between theology and politics was so enormous that those engaged in their respective enterprises seemed to speak altogether different languages even as they used similar words like "power" or "sovereignty." As I note in my Gifford Lectures, published as *Sovereignty: God, State, and Self*, even in the realm of normative political thought the "religious thinkers," with few exceptions, were missing in action. As well, the religious dimensions of those thinkers who were central to the canon were often ignored or diminished. For example, John Locke's scriptural references from his classic *Two Treatises on Government* were often eliminated from consideration, as if it were obligatory of Locke to add that sort of thing, given the historic moment, but one should attach little meaning to it. The thinkers whose religious commitments couldn't be scraped off like so much stale icing from a two-day-old cake were admitted to political theory in excised form. Perhaps portions of St. Augustine's *City of God*, but, Heaven forfend, nothing from his *Confessions.*

With concepts such as "sovereignty," whose religious meanings and origins are potent and ubiquitous, political science still managed to sever the political study of sovereignty from God's sovereignty or the sovereignty of kings, because that meant one was slipping over into territory that showed the connections between "church" and "state." So it was not a hospitable terrain for the student of Bonhoeffer who happened to sit in a political science department. But that did not trouble me unduly as I approached the Bonhoeffer event all those years ago, assuming that we would focus primarily on Bonhoeffer's role in the conspiracy to take Hitler's life that wound up with Bonhoeffer losing his own, plus the lives of relatives, friends, and compatriots. They had held fast in the midst of a story Bonhoeffer had depicted so vividly:

> Today we have villains and saints again, in full public view. The gray on gray of a sultry, rainy day has turned into the black cloud and bright lightning flash of a thunderstorm. The contours are sharply drawn. Reality is laid bare. Shakespeare's characters are among us. The villain and the saint have little or nothing to do with ethical programs. They arise from the primeval depths, and with their appearance tear open the demonic and divine abyss [Abgrund] out of which they come, allowing us brief glimpses into their suspected secrets. [1]

So I anticipated a pointed, hard-hitting discussion. The film concluded. Lights went on. The chairwoman of the evening introduced who was to lead the discussion, one Diane P. Correct (not her real name), a well-known militant Quaker activist in the area who seemed to lead one protest or another nearly every day. Despite her own militant pacifism, I hoped she would be able to approach Bonhoeffer's participation in the July 20 plot with some charity and historic detachment given the nature and desperateness of the situation. Not so, as it turned out. Ms. Correct's first words were:

"Okay. The tragedy of Bonhoeffer is not that he lost his life because of his role in the conspiracy. The tragedy is his involvement in the first place. I would like to discuss how and why Dietrich Bonhoeffer went wrong in abandoning non-violence."

A long silence ensued.

I then raised my hand, rather timorously, for Ms. Correct was formidable and known to bear grudges, and one didn't want to get on her wrong side. But I couldn't let this stand. I said something like:

> "But this way of beginning proceeds from the presumption that Bonhoeffer was wrong, period, and we just have to say why. Wouldn't it be better to try to approach his deepening involvement step by step, what was going on, why, finally, and how he decided on the course of action that led to Flossenbürg?"

A furor ensued, but I do not recall anything of substance being discussed, finally. Instead, the conversation was dominated by the methods of protest for contemporary protestors. Mid-twentieth-century Europe faded into the background quickly. Now, all these years later, I have been given the opportunity to make good on what I put forward so tentatively nearly forty years ago. As a political theorist who, for twenty years, has taught in a Divinity School, my scholarly life is one of sanctioned border crossings when before it was considered a dubious and unhelpful business to indulge that sort of thing. For those of you who want more on these issues, I refer you to the opening pages of my *Sovereignty* book.

Let me begin with the fundaments of what is required, what is rock-bottom, if one is to be within the universe of political theory or touch it in significant ways. A thinker must touch on questions of power, order, free-dom, justice, sovereignty, the state, civic life, legitimate and illegitimate uses of force, peace, war, and human nature itself. Bonhoeffer clearly meets this standard, and his thoughts are especially important and provocative on the limits to freedom, on the nature of government (and the mandates more generally), on what it means to speak the truth, and on appeals to nature or the natural.

What everyone wants insights into, of course, is Bonhoeffer's role in the conspiracy. But this cannot be understood apart from consideration of his struggle with questions of lying and deceit, as well as decisions about when and how to act in situations of danger, horror, and destruction. Politics is a world human beings inhabit before the last things. Politics is part of the penultimate, not the ultimate, sphere. It is in claiming ultimacy for politics that opens the space for the demonic to rush in—if we stay with Bonhoeffer's vivid imagery. So in order to understand Bonhoeffer's protest, we must understand his general account of ethics.

For the purpose of one short paper, we can only touch on a few key questions. These, in turn, will lead us to the matter of tyrannicide, and here I wish to distinguish between political assassination or murder and tyranni-cide. Losing that distinction means we lose much of the rich historic and theological backdrop to Bonhoeffer's deed; we distort the meaning of the conspiracy. I suspect that the major contribution of my paper will lie in unpacking this distinction, but we must provide some detailed backdrop be-fore I "go there," so to speak.

Let us begin with Bonhoeffer on politics and the state. Keeping in mind that Bonhoeffer was not *per se* a political thinker, he nevertheless wrote and thought in a politically drenched vocabulary, rich with political implication and meaning. There is a gulf between politics as an ethical enterprise—concrete, embodied, multiple, plural, taking shape within the framework of concrete institutions—and politics as a triumphalist enterprise dominated by the Omni—competent state that destroys any possibility of authentic poli-tics—a politics that must abide by certain limits.

How does Bonhoeffer, drawing upon his theological sources, carve out a space for decent politics? Bear in mind that, for Bonhoeffer, the state must never become a source of ultimacy, the be-all and end-all of human existence. For that existence is lived entirely in the here-and-now, the penulti-mate realm. When that realm aspires to ultimacy, it violates its God-given mandate, its very right-to-be. How did things go awry? When did politics start to aspire to ultimacy? Bonhoeffer indicts the French Revolution, which brought into stark relief

> Western godlessness. It is totally different from the atheism of certain individ-ual Greek, Indian, Chinese, and western thinkers. It is not the theoretical denial of the existence of God. It is itself a religion, a religion of hostility to God. It is in just this that it is western . . . the deification of man is the proclamation of nihilism. [2]

The error at base, argues Bonhoeffer, is an anthropological one. The French revolutionaries embraced notions of human innocence and human malleabil-ity: human beings are clay to be molded by architects who know where history is going and what must be done to get there. They embraced a radical view of human self-sovereignty and self-creation, disdained the God of crea-tion who reminds human beings of their dependence and creatureliness, and embarked on a course of destruction as a perverse mimesis of God's genera-tivity under the presumption that the categories of "good" and "evil" did not apply.

Bonhoeffer claims that one cannot set aside questions concerning "the nature of man" and in what his and her freedom consists. Freedom is not a word that is its own principle of justification: sooner or later, the anthropo-logical questions are going to come up. Sooner or later, a debate must occur on the adequacy, or not, of contrasting anthropologies. Bonhoeffer never forgot that it is only through foregrounding the anthropological question—what does it mean to be created in the image of God?—that theology can prevent its assimilation into a variant of an ideology external to itself, can forestall its sublimation within some political doctrine or plan or scheme, whether Bolshevism, fascism, or even liberalism.

It would be constructive to contrast Bonhoeffer's insistence on anthropol-ogy with the political scientist's demand that we can altogether prescind on the human nature question, that all we need to know is that behavior is caused—there is a stimulus and a response—and people are in principle predictable. For Bonhoeffer helps to explain why all reductionistic treat-ments of human action, behavior, thinking, and feeling must fail. A longer argument could be made here, but limitations of space mean I must press on.

A compelling anthropology should help us to contend with the complex-ity of human nature as well as challenge and question our culture's preoccu-pations in order that we might embrace that which is worthy. Bonhoeffer departs decisively from celebrations of human self-sovereignty: no one is sufficient unto himself or herself, and to presume such is the sin of pride. We are always living with, and within, a limit. Let me unpack Bonhoeffer's views in this matter with an eye toward displaying what Bonhoeffer calls God's "yes" and "no" to the world and our own "yes" and "no" to modernity.

God's "no" to the world is signified by crucifixion: God condemns the world for its sins. But resurrection is a resounding "yes": the world is forgiven and redeemed. Working with the "yes" and "no" dialectic, Bonhoeffer says, "yes," we cannot do without notions of human freedom and emancipation. But the "no" is equally decisive: we face an unprecedented mechanization of life, on the one hand, and the proliferation of what Bonhoeffer calls "vitalism" that posits life as "an absolute, as an end in itself," a view that "cannot but end in nihilism, in the disruption of all that is natural," on the other.[3] The problem here is the absolutizing of an authentic insight, namely, the insistence that life is not only means but also an end in itself. The key questions are: how is that end construed? How is it misconstrued?

It is misconstrued if the human being sees himself as his own principle of justification and embraces an image of human completeness and self-sovereignty that forgets mutability, temporality, contingency, and finitude and leads to prideful self-absorption. Acts of freedom, undertaken from faith and in love, are acts that recognize a limit. But what is that limit? What is the horizon within which human freedom is realized? In modernity, the tendency is for that boundary to be set by collectivities like states as human beings are sacrificed to ends determined by rulers, or, alternatively, defined by the putatively sovereign self alone as I make my choices into absolutes: so long as a choice is mine, it trumps all other possibilities.

In this way, human beings misuse freedom and transmogrify into destroyers. Actual freedom is always situated and concrete, and it implicates us in acts that signal at one and the same time our ability to bring about change as well as our inability to even remotely approach total transformation, whether of selves or situations. But this recognition of the limit of our freedom still begs the question of who and what sets or affords, that limit that we are called to recognize.

Bonhoeffer works in several ways to articulate the notion of a limit. The first is to argue that we must take account of that which is given or natural, categories that have fallen into disrepute among us and, on Bonhoeffer's account, already been discredited in Protestant ethics and been preserved almost exclusively within Catholic thought. This is unfortunate, he claims, as we require some appreciation of that which is natural or given in the order of things. But do frail human minds have access to such a standard? Is not any such possibility spoiled by the noetic consequences of sin?

Bonhoeffer's response is to argue that we do have access to the natural "on the basis of the gospel." In his move to redeem a concept of the natural for Protestant ethics, Bonhoeffer argues that we enjoy a "relative freedom" in natural life. But there are "true and . . . mistaken" uses of this freedom, and these mark "the difference between the natural and unnatural." He throws down the gauntlet: "Destruction of the natural means destruction of life . . . The unnatural is the enemy of life."[4]

It is hard to overstate the importance of the natural-embodied for Bonhoeffer. He saw around him arguments that demeaned or diminished embodied integrity and came to fruition in evil practices. The first step down this road lies in finding no value in life itself. (Recall here that value in the behaviorist-positivist political science scheme of things is never intrinsic, never something we can come humbly to understand but, rather, that which is applied according to whomever has the wherewithal to make their view of "value" stick.)

In the totalitarian order, the state could determine which lives had value and which did not. Bonhoeffer understood the importance of maintaining firewalls of a conceptual, theological, and ethical sort to forestall such depredations. The prevalence in our time of crude utilitarianism affords examples in abundance of the sorts of arguments and claims Bonhoeffer repudiated and saw as evidence of nihilism—hatred of God and creation yielding hatred of the human itself.

The other limit to distorted misuses of freedom is one I will call, following Bonhoeffer's lead, "existential." Bonhoeffer stressed unceasingly the existence before me of a concrete other, not some abstraction I can simply wish away or manipulate or take account of as the mood strikes me. When I deal with another, that other is not an abstract category of discourse hypostasized to archetypal proportions, but a real, flawed, finite, complex human being, one of God's creatures. I am not permitted to wish him or her away, one of God's creatures. If I am not permitted to wish him or her away, neither am I permitted to incorporate this concrete other into my purposes in such a way that his or her autonomy is effaced.

Bonhoeffer uses the term "existential" to characterize the way that Christ can be thought of. How so? Because "Christ is not first a Christ for himself and then a Christ in the Church . . . Christ can never be thought of as a being for himself but only in relation to me."[5] Analogously, the self and other are not presented as opposite and commensurable principles but only in relation. "Contempt for man and idolization of man are close neighbors"—that is a tragic truth and a persistent fact of modernity.[6]

We can see clearly the implications of Bonhoeffer for politics: a politics of limits but a politics that speaks to the complex nature of the human person. There are legitimate ends and aims of government, but government must never aspire to totality, for then it becomes murderous. In modernity—with its promises of power and control, its ever-present allure of nihilism, of throwing over all limits and embracing the meaninglessness of it all—the temptations of overreach, or claiming ultimacy for our penultimate and limited projects, may, at times, be overwhelming. As Bonhoeffer notes:

> Those who act on the basis of ideology refuse on principle to ask the question about the consequences of their action. This allows them to be more certain about their own goodness than those who act responsibly, within the limits of their abilities, after having seriously considered the consequences. Those who act on the basis of ideology consider themselves justified by their idea. Those who act responsibly place their action in the hands of God and live by God's grace and judgment. [7]

Surely, for Bonhoeffer, working with others to eliminate Hitler was to act responsibly, to place one's action "in the hands of God." For some, this is simply sacrilege. How could God possibly sanction any conspiratorial effort to murder a human being? Perhaps one could make some sort of legalistic argument for taking out a Hitler, but surely one should leave God out of it. For Bonhoeffer, one can never leave God out of it. Christ lies in the very center of our existences, not on the fringes of life. He is the very heart of our action if we are acting responsibly according to his will.

But let us parse this further. I indicated earlier that I suspected the major contribution of this paper would be in the matter of unpacking the conspiracy and adding something new to the discussion, or offering, perhaps, a somewhat different angle of vision from which to view these frightening and terrible events. So let me explain what I have in mind. Most often when we think of the conspirators and their actions, it is in highly personal terms: they aimed to murder Hitler. They were out to get Hitler and, if possible, a few other top Nazis, like Goebbels. This was a plot to culminate in a murder, an assassination.

But is that really the most apt description of events? Think of the difference between murder and assassination and, by contrast, tyrannicide. Colonel Claus von Stauffenberg, a leading conspirator who actually placed the suitcase containing the bomb that was to kill Hitler, did this. A devout Roman Catholic, von Stauffenberg evidently met with a priest, a Monsignor, to explore Church teaching on the matter of disobedience to the head of government up to the point of killing him. In these discussions, surely, the discourse of tyrannicide was central. John of Salisbury, the twelfth-century theologian and theorist, held up the hope that God would lift up a single man to rid the world of a tyrant. He advocated tyrannicide in this sense. But the controlling discussion for Catholics was that of St. Thomas Aquinas, *De Regimine Principum* or *On Kingship*. Given Thomas's basic Aristotelian orientation, his view of kingship was teleological. The king is not just someone who wears a crown. He is someone directed to set purposes, and we evaluate the king by his ends. Because human beings are not meant to live alone, but in association, it is epistemologically necessary to bring many into discussions for no one man can arrive at knowledge of all things through the use of reason. We live in society so one person can help another by employing reason in different ways.

Here comes the crux of the matter and why the distinction between assassination and tyrannicide is so important. Assassination is essentially privatized. A person or conspiratorial group is driven by their own lights—most often the fuel is ideology—to kill a leader in order to take power themselves or put in place some other leader. They seek a private good, not a public good, a common good, which is the legitimate end of politics.

If the ruler rules for his own private good, it is unjust and a perversion. But it would be similarly unjust to murder him for private reasons, like the killers of Macbeth. Because kingship is, for St. Thomas, the best form of human governance, its deformation is particularly despicable. The true king rules for the common good of all and not his own benefit. The right name for someone who rules a perfect community is a king; someone who directs a household is a father. If the king ceases to rule for the common good, the deformation we call tyranny occurs, and it is the worst possible type of government—if indeed we can even call it "government."

Tyranny seeks the good of only one person and is the most unjust form of government. The tyrant undermines virtue, threatens spiritual welfare, sheds blood for nothing, prevents public spiritedness, prevents bonds of friendship from developing among his subjects, and stops the enjoyment of mutual peace. He sows discord and promotes dissension. People brought up in fear become servile so all people are lowered by tyranny.

What can one do if the king becomes a tyrant? Because power must be bound and limited, the tyrant's power must be rebound and relimited.[8] It is not unjust for the community to depose the king or restrict his power if he abuses it by becoming a tyrant. In most cases, one should endure and pray to God. But there are some situations that are so egregious, so beyond endurance, that tyrannicide—a public act to a public end—may be justified.

I suspect that even those who support Bonhoeffer's deed sometimes distort it by thinking of it along the lines of political assassination rather than tyrannicide. And that tends to privatize the deed, something one can readily see because so much of the planning and plotting is secretive and outside the glare of publicity, so to speak. But if one follows Aquinas, the culminating act of deposition must flow from a careful process of ratiocination, of consultation between and among the king/tyrant's courtiers, associates, and administrators. It cannot be the act of the proverbial "lone assassin"—a locution that captures the essentially privatized nature of assassination. Tyrannicide is the action of a particular "we" on behalf of the wider community. Their action is purposive and aims to restore the true *telos* of authentic kingship, of rule for the common good.

Because Bonhoeffer wrote no apologia for his actions, no list of factors that, when added up, equaled "kill Hitler," we can never know for sure what all he was thinking and anguishing over as the hours ticked away and the time approached for the deed to be done. We do know that he placed his all, his very self, in the hands of God. He would act concretely, in this time and place, according to the will of God that came, always, as a concrete call, not an abstract, moralistic injunction. And that he did. I submit that we can better understand his act if we think in terms of tyrannicide rather than assassination, although the philosophical and theological bases of Bonhoeffer's thought overall are quite different from St. Thomas's Aristotelianism.

In our age where private ends, means, and purposes trump nearly everything else, it is all too easy to think of the conspirators acting for personal or private reasons. This presumption clouds our understanding, distorts the deeds and dangers involved, and deepens further the difficulty we have in truly thinking about politics in terms of a common good.

NOTES

1. Dietrich Bonhoeffer, *Ethics: Dietrich Bonhoeffer Works, Volume 6*, trans. Reinhard Krauss, Charles C. West, and Douglas W. Scott, ed. Clifford J. Green (Minneapolis: Fortress Press, 2005), 76–77.

2. Dietrich Bonhoeffer, *Ethics*, trans. Neville Horton Smith (New York: Touchstone, 1995), 103.

3. Bonhoeffer, *Ethics* (Touchstone), 148. See also part I, ch. 1.

4. Bonhoeffer, *Ethics* (Touchstone), 144, 147.

5. Bonhoeffer, *Christ the Center*, trans. Edwin H. Robertson (New York: Harper Collins, 1978), 47.

6. Bonhoeffer, *Ethics* (Touchstone), 75.

7. Bonhoeffer, *Ethics* (Fortress), 225–26.

8. In her manuscript, Dr. Elshtain made an unidentifiable reference to "On Tyrannicide." She may have been referring to Aquinas's *Summa Theologiae* II-II, q.42a 2c.

Chapter Six

Interview with Jean Bethke Elshtain

On 24 September 2009, the editors of this collection sat down at Trinity Western University with Dr. Jean Bethke Elshtain for a wide-ranging interview in which she responded to questions about her life, her scholarship, and her influences. The text of the interview follows. Both our questions and her answers are provided.

JD, PR, JZ: In past interviews (with *Democratiya* 2008 for instance), you have freely shared the family influences and growing up in a small rural community in Colorado. Could you also share with us the intellectual influences that inform your thinking? Who are some of the most influential thinkers that have shaped your intellectual path of discovery and affirmed your practice of applying rigorous ethical thinking to concrete practical issues which confront us all?

JBE: Well, there are certain thinkers that just pop into my work all the time that I clearly make reference to and there is a certain repertoire that I draw upon. Augustine is obviously one, and I think he is the only "thinker" about whom I have written a book—the little book on *Augustine and the Limits of Politics*. Camus is a very important thinker for me. I discovered Camus when I was in high school. I was going through some of my own issues about faith and putting the question, which I suppose a young Christian who's going through something of that sort would put, which is: "Can you be a good person? Can you not be a Christian but also be a good person?" That seemed to be "the question" of that moment. I don't think it is "the question" any-more, but at the time it seemed to be the question and the answer to that—and I'm glad—was "Yes, you can be a decent person in the world without being a Christian." So then that for me raised questions in my mind about

faith, which I won't go into any detail here. But at any rate, here was Camus
with this pretty poignant engagement about belief and unbelief. It just struck
me that he represented—in a sense embodied in his person—some of the
strands of the Western Tradition in one person, that sort of dialectic of faith.

JD, PR, JZ: We think your reading of Camus is interestingly optimistic or
hopeful in the sense that Camus is often looked at as a very pessimistic
character, and his work appears to be dystopian or absurdist. But your perspective on him sounds rather different.

JBE: Well, I do think it is a terrible misreading to see him as a pessimist or to
think that the absurd is the end point of Camus. He made it very clear that his
early work was a way of moving through this notion of the absurd—that life
has no meaning and purpose and so forth. But one doesn't stay there: one
explores that possibility, but it is not the finishing point. He saw his work as
going in cycles. The first cycle was with *The Myth of Sisyphus* and the novel
The Stranger. That was the stage of the absurd, but he then moves on to the
next stage, and he was trying to articulate a sort of positive ethic at times—an
ethic of limits such that if we shut the windows of transcendence, if (as he
puts it) there is only an empty sky, then what are our standards or how are we
to live in the world? That he explores in *The Plague* and *The Rebel*, and so
on.

JD, PR, JZ: So there is a sort of reconstruction that follows the absurdist
phase.

JBE: Exactly. And people often just leave him with the deconstruction,
which irritated him extraordinarily because he insisted throughout his life
that he was not an existentialist. He didn't want to be called that. He didn't
see himself as that. I had a long conversation with his daughter a couple of
years ago after reading Camus. She is his literary executor, and she said that
this was just one of the many directions of his life, that he was put in the
same camp with Sartre. But he would find himself as just the opposite of
Sartre in most respects. So Camus is one of the more important figures in my
work. Bonhoeffer clearly comes up all the time, but I know you'll have some
more questions about Bonhoeffer later, so we'll get into some more detail
about him. I would say that Pope John Paul II is a figure I have found
intriguing from the very beginning as a philosopher and as a pontiff. A
number of his encyclicals and his book on the acting person are quite powerful documents, and I have found those very instructive. Hannah Arendt is
someone else that I reference rather frequently. She is an irritatingly elusive
thinker, and anyone who has encountered her knows what I mean when I say
that. But there are some powerful moments and concepts in her work. It also

strikes me that she is struggling to do what so many of the really philosophical thinkers of the twentieth century have struggled to do, which is to articulate some philosophy of limits in a world of great skepticism of religious belief which would otherwise provide these limits.

As someone who was raised as a Lutheran, Luther's been a person I have really tried to come to grips with in my life and in my work. Luther is always in the background. In addition, there are numerous novelists, writers who are not officially philosophers that have been important to me over time. The American novelist Nathaniel Hawthorne is someone I've always found quite powerful. He has a very well-developed sense of sin and of human failings and human shortcomings. He powerfully answers utopians. He sees right through certain arrogant schemes to transform the world completely and does a beautiful send up of utopian experiments in his book *The Blithedale Romance*, which is poking fun at this utopian experiment that some New England intellectuals tended to get caught up in, the so-called "Brook Farm." His short stories are brilliant on many of these issues, including one that I've used going into this discussion about genetic engineering and the search for physical perfection. It's called "The Birthmark." It's a short story where a fellow who is a forward-looking scientist for his time marries this beautiful woman who has this birthmark that he can't stand, that she would be perfectly beautiful if she didn't have this little birthmark. So they have to find this way to remove the birthmark, but it kills her in the process. You know, he's writing this in the 1850s, but he had a sense of so many of the things that we're grappling with now. The American woman novelist, Willa Cather. Her novels about pioneers are very touching. My favourite is one called *My Ántonia* because the protagonist, the major character, reminds me a little bit of my immigrant grandmother. But her evocation of the land—she grew up in Nebraska; I'm from Colorado—of people grappling with the land. That always struck a very common chord with me.

And then for a number of years, if you found me reading a book, it was most likely a murder mystery. What I've found is that many of the people who write in the genre—procedurals and all of that about detective work and such—are those to whom one should go to find writers with a well-developed sense of justice and evil in the world. I mean, the horrible things they have to confront: how do you deal with that? What made you do it? And when sin and evil has fallen out of our vocabulary, they unhesitatingly use that language. The British writer P. D. James has a wonderful series with Adam Dalgliesh, who is a poet and now a commander in Scotland Yard (he wasn't always a commander, but he rose to that position). I love those books. There is a Scottish mystery writer named Ian Rankin who's wonderful. There's a Swedish mystery writer named Henning Mankell and the American writer named Michael Connelly. What these books seem to have in common is that their protagonists, their heroes—these damaged men who are dealing

with all these horrible things in their lives, homicide and so forth—still cling
to this idea of justice and fairness.

JD, PR, JZ: In *Who are We?* you refer to Leon Kass and the "wisdom of
repugnance." More specifically, you address mystery stories and how mysteries reveal the existence of good versus evil. Do you think that it is a
problem that in modern society we have accepted a higher level of gore, that
in the era of Quentin Tarantino we've accepted a new genre characterized by
gore rather than repugnance? Is there any sense in which that is eroding our
understanding of repugnance?

JBE: That's a good linkage. That's a good connection and the answer to that,
I think, is yes. To the extent that these images have been repeated over and
over again, their capacity to shock us diminishes, and what is retained in
these murder mysteries is that capacity to shock is still there. The scene is so
horrible sometimes that seasoned policemen vomit at the sight. You still have
that sense that a horror has occurred, that there are people lying dead who
ought not to be in that condition. So that repugnance is still there, that
capacity to experience that. And I think that's one reason that I've gravitated
toward that genre for the last decade when I read for fun. I think that this
wisdom has been less understood by critics of Kass who think it's just an
aesthetic reaction, when the critique actually runs much deeper than that. It is
something that really offends something very deep in us: the way that scenes
of corpses piled up at death camps can, that this just ought not to be. That
something really deep and fundamental has been violated. I think I for one
can still find this sense of violation, interestingly enough, in some of these
works that I have mentioned, despite that fact that these are people you
would think would be completely inured to it. And yet they're not. I mean,
they're often tragic figures because they've seen so much that they're
haunted by it, but they're still shocked in a way that differs from the common
viewer's reaction. From the comfort of a movie theater chair or the couch in
the living room you're not that shocked by the images.

JD, PR, JZ: So there is something about the written word as opposed to
visual images that communicates better the repugnance at the violation of
human dignity

JBE: I think that remains the case. Because when some of these stories are
turned into television productions—and I've seen British productions of P.
D. James—it doesn't work in the same way. Again, the capacity to shock and
to get the mind reflecting on things is not as acute as when you are reading,
where you get a lot more of the inner dialogue of the protagonist.

JD, PR, JZ: To follow up on this: the images that appeared on TV during the Vietnam War like that of a real-live execution of Vietcong guerillas and the shocking image of the naked young girl Kim Phuc running down the village road after a napalm bomb attack transfixed the minds of viewers across the world to the horror of modern warfare. You show those types of pictures today, and it doesn't faze an audience conditioned to pictures and movies of violence. You can now watch episodes like this on any kind of serial TV show. For those of us who saw those images at the time, they were horrific because it was the first time that they were identified as real pictures of real people in real time.

JBE: You're right; it is horrific. I mean, the aftermath of My Lai massacres—it's almost unbearable. Again, I don't know how to account for all of it, and I don't want to be in the position of saying, "Oh, our young people today are all going to ruin." But there is something too that's been going on that—and I don't want to overuse this word—but that desensitizes and creates a barrier between yourself and the images, so it's much easier to look at them and not become profoundly disturbed in some way. I think that's true, and I suspect it's because the barriers keep coming down as to what can be represented. I remember when the first time—it was a Swedish film, I forget the name of it—the first time a woman had bared a breast in a film that was not a pornographic film, but a mainline film. I was thinking, "Oh my goodness; how can they do this?" And now you know that full-frontal nudity is nothing and it's done casually—not pornographically, but causally. You're not that sensitive anymore, it's not that big a deal anymore.

Some of these things should be big deals. How can one retain that sense? I mean these are not little things—these are major things, and they should be occasions for very deep moral reflection—in some cases, anguish—but certainly for thought. If we lose that capacity collectively, I'm not quite sure where we'll wind up. It's a very frightening thing. If you think of some of the crimes that are committed—even by very young people—that show a sense of real cruelty. I think they are particularly alarming, not just because they involve killing another child—most serial killers start out killing and torturing animals—but that in this particular child, the capacity to identify with another living being is absent altogether. This is just stuff I can do, and so I'll do it. Now those are anomalies; those are rare cases, but is there something more general that is inuring us to this level of violence that is shocking?

JD, PR, JZ: So recently, certainly you're aware, where another [student] walks into a school [with a gun]. They're not jihadists. But what they often do is they'll put headphones on and stay in some kind of disconnected bubble—the sovereign self, that's the word—so that you do not have this connection, you do not look beyond yourself, you do not have to look the victim in the face.

JBE: They're in their own world, and it's this sort of self-naming, self-defining, self-justifying world. And you don't have to engage.

JD, PR, JZ: So what is this bizarre thing that before you partially advertise this on a blog? So that what, you *are* in community with somebody?

JBE: I think there's this strangely inflated sense of self-importance. It's like, "I'm going to announce to the world my great plan of massacring my classmates." So I do my blog, and then I march out and undertake this. It's this notion that someone, somehow, out there people will recognize my audacity.

JD, PR, JZ: So it's the perverted hero.

JBE: Yes, a perverted hero. "I dare to do this." Like the kids that carry out the Columbine massacre, such as the leader of the two. It was this perverted sense of, as you say, heroism: "a lot of people talk the talk but they don't walk the walk. I dare to do this." And in his emails and in blogging, he really talks about being inspired by the Nazis and being drawn to Fascistic ideology and what he's trying to do and people on his list that he executed. It's really, again, this: "Look at me; look at what I dared to do. All the rest of you may talk: 'You know, I'd really like to murder this teacher.' But you'd never dare to do it; but I do, and I will."

JD, PR, JZ: Let's turn to a question about Bonhoeffer. The German theologian Dietrich Bonhoeffer frequently comes up in your writings. In *Who are We?*, for example, you compare his reading of the fall with John Paul's theological anthropology. In your Gifford Lectures Bonhoeffer features, beside Camus, as an example of an incarnational thinker. Why are you drawn to Bonhoeffer (if that's a good way of putting it)? For what reason(s) do you think he is an important thinker for current debates in ethics and politics?

JBE: Well, I was initially drawn to Bonhoeffer because of his heroic life and sacrifice, and I read the truncated version of *Letters and Papers from Prison* that was originally published in the States. And then I got the even longer version. So I was drawn to that. And coming from a German background myself, there was this question in my mind about what had happened in Germany in World War II and especially in the capitulation of the state Lutheran Church to Nazi ideology. Here was this man who was a thoroughgoing Lutheran, who helped to set up the Confessing Church and departs, in this very dangerous situation, from the official stance of the German Christians, and so forth. So that's what I was drawn to—an example of a life more than anything else. From that point, I started to read the more dense theological texts—just on my own because I don't have an official theological training.

I remember working through *Act and Being,* which is not that easy at all—you can't just go through it once; you have to go back. And then, of course, the *Ethics.* And then I started reading some of the other works like *Creation and Fall* and *Life Together*, and so forth. I think part of what Bonhoeffer represents is the capacity to work within a tradition and to explore its resources and to come up with creative possibilities within that tradition. He never abandons Luther. He never says, "I am an anti-Lutheran." No, he says, "this is what Luther really is all about." So that's definitely interesting. You don't have to [abandon tradition] in the process of engagement or rethinking things. The stance of my generation in the United States [was] the stance of "abandon this and abandon that" or "trash this and trash that." No, there is another way; there is this process of critical engagement that is possible within a complex tradition. So it struck me that Bonhoeffer represented that. And then also the ecumenical encounters, especially what he was learning from Catholicism—things about community and ecclesiology are interesting. And I also—you're going to laugh at this—I had fantasies in my mind that I had some kind of connection with him because Eberhard Bethge was his best friend and "Bethke" is my family name. Before I got to know Eberhard Bethge, I asked him about this. People kept asking if we were related. I get letters from Germany where the "k" becomes a "g" because my family had changed the name to a "k" when they immigrated to the States. Anyway, I asked Eberhard about this, and he said that we could possibly be related because my father's people came from the same area that his family was from. But I've never explored it beyond that. So I have this sense that I have this personal connection—partially with the name, but also a kind of strange intimacy that I imagined.

So Bonhoeffer became sort of inescapable. When figures start to show up in your dreams, which he does, and you begin having conversations with them, you begin to think that they may have become pretty important. I also think about the grappling that Bonhoeffer was doing with the question of nature. He was saying, "Protestants abandoned this. There are lots of Catholic moral theologians who talk about nature and natural law and body questions. We've got to start doing this, see what's there, what we're supposed to do with the notion of nature and natural." And he didn't get to do very much because of the way his life ended. But he was starting off in this promising direction. So I was drawn to those concepts, as well. I think his amazing essay *On the State* has been insufficiently discussed—the nature of the State and the government, and I think there is more to do in that area with him.

JD, PR, JZ: May we follow up on Bonhoeffer's notion of nature: you have mentioned that you're pursuing a somewhat determined meaning of the self that developed according to our human nature. Yet how we interpret human nature is never a view from nowhere; so we were wondering what, if any, are your presuppositions for talking about "human nature." As a theologian, Bonhoeffer, of course, would define that christologically. So what would you say to someone who says, "You're talking about common reason and human nature, but you're loading it with a theologically-colored notion of what nature is."

JBE: Well, I think you could begin by exploring what common ground there might be before you start to bring the Christological context in about our human nature. It strikes me that if you're going to admit that we can still talk that way—that there is some "there" there—that we're not just the products of some kind of social construction, then you would have to start with certain very fundamental things about human finiteness, about finitude, about our embodiment, the fact that we are in the world in a particular way as creatures of a particular kind. And I think you could get pretty far, working on that level in the presence of people who do not look at nature through the lens of Christology at all. I think for the purpose of the physical life, not for the purpose of theology or philosophy, but for the purpose of political life, that there is enough that could be shared there that it would help to provide a sort of basis for a concept of human dignity. We are creatures such that certain things shouldn't be done to us by the more powerful. And it would also ground them—not just what shouldn't be done to us, but what should—by way of what Bonhoeffer says in certain areas of life it helps to think about, about the taking of license and what should be provided for people or offered to people. The fact that because of our bodiliness, it is in our natures to be creatures of a certain kind. So I think there, in a political sense, if you could get enough agreement there, you could avoid the charge that when you say "human nature" that it is Christologically-loaded, that it has no bearings, that I have nothing to say for anybody who isn't a Christian. I think we don't want to do that work most of the time.

JD, PR, JZ: This veers away from the topic of Bonhoeffer, but we would like to follow up on the question of human nature to ask a more specific question on gender and human nature. Do you think there are essential differences between men and women in the way that we understand it or is there a single human nature and yet, only the contingencies and vicissitudes of history and biology can be understood as male and female?

JBE: Well, I think it's both. I think there is a common human nature—that we share more things than we differ in. But maleness and femaleness are not just arbitrary lines that have been drawn, but in fact express something fundamental about the two kinds of human beings. Of course there are anomalous cases where a person might physically share the characteristics of another sex, but people who pay attention to biology and physiology to know that there are significant differences between men and women in many ways. The brains are different in interesting ways. You know, this has now been demonstrated beyond any doubt, so you know the question is what do we do with that, with those differences? How do we imagine social forms based on these distinctions? I think that we understand males and females in relation to a shared human nature, but at the same time, there is some integrity to notion of maleness and femaleness. And then again, you argue that these differences become the basis for insidious comparisons that we're to disparage one sex in relation to the other. I think that's been the issue historically. The radical feminists in the 1970s got completely wrong when they argued that the problem is male/female itself, and that just by the virtue of being female you are oppressed by definition before you talk about anything in the social order. Just being female oppresses you. So you're kind of ontologically "cheated," so to speak, by being born into the world as a female. And I can never figure out why that was the feminist position. That seems to be only resentment.

JD, PR, JZ: Could we back up a bit? Would you call yourself a political feminist? Why or why not?

JBE: Well, I've become more and more wary about applying labels onto myself, but certainly to the extent that feminism has to do with the status and dignity of women, I would say, "Yes, I am." And that's the way I like to think of feminism, not as an all-encompassing ideology which has answers for every single question in the world, but as a concern with what's happening with women in different societies. To that extent, when I think about, for example, in Afghanistan with the Taliban, one of the first things I think about is what's happening to women: the sort of systematic abuse that was meted out against women. If one's thought tends in that direction, I think that probably makes you a feminist of some kind, when those are the big questions that come into your mind. But it's become such a hopeless discussion, in many ways, this discussion about feminism, because it's turned the state of it into a checklist of the things that you agree to, including abortion-on-demand, and so on, and I'm not for that. So, it's an almost impossible discussion, at this point. But if it's the way I've elaborated it to you, I'd be happy to have "feminist" attached to my name.

JD, PR, JZ: Turning now to your relationship with and your thinking about similarities and differences in your perspective and writings from that of Charles Taylor. There are many comparisons that can be drawn and have been drawn between your concerns about the person and authentic self-hood and those of Charles Taylor. Yet there are also profound differences. Could you elaborate on some of the key similarities that you share with Taylor and perhaps where you mark your differences?

JBE: That is a very interesting question. I really haven't explored that in any systematic way. I think there is probably still a way that I would say that Taylor's view of selfhood still often seems to me somewhat cerebral and rarified, and mine is a little more down-to-earth, sort of very, very basic stuff, you know, about what happens to the body of infant as it enters the world and what kind of world it is. Is it a welcoming world? Is it a world that brings love and care? Is it a world that's full of menace and dangerous and cruel? So I'm constantly drawn back to this very basic thing, and I think that his grand view in many ways is essentially a self-reflective self. That the self can ruminate almost endlessly on who the self is, and I don't even agree with that. But I think that my points of emphasis are perhaps a bit homier and a bit more down-to-earth.

From my Protestant background, I would certainly say that I would bring some dimension to discussions of selfhood which you don't find in Taylor. Although, he does acknowledge that one of the achievements that resulted from the Protestant Reformation was affirmation of ordinary life, where the distinction between vocation, the spiritual and non-spiritual vocation, that the distance is hazy. That's an important thing to mark. I think I would elaborate more on that—what is involved in that ordinary life—to focus more on that and make it ever more concrete. And I think I do a bit more of that than he does, to be honest. I think also that he finds some of the markers of selfhood in works of art and music and so forth. Again, I don't disagree—it's terribly important—but I also look at some very down to earth stuff about the transformation of certain technologies that altered forever people's relationship with the land, different views of time that emerged with the coming of the Industrial Revolution, where people's sense of what it means to locate themselves temporally altered dramatically. So I think there are just some different emphases that we regard there. I haven't done this systemically at all. I'm glad that you brought that up.

JD, PR, JZ: One of the criticisms that's been made of Taylor is that his self is really a rational self in the Kantian sense. And it strikes me that in that sense, it is almost a sovereign self.

JBE: Yes, I think the Kantian self is a sovereign self.

JD, PR, JZ: And then on the other hand, your talk seems to be more focused around those who have vulnerabilities, and therefore we require community in order to be whole.

JBE: Yes, I think that's a fair enough observation. But I don't think that Taylor is a Kantian. I do think he's more of a Hegelian than a Kantian. But I do think there is a kind of enshrining of intellect that is very much a part of that, although he's very aware of these other questions. But he's a philosopher, and philosophers focus on philosophers, for the most part. And, of course, he does it brilliantly. But I would not interpret him as Kantian; I think what he really highlights so much in his view of the self is the capacity for rational self-critique and thought. And I have already explained where my empathies start in slightly different places.

JD, PR, JZ: Moving now to some of the questions that surround democracy and sovereignty, we wonder if that might begin to frame some of the questions around religion and civil society. We're interested in pursuing this question. In *Democracy on Trial*, you refer to the inspiring story of *las madres*, the Mothers of the Disappeared, in Argentina, as having "jolted me out of my own complacency about rights and public freedom." You write: "Human rights was, for them, a way to express the timeless immunities of persons from the depredations of their governments rather than as a vehicle for entitlements, as we Americans more and more see things" (134). Elsewhere in the same book, you criticize the increased "translation of *wants* into *rights*" (16). Has anything in the years since your concerns were written in *Democracy on Trial* given you greater hope for the future of responsible rights talk?

JBE: The simple answer is no. Let me explain a little bit by what I meant about being jolted out of complacency. There was a core group of people who were cultural critics who were very critical of rights and rights talk. And I had sort of joined the chorus on that. I think that's very easy to do when you're a member of a society where rights are simply assumed and where you take it for granted. This experience really alerted me to the fact that human rights is sometimes the only weapon that people have in these terrible situations to say, "We're human beings too. We have rights, and they've been violated in the most egregious way." I promised myself I'd never talk casually about rights ever again, and after that encounter, I have tried to keep that promise.

At the same time, I think it's important to worry about the trivialization of rights, where people have a long shopping list of rights, from trivial stuff to something fundamental like not being hauled out of your house in the middle of the night and "disappeared," never to be seen again. How do you preserve

the power and solemnity of rights in that fundamental sense, speaking directly to the dignity of the person from rights as, and again I'm expressing my
preference as the political scientist might say, my wants at any given point in
time. As far as I can see, that dynamic, that translation of wanting the rights
is still going on in Western societies. So it's almost become a right not ever
to be criticized, not to have anyone ever say anything that makes you upset or
makes you feel uncomfortable and so forth. I think part of being an adult in a
social world is that the world isn't cut to your measure, and people are going
to have profound disagreements with you. There are going to be plenty of
folks who say things to you that you find troubling. Am I to be positive and
encased in a little bubble and never have to deal with that? And then somehow address this in the language of rights? I think that's a terrible problem
for us in modern liberal democracies and I think it makes it difficult for us to
really respond with the appropriate sense of shock and horror when there are
these situations where these rights have been violated in the most horrific
possible way. It is their absent fundamental rights that make some of the
things that we whine about look pretty petty.

JD, PR, JZ: So is the discussion surrounding human rights a useful but
ultimately insufficient way of understanding the problem of human dignity?

JBE: I think that's right, and I'm not sure exactly if you do the kind of work I
do, where one goes, other than constantly talk about the issue and remind
people that there is an issue here and to spread about the kind of loose talk
about rights. Let me give you an example of that. I think we talked about it
before in *Who Are We?*, about the possibility of human cloning: when that
first hit the news, immediately this Harvard Law professor rushes into print
with an article about how we should not violate the rights of clonees. "Imagine future clonees and what rights they might have. How can we violate
their rights by saying that people couldn't clone themselves: it would prevent
a clonee from coming into existence." So somehow I have violated the rights
of prospective clones. And this is the big human rights guy at Harvard named
Laurence Tribe. This is just crazy talk, where you're abstractly attaching
rights to a thing that doesn't yet exist, whose rights would be violated if you
said you couldn't clone. And you attach that to things that people are saying
about Iran too—what's happening to the protesters, against Ahmadinejad,
and the other trouble spots in the globe, which is mostly sub-Saharan Africa,
unfortunately. What's happening with people and their rights and there's
something quite disturbing about that disconnect.

JD, PR, JZ: Are you familiar with George Grant?

JBE: He was a Canadian political philosopher.

JD, PR, JZ: Yes, and a critic of the Rawlsian version of rights. Do you accept that Rawlsian Liberalism finds its logical conclusion in a space of political and moral relativism which is concretized in the right to abortion on demand? Where does the relativism associated with contractual liberalism lead us?

JBE: I'm not sure that I would use the language of moral relativism in criticizing Rawlsian liberalism. It might just factor into something like that. I don't think that Rawls finds himself at all as the moral relativist

JD, PR, JZ: Agreed.

JBE: And he believes that he has in some ways a profoundly moral vision of justice. But nonetheless, there is something about the way the terms of his contract gets developed and set up when you disarticulate the procedural dimensions of the policy from the constitution from any grappling with question of the good. That opens the door to all kinds of possibilities, including abortion on demand. Which if you counter it as a kind of procedural right, if you will, then you're accused from the Rawlsian position of speaking from a comprehensive view of the good. It's somehow incompatible with the procedural terms that sustain the view of democracy at the time. I think that critics of both Rawls and abortion on demand have encountered that kind of response from the Rawlsians. And I'm not sure moral relativism is the right way to speak of Rawls. But an incapacity to speak within the Rawlsian framework—it's very difficult to find the ground on which you would begin to criticize something like abortion on demand so long as the right regarding the procedures are set in place correctly as such that this determination about abortion was made. And there's nothing in Rawls that I can think of that suggests and articulates the limits to what I call self-sovereignty. I can't think of what that word would be, actually. So the Rawlsian is not surprised therefore that the prominent student of Rawls—I cannot think of a single one of them who would have raised questions about the abortion regime, for example, in the United States, which as you know is the most permissive in the entire Western world. There are more restrictions in other Western democracies.

JD, PR, JZ: Would you speak to your role as a public intellectual? In his book *Public Intellectuals: A Study of Decline*, Richard Posner writes: "Not all intellectuals are professors, even today, but most are. Today, then, the typical public intellectual is a safe specialist, which is not the type of person well suited to play the public intellectual's most distinctive, though not only role, that of critical commentator addressing a nonspecialist audience on matters of broad public concern. That's a niche role, perhaps little more than a walk-on part in the play of politics, culture, and society. And often the wrong things are criticized. But it is something, and something for which few modern academic intellectuals have the requisite perspective, temperament, character, and knowledge" (5). Our first question is, do you think the public intellectual is in decline? Secondly, do you think one way to solve this dilemma, if there is one, is to provide degrees in public intellectualism? And finally, can someone be trained to be a public intellectual?

JBE: I want to respond to the later questions first. That sounds to me kind of desperate to be trained as a public intellectual. It's not a technical thing; it's not something where there are certain steps to go through. It strikes me that the professional life is the responsible thing to do because the whole notion of the public intellectual as someone who is, in some sense, regarded by others as an intellectual who nevertheless engages the public. Not every day about every thing, but some days about some things. Because if you're serious about that engagement, you realize you are not universally competent. You cannot speak about every single question. I would be very loathe to engage complex economic issues, for example. And there are probably some public intellectuals who would be quite pleased to talk about some of these economic questions. I am in the position of reading one economist who can say "that makes sense" and another who completely disagrees and says, "that [other idea] makes sense," but I can't distinguish between some of these positions. Again, I lack the competence in that area. The notion that you can have a uni-competent public intellectual seems to be kind of an odd idea.

On the positive thing about decline: I'm not sure what Richard Posner's going on about. I think it depends a little bit on what the point of reference is. And certainly, Posner's right if there are fewer non-specialist intellectuals running around than there were perhaps in the 1920s, or at other points in our history in the United States, and that most intellectual life takes place—for better or worse—within the academy. But I'm not sure this is a story of decline, but a story of a change in the intellectual environment. And moving in the direction of actually providing ever-greater access to higher education for all kinds people, who at one point may have been really smart folks who read the newspaper at some café and pronounced something, and now they can actually get a PhD and get a job in the academy, which is probably what they would have liked to have done earlier, but the doors were slammed shut to them for one reason or another. I made the quip at one point that there's a danger that a public intellectual can become more and more public, and less and less intellectual. He's out there all the time pronouncing, but he doesn't go back and renew his intellectual resources and spend some time in contemplation. I think that the intellectual should be someone who has a foot in the deep end of both contemplation and the public realm, as Arendt might say. You've got to achieve some balance. I think to become a professional public intellectual, that balance is lost altogether. And it becomes more of a technical thing. Like how do I break into print? Or should I get an agent?

JD, PR, JZ: Following up on that: in Canada in particular, but also in the United States to some degree, the professional journalist seems to have taken on this role because they're reporting anyway and they're always being asked to comment on this, rather than having people from the academy. TV hosts, newspaper editors are afraid that people from the academy won't be understandable.

JBE: I think there is a kind of layer of innate opinion occupied by journalists, who have developed some intellectual preoccupation. They're not just reporters; they're folks that are in between being a reporter and an academic specialist. I do think that with the coming of cable and its triumph that more and more of those people are springing up like mushrooms overnight. And I think that's inviting a kind of decrease in the need to call upon academics to make certain kinds of pronouncements. Because you have some who are really smart—many of them are, they're really smart—and some of them have degrees that they've earned as journalists, not to blight the academy. And they're available, and you don't have to tell them to look at the camera. If you bring in someone from the academy, you don't know if they're going to freeze in the light. But here you get someone who knows how to do it and is really smart. And I think it's a whole lot easier than having to bring in a bunch of academics. And to watch them sort of stammer because they become afraid when the camera goes on. So I don't know. I don't have any sort of systematic study whether there are fewer academics being called upon to make pronouncements outside of university campuses than ten or twenty years ago, but I suspect so because of the growth of all these different kinds of markets and target audiences. There are all these different kinds of audiences and all the different kinds of experts from these different groups that you can find to speak on these different issues. And I think that tends to leave a kind of academic generalist, a public intellectual in a kind of strange no-man's or no-woman's land, where people aren't quite sure what they need to do.

It's become increasingly difficult for me because if you're heterodox, if you can't be counted upon to take the hard or direct position on it—I think there are journals who, at one point, have closed their doors. Maybe I disagreed with them on something or one of the editors had an attitude about something. And then your other possibility is to say, "Well, but I don't agree with their editorial position and yet they have lots of good articles." And I think that over time you think, "Well, should I start writing for the *Weekly Standard*?" It's a really good journal, actually. They have some really good writers. But you're immediately a neo-conservative if you write for them—and a lot of people call me that as it is, but I don't think I am to that extent. But that would be a far more welcoming place than the *New Republic*, where I wrote things for a number of years, and that paper is shut to me now. So I suppose because I'm not gung-ho on gay marriage—I guess it's become one of their big issues. I'm not sure. When people start not taking your phone calls, you know what's going on.

JD, PR, JZ: The trend toward professionalization is not unique to the media but is ever more becoming an issue for higher education. Given your interest in selfhood and its formation through institutions, are you concerned about the universities' trend toward pragmatism? As a public intellectual concerned with the fate of our culture and its ability to foster human ways of being, what vision would you uphold for the university and what course of action would you suggest to students, faculty, and university administrators for accomplishing this vision in light of the continuing trend toward pragmatism?

JBE: It has been for a long time, yes. Well, I teach at a university, as you know, where the core curriculum has never been abandoned—at the University of Chicago. It's been tough because the demands were considerable and people's sensibilities and such, but it's still there. You have a core that no student can escape. You *have* to do some work in philosophy; you *have* to do some work in the basic sciences, some basic work in literature. So the students share a common culture when they come to Chicago, or they end up sharing a common culture. And it gives them a chance to have discussions in their dorms and such, because they're reading many of the same texts. And these are your basic, classic works: Plato, Aristotle and on down—if you're thinking of traditional Western philosophy and Western political philosophy. And that's one thing that I would certainly use. And I could go on and say this is what you should use. There should be something like a core curriculum, and it should include many of the basic, fundamental great works. The idea that we're somehow preparing students for the world by denying them an education in these texts, without making them aware of them—I know some divinity schools where you have to have read certain, in some cases, pretty wild theologians, but you can get out of there without having read Augustine or Aquinas or Luther or Calvin—that doesn't make any sense whatsoever. So you've got to grapple with some of these works—it doesn't mean that you have to like them or even agree with them—in order to understand what your options are in all positions. I think we really cheat them out of something when we think we're sparing them, enlightening them, all of that nonsense. We just wind up making them stupid because they don't know their audience or have any sense of where they, as children of the West, have come from, and what the West historically has held. There is no substitute for doing that in the classes. I mean, the classes that are being taught, that's the heart of it.

What do we offer? What do we think is so important that every student has to partake in it—it's that important. It's not just a smorgasbord, where you can do the construction of basket weaving in Samoa. It's not like that. You know, I'm thinking about some of the curricular debates in the Middle Ages. They had these debates too, about what students should be learning and what the curriculum should be. And you already have the tension emerging between the more technical/scientific and the more humanistic. So, I suspect that's the tension that's there. In the university, we should seek to embody that tension, not avoid it. This is especially true in the ways the different areas of emphasis can learn from one another. That way we don't have the C. P. Snow phenomenon of one hundred years ago saying there are two fundamental cultures and we can't speak to one another. It doesn't work in terms of rational versus humanistic. How do we bring them together in a kind of mutual dialogue?

JD, PR, JZ: Yet even this dialogue has to have a goal. Postmodern criticism has pretty much destroyed former humanistic aspirations to universal knowledge, but now we are stranded without any universals, without any overall goal; especially liberal arts universities sought to educate toward wisdom, moral formation, and the common good, but we have lost a shared notion of the common good, have we not? What does this mean for university education?

JBE: We have lost that. I think we've completely lost that. Alasdair MacIntyre said something along these lines in his discussion on universities. And one of the arguments that Alasdair has been making is that unless the university has some understanding of the good that is to be attained by a student in spending four years here, the upshot will be general incoherence. I think that's too strong, but it makes a point. His view is that if you don't have some sort of sense of the good, and you're taking all these courses that it's pretty much up to you, that what students will do is reflect the preoccupation of the zeitgeist, and they will tend toward the directions of the most profitable and the most useful in a pragmatic sense, including what we know of as success. The upshot will be that they will lose most of what we know of as the humanities because they revert to what society most values at that point in time. So that gives us the sense that, I think Alasdair MacIntyre would agree with me, that the universities need to become Thomistic. But he does suggest universities need to do more thinking than they do about "What do we represent here? What are we trying to do here? What are we going to offer here? They should also consider seriously their role in the ongoing moral formation of young people. You know, an eighteen-year-old is still pretty young. When I was eighteen years old, I didn't think I was. But you realize later you were. And there is still a lot that's still going to be shaped and formed and learned, and professors are playing a role in that. And that's the kind of responsibility. The question is how do you understand that role? Is it to shock the hell out of them? To disabuse them of everything they've learned? Is it to begin with them where they are and help them to explore the responsibilities perhaps they've never considered before, but to never do that in a way that assaults them, that you can guide them through some of the great celebrations of the human spirit and of the human good and so forth that we have available to us as part of our heritage? Is that what this is about? Or do we think we just have to throw to them a lot of technical knowledge about being good professionals, good XYZ? I don't think those kind of questions go on for the most part.

JD, PR, JZ: Let's shift to the question about sovereignty. You're arguing from within a Western Christian context. How does this narrative from a realist or participatory ontology work in a different context, such as the Islamic Shari'a tradition, Eastern and Hindu notions of law?

JBE: Well, I'm not exactly sure. I think that I know something about the Islamic Shari'a tradition, given that I've been studying it academically for about a decade and given some of the discussions that I'm a part of. And there I would say that one way to find out how this works would be to think about the ways in which one might structure certain kinds of engagement, such that certain perspicuous contrasts might emerge. And one could get a clear sense of that. I have a friend who, for about three years, was asked to be a provost in a newly emerging university in Iraq where the students are clamoring for Western humanist texts and work. That's what they want to study. They want to study the stuff that was utterly forbidden to them and learn more about that. The same fellow at that time, in one of the Emirates—I forget which one—teaching students St. Augustine and so forth. They find him really interesting. That's a little jarring but still you have these key kinds of engagement. There I would say there's no substitute for trying to offer what one has to offer and to see how others respond. The question would be the context in which that might happen.

JD, PR, JZ: It suggests that other traditions may be going through the same process, in their own idiom, dealing with nominalism and the issues surrounding it.

JBE: I have to believe there's probably something to that. But I don't want to overstate it because it does strike me that there's something about the Western Christian tradition that's so extraordinarily self-reflective from the beginning. You've got Augustine saying "Well, how do I know that I exist? I know that I exist because I can ask questions. I can doubt," already anticipating the Cartesian, Kantian flow—you know, "I doubt, therefore, I am." That strikes me as probably unique in a certain respect. It spurred along centuries this kind of complex give and take within a single tradition. And that's why we have some different variations of it, really, which we perhaps don't see in some of these other traditions. But I don't want to speak out of turn because I just don't know enough to know for sure. But I do think that in every tradition, there is a process—there have to be questions from within it; there have to be people to respond to those questions, and people have to react to that response. I think then the question is what is built on that: Is this process ever going to end at some point? Is the door slammed shut and you say that's it? Or is there an ongoing openness to continued engagement? And there, again, I don't know enough to know what these other resources would be within some of these other traditions.

JD, PR, JZ: What is the role of religion for the development of these resources? Within the Western tradition, for example, do you think that the concept of the incarnation is important in their development? You have called Camus an incarnational thinker. Charles Taylor talks about the excarnation or disembedding of Western self and thought from transcendent horizons, a concept you also use. Does not the idea of incarnation have something to do with the way Western thinkers conceive of reason and its relation to faith? Could the Western ability for self-criticism you just mentioned possibly depend on this notion of the Incarnation, which other religions may not have? Have you given this any thought?

JBE: I haven't given it any systematic thought. It certainly has crossed my mind because when you reflect on what is it about the West as such that these kinds of discussions have occurred at a very high level. This struck me when I was working on the Gifford lectures, the extraordinary complexities of these discussions. It's humbling, really. The level on which they're taking place, and you realize not every tradition yields something like this. So what is it about Western Christianity that did? It strikes me that it does take me back to the moment of Incarnation, the breaking through of the divine—the unveiling of God into history—which gives history itself a shimmering importance. In a way in the light and dark of creation, you can see the magnification, the importance of this world through all of this. And I think that kind of helped spur these kinds of reflections over time, precisely because of the heavy burden put on human beings because they're created in God's image and in fact because the *imago dei* is profoundly reaffirmed with the Incarnation. The notion of the being of a certain import is essential to all of this. Can you have that without that moment of Incarnation? That's a question mark. I just don't know. I know other traditions—like the Islamic tradition of jurisprudence—some of those traditions went dry at some point. Again, there is tremendous complexity and lots of interesting discussions.

JD, PR, JZ: A related concept of incarnation is the idea that just as God has revealed himself within a concrete person, language and history, so all human knowledge and truth is mediated. For Christianity and the West this view has made a fundamental hermeneutic difference. In contrast to Islamic tradition, for example, the biblical text is not literally God's revelation, but its mediation through text. Therefore translation of the biblical text, in contrast to the Koran, is not viewed as an inherently imperfect rendition of God's revelation. Luther spoke in this context of a Word behind the letter of scripture. Hence mediation and interpretation are intrinsically part of Western religious discourse. Do you think this concept of mediation makes a cultural difference?

JBE: Yes, in Christianity there's a point of mediation. From what I know, I would say that's right. The issue would be what does that cash out as? What is the fallout from that? What are the implications of that? And to that I'd have to say that I haven't thought systematically. You and I were talking about this earlier, and I said it's certainly not simply an accident that human rights and democracy have emerged in the West. It has to be tied to Christianity in some fundamental way. One of the ways you can evaluate traditions, is what kind of institutions do they yield? What's the nature of those institutions? Do those institutions enhance or diminish human dignity and human possibility. Those are the kind of questions one needs to bring to tradition, it seems to me. Certainly if you are a woman, these questions often take on an added poignancy or force because, certainly by contrast to many alternatives, in the Christian West, women have moved up and in an extraordinary way. People with education could run separate institutions during the Middle Ages, wrote under their own names, could be critics of Popes, so on and so forth. Then you read reports of visitors from the Islamic world are horrified by women doing these kinds of things, like women sitting at a table with men and eating at the same time. So if you're a woman, you take note of those kinds of things too and what happened. Even the stuff you know from our history about the vote and suffrage—still, there's a big difference, when you think about women and their roles, their status, and their significance. That's all part of comparing traditions for me.

JD, PR, JZ: One of the questions we had while reading *Sovereignty* is a reflection upon what you say in *Who are We?* One of the hallmarks of both fascist and communist totalitarianism however was the subordination of the person and the state to a monistic notion of self in relation to others. I wonder if we can relate that back to your ideas on self-in-relation. What relieves our mutual dependencies from becoming a sort of tyranny just as narrow as extreme state or self sovereignty?

JBE: That's a very good question. I would have to say more, and I do say some stuff in the book that I couldn't bring in the first lecture last night, about the rejection of self-sovereignty. The rejection of self-sovereignty doesn't mean self-abnegation. It doesn't mean that the self is relinquished and folds itself into a system of dependency such that there's no self that can be carved out of that, you sort of subsume yourself to the group and the group defines you altogether. There I think that what spares my view from going in that direction, sort of the unChristian direction of the totalistic ideology, is precisely that notion of the self-respecting self—the self that isn't simply a tool in the hands of the others but has a sense of her own dignity and, we would say in our language now, understands her own rights, but is well-aware of the intrinsic sociality of human being as such. In fact to go in Hannah Arendt's direction—some of her analysis is very powerful. One of the hallmarks of totalitarianism was precisely to separate persons from community, to break them down into isolates, to destroy family, to destroy subsidiary institutions, to redefine them all in monistic direction, and then to provide an alternate identity to people through what Arendt calls the "iron band of terror" wrapping around them. The best protection against that is precisely the bond of mutuality—a robust engagement of one person with another, and maintaining all these other kinds of institutions so that they're not so easily suborned and overtaken by some monistic or totalistic project.

JD, PR, JZ: We are also interested in how nominalism engages in your understanding of just war theory. The question we have is: What does an unreasoned nominalist state mean for just war theory? Can the nominalist state engage in just war articulated outside the boundaries of the state? And to provide you with an embodied example: assuming World War II was a just war, did the Soviet Union conduct a just war if it was a nominalist state?

JBE: Let's take that last question first. That's a very interesting question because the way that it's usually analyzed is that yes, World War II was a just war and the Soviet Union was fighting against Hitler, which was an important thing to do, so on the *jus ad bellum,* the occasion for war, yes, it was justified. But where you get into trouble with the Soviet Union was how they fought the war in many instances. There was the brutal treatment of

German prisoners of war. The Soviet army was the raping army, systematically raping many of the women. In terms of raping women, the stories are
absolutely horrific, almost unbearable on the part of the Soviets. The massacre of Katyn, all of these things committed by the Soviets. So an unjust war
in that sense was perpetrated by the Soviet army.

You're suggesting something beyond that. That is, if you're a nominalist
state defined entirely by will, could they ever engage in a just or justified war
as such? It's hard to imagine the Hitlerian regime engaging in a just war; it's
hard to imagine the Stalinist regime doing the same thing, given the particularly perverse nature that their politics of willfulness took. Prior to World
War II, the Soviets were fervently preaching world conquest under the ban-
ner of the triumph of Communism. That was their justification for how they
were going to crush people here, there, everywhere. So you hear Churchill
saying I would make an alliance with the devil himself to fight Herr Hitler.
Well and good, but the aftermath of those critical alliances is often deeply
troubling and frantic, and I think we found that out with World War II. So to
the extent that you have a state that's overtaken by the sort of totalizing
ideology which defines all it's enterprises by its exercise of the imposition of
will over others, then I don't see how criteria for just war would be in play in
those kind of circumstances. The kind of criteria for justifiability would not
be criteria they would take seriously at all. It would just become an irritating
blemish they want to get out of the way.

JD, PR, JZ: Let's move onto another nominalism question. In the Gifford
lectures, you mention nominalism as a late medieval theological development that changes views of the self and the influence of that. As you well
know, this is a story you get a lot in predominantly Catholic accounts on how
we get to modernity. Louis Dupre has called this our particular Western
"Passage to modernity." We would like to hear more, how definitive you
think this is. Is there a certain mentality or cultural attitude that comes about
through nominalism? Briefly outline why you think it's so important. If
that's what we have, do we need religion or theology to change it back? How
do we change this attitude which has led to univocity and voluntarism?

JBE: There, I think that the one point we would have to make is that the
discernible shift is never entirely total. It's not as if previous understandings
just disappear—Thomist realism, if you will, and the understanding of the
nature of the human in a pure Trinitarian lens. None of that goes away. You
have a different emphasis that emerges. And yet, at the same time, you have
certain institutions they have set up, including some political institutions, that
represent not so much the triumph of nominalism as a kind of modern (in
their own context) version of that older tradition. I would say the Constitu-

tion of the United States is an example of that where one of your major intellectual sources is Locke, and Locke is defecting from the system that Hobbes is savaging. Hobbes the great nominalist is assaulting and Locke is still kind of in that old-fashioned natural law, higher law tradition. This is essential in helping to form the basis for certain institutions, not just in Great Britain, but also certainly in the United States.

So the turn is never complete. The nominalist temptation is very strong and powerful, and really did triumph in some places, and is carried in a variety of modalities, but there always seems to be an ongoing engagement or tends to be. When there's a thoroughgoing triumph of the will, and people see the fruits of that, they recoil from it and then start to look for alternatives to that. I certainly don't want to saddle William of Ockham with Nazism or anything like that, but you can certainly trace that nominalist strand and see how that can lead to more and more of certain behaviors when the constraints fall away and lead to this unadulterated view of a certain vision of self that is to triumph—this purely voluntaristic self.

Now, I see more of that nominalistic notion of self creeping certainly into the United States in the last four decades. I think it tends to come not quite so much as a militant way, but as expressive individualism. I talk about it as soft self-sovereignty in my book. It's this idea that "I want to be me." It's a kind of happy-go-lucky-ism, but in its own way it's a sort of nominalist strand in that there are no strong values that I want to affirm because they'll limit me in some way or they'll be limiting to other people. So it's not so much I'm going to go crush them, as "Nobody has a claim on me; I'm happy, free, doing my own thing." So it can go off in a number of directions. And I do think when I was working on that, by the time I got toward the end of discussions of the self in the lectures, I thought that there was a lot more to say about this, but I guess this was going to have to suffice for now. I will probably have to go back and rethink some of this at some point in time and develop more clearly distinctions in strong and soft versions of sovereignty to the extent that people are interested in it. It struck me there's some kind of strain in my own argument that I hadn't quite developed as of yet, or as I would liked to have done. But as I said, at some future point I'd like to come back to it.

JD, PR, JZ: In 2002, you were a participant in a conference "Pluralism, Religion and Public Policy" at McGill University. In addition to giving a paper entitled: "Persons, Politics and a Catholic Understanding of Human Rights," you also were the respondent to The Rt. Hon. Beverley McLachlin, chief justice of the Canadian Supreme Court. We refer you to the substance of her argument that the rule of law in Canada is a totalizing system within which freedom of religion was allowed for citizens and your response to that was critical. To quote only a short part of your response: "Law is enjoined to recognize the space that faith occupies. A good bit of the history of the West is a story of the ongoing struggle over what we now routinely call church and state, and their respective purviews." Would you elaborate a bit more on that?

JBE: Well, that's a very strange opinion because she is very bold in her argumentation. She started off by making it clear that everything is to be evaluated from the point of view of the state. So, how much freedom of religious expression can the state permit or allow? So there was this privileging the state right off the bat in her comments, and I thought that was interesting—because it puts religion in the point of view as being a kind of supplicant at every point. *"Please please let us have more freedom!"* And the reason she does see things that way is she saw the state and any sort of religious thing as being in necessary competition with one another because they're two totally comprehensive worldviews and so forth. I believe in my remarks I mentioned Jesus and the coin—Caesar's coin. You know, "Render to Caesar what is Caesar's and render to God what is God's." She said at dinner later that she'd always found that completely incomprehensible. But [this passage] really does suggest that we're obliged to think about what's Caesar's and what's God's, and that Caesar is not always in the position of telling us what's God's. This totalizing drive that she saw struck me as a bit scary when it comes to matters of the state, because it suggests that the state's drive is to dominate over civil society, churches, and so on, but that the state can refrain from doing that, even though it's driven to do that, by again, saying, "how much can I and will I permit?"

JD, PR, JZ: William Cavanaugh makes the assertion that the state is inevitably going to be dominant towards civil society. Do you think that this is an inevitability?

JBE: I don't think that every state necessarily has that aspiration. One wants to distinguish between state and government in there also. If there's an appropriately modest view of government instead of *the* state as this big all-encompassing thing, I don't think government is driven in that direction. Modern statism is. But I think there are ways to soften that modern statism. In the United States, I think that because of the Constitution and all barriers that were set in place because of the Bill of Rights and because of the First Amendment of the Constitution, which built in both the non-establishment and free exercise of religion, you have that enshrined from the very beginning. And then you have that whole history of jurisprudence in the United States, carving out what that history of free exercise means, and it's a very robust understanding. If any representative of the American government made a statist claim that there's only so much religion that the state will permit, I think the cries of horror would be deafening. That's not the perspective that we approach this from. So I understand what Cavanaugh is talking about, and I think there is that potential addiction of power over the last couple of centuries on the part of the State. I think that's part of this angry debate in the states right now on health care. It is: how much is the state going to take over? That's really the heart of it. That's why people worry, and I think in many cases appropriately, that once you have state control of certain things, then they're going to get to define costs and benefits and to determine when to cut off medical assistance to the elderly. And we don't want to let the State do that. And I think that's where the heart of this debate comes in, although I don't think it has always been presented that way. So there's a wariness about the state in the United States and I think that that has really tamed that focus, that drive over time. At any rate, I think that my view of the role of the state is more in the tradition of subsidiarity: the state is there to serve rather than to dominate over institutions of civil society. The state is there as a kind of dialogic partner of the voice of the people and through them, their plural institutions. A kind civic totalism is so often the frame for the state's aspirations. That is something one really has to struggle against. So it struck me that Right Honourable Beverley McLachlin was representing that, rather than offering anyone a way to struggle against it. So that's quite a striking occasion for me. I had this sense that she was really finding my comments unintelligible. And I was finding her kind of scary. It was an interesting moment.

JD, PR, JZ: I wonder if we could conclude our conversation by going back to reflecting on your overall work. Did you have all these interests planned, is this a planned path of research or did events and occasions guide you in this development?

JBE: I think it's a little of both. I think I've been pushed and prodded by events more than anything. Freud joked at one point—Freud's another thinker for me by the way. You might not know it, but I have found him endlessly fascinating as someone who is grappling with how to generate a moral sensibility with the complete absence of a transcendent reference, but I digress. He quipped that if we're lucky, we have two or three really good ideas in a lifetime. And it occurred to me that that's probably true. If I look back on my work, there were certain preoccupations throughout the whole thing: the public/private distinction—how one works in that, the question of how we think about ourselves in relation to the world of which we're a part. And then the whole issue of force and violence: when is it ever justified? How does one orient oneself to this given that we don't know of any society anywhere that has ever existed without violence?

I'm going to co-teach a course in the spring at the University of Chicago with a colleague of mine from the medical school actually. He is a pathologist, but he has a PhD and is a Thomist. It's going to be about murder, that is, how murder is foul. And we're going to talk about the different angles in which people think about it: theologically, legally, sociologically, medically, and psychiatrically. So we're organizing the problem of how we think about something that is endemic to human culture and is horrible, but we tend not to think about it systematically. But I'm not quite sure where any of this came from, but I can't think of a time when I wasn't interested in context in which people were in visible danger, or who were in extreme moral situations; you know, the question of who were the heroes? Who were the villains and how that sorts itself out.

So I think that's where my work on just war emerged and in some other places such as the book on the aftermath of 9/11. If 9/11 hadn't happened, the book *Just War Against Terror* would have never been written—that was occasioned by the attacks. There are other works that have been occasioned by my dissatisfaction with the direction of where we're going in feminism. So it's my reaction against some of that. If directions had taken a certain different turn, there would have been other books I might have written. For me, it's not simply me sitting around having my own thoughts, but when you engage the world, there are thoughts that come to you. The world's great events are the direction your thinking takes. At the same time, I have a sense that there are certain things you want to do before you "shuffle off this mortal coil" and things you want to bring about.

For me it's also a wanting to express some depth of gratitude toward certain thinkers. I want to make sure that I'm paying sufficient tribute to thinkers that have been important to me. You know, I've talked about Augustine and Camus, so I want to make sure I do that—show an appropriate amount of gratitude to them in my work. I want to find ways to do that. So we'll see. There are some folks who think I should do some kind of memoir, and partly because there have been a lot of books by polio survivors recently since we're getting older and since this thing has been largely eradicated, so some reflections on that. I thought that would be an interesting thing to do. There are lots of very interesting questions that emerge when you're forced at a very young age to deal with issues of vulnerability, physical limits and of that sort and then how society responds to that. I've been thinking of something along those lines. I'm thinking about doing a book on film, because I'm a film fan and think about whether films can be a moral educator or not. We talked about how images can inure you to certain bad things, so how do we distinguish between films that are the occasion for moral reflection and thought rather than those that may quash our moral capacity? That's another direction I might go. So there's still quite a lot to do.

JD, PR, JZ: Thank you very much Jean for sharing of yourself with us.

II

Sovereignty through the Ages

Chapter Seven

Mars Bound: Limited War and Human Flourishing

Marc LiVecche

THE BISHOP OF HIPPO IN LONDON

In the Sainsbury Wing of England's National Gallery resides *Venus and Mars*, an early renaissance painting by Florentine master Sandro Botticelli, depicting the post-coital deific pair reclining opposite one another in an arboreal alcove and surrounded by a small fold of rather frolicsome satyrs. The work is generally taken to symbolize the platitude that love conquers war. The immediate presentation seems to bear this out: Venus, goddess of love, is clothed and awake, watching naked Mars, the war god, who is very much asleep, unarmed and unarmored, captive perhaps by the placid bonds of *la petite mort*. However, initial appearances aside, prolonged inspection leaves us unsatisfied. Discontent deepens upon learning a facsimile hung in the Oxford rooms of C. S. Lewis;[1] unusual given most walls in his office and home were apparently unadorned.[2] It can scarcely be believed that Lewis, unlikely to overlook simplistic aphorisms and self-confessedly unenthusiastic about paintings in general,[3] would include among the few for which he did care one so sentimental. Happily, there can be found in Lewis a pair of promising explanatory keys.

The first is located in a letter Lewis wrote in 1925 to the historian A. K. Hamilton Jenkin: "In a certain juncture of the planets," Lewis mused, "each planet may play the others' part." Turning back to Botticelli we see this suggestion has some purchase. Mars has lost much of the martial aspect. The satyrs have taken possession of his armor and his lance—euphemistically unmanning him—leaving him defenseless as he slumbers nearly completely exposed save for a strip of cloth draped with modest precision across his hips. Venus, however, appears to have assumed the martial character. We suddenly realize she may not be merely *watching* Mars but watching *over* him as well; she has acquired her lover's helm and lance, which thanks to the satyrs have now been visually repositioned so as to suggest *she* is wielding them. Truly, each does seem to play the other's part.

Yet the reversal is incomplete. Venus is still Venus—evidenced not simply by the sated repose of her lover and by her own continued physical beauty but by her beauty's presentation, particularly how it is delicately eroticized by her diaphanous gown, which not only teasingly hints at the sensuously comely form beneath but which Venus happens to be presently drawing up her leg—one can see the folds of garment just beginning to gather beneath her fingers as she pulls. Precisely what she has in mind is, of course, speculative, but the satyr near Mars's head appears about to wake him[4] by sounding a conch shell in his ear. Is Venus having him roused in order to continue the diversions of her divine purview? Mars, for his part, is still recognizably the war god: powerfully muscled, his strength remains at hand, however immediately latent—indeed, his very nakedness, while at one level suggesting vulnerability was, in the Renaissance imagination, a sign that he was unafraid of danger even *when* most vulnerable.[5] Mars retains, as well, possession of a portion of his armory as he rests on his sword and cuirass. The satyr behind him, try as it might, is unlikely to strip him of them.

To account for the lover's resilient self-possession we now turn to Lewis's second explanatory key. In a literary analysis, Lewis described how Renaissance depictions of inverted relationships in images of cosmic order were meant to convey mutual *reconciliation* rather than a triumph of one over the other.[6] The Romans alluded to this idea in the name of Venus and Mars's most noteworthy offspring, their daughter Concordia—the personification of harmony.[7] Venus and Mars—love and war—embrace and reform one another in mutual self-giving without either annihilating the other. Now *this* is something with which Lewis could truck.

It is also something upon which we can build a reflection of Jean Bethke Elshtain's view of war and the martial character. On this topic, Elshtain and Lewis both stood in the Augustinian stream of Christian realism. Among much else, the Augustinian realist does not judge the martial nature something to be overcome, recognizing instead that given the conditions of this world, martial power, including coercive justice, is a basic, even salutary, property of political life. However, because human beings are motivated both by love and kindness as well as selfishness and cruelty,[8] the use of force must be viewed with skepticism[9] and deployed within carefully prescribed constraints. This recognition is exemplified in the just war tradition, a way of reflecting on the necessity and limits of force that accounts for, and subsequently seeks to reform, the presence in human beings of "two different states of nature: the state of integral nature and the state of fallen nature,"[10] alternatively cast as original innocence and original sin. These twin anthropological realities issue in two kinds of competing freedoms: *cupiditas,* which enshrines a form of self-love and tends toward the domination of others,[11] and *caritas,* an orientation to the good and love of the neighbor, including a recognition of one's own interdependencies[12] and subsequent understanding that "dependence on others is not a diminution but an enrichment of self."[13] Insisting human beings are not limitlessly free,[14] Elshtain argued against overly voluntaristic construals[15] of freedom—essentially arbitrary willfulness refusing to recognize intrinsic constraints[16] —which, paired with *cupiditas,* fuels the estrangement, conflict, and tragedy that constantly feature in human relationships.[17] She supported instead the Augustinian notion of freedom as acts recognizing a limit undertaken in submission to something beyond the self[18] —namely, the character, requirements, and aspirations of divine love.

This then is the salient connection: Botticelli's *Venus and Mars* supports an Augustinian reading in which love *qualifies* but does not eradicate war. That the painting does so can only be because it is a product of a Europe that still remembered she was a child not only of the ancient Greek and Roman worlds but also of Judaism and Christianity,[19] a patrimony, Elshtain lamented, increasingly disclaimed. She observed, as did Lewis, that the just war unity of Venus and Mars is persistently divorced by those who see the combative side of human nature as pure, atavistic evil on the one side and, on the other, those who decry the insertion of love into power politics as immaterial sentimentality.[20] Grounded in Elshtain's Augustinian realism, this chapter argues the value of the just war inheritance as a support for human nature, its intended ends, and its attendant obligations—including meeting the terms and responsibilities of both love and justice.

I proceed by extending Elshtain's brief reflection early in *Sovereignty* on William of Ockham's nominalist view of human freedom. The pursuit of happiness—human flourishing—was, from the Greeks down to the medieval Scholastics, *the* primary moral question of every philosopher of note. With Ockham the connections between freedom, virtue, and happiness were severed.[21] Against this, I draw on Thomas Aquinas's view of freedom as excellence, which, *pace* Ockham, grounds freedom not internally in arbitrary will but in teleological flourishing—that is, human freedom is defined externally by the intended purpose of human being itself. I go on to consider how the just war tradition shapes men and women toward their flourishing, individually and collectively, by rousing the martial character within limits against injustice. But I start with something more preliminary. Elshtain limns the just war tradition as premised on a few basic assumptions, including the existence of universal moral dispositions, if not outright convictions.[22] To flesh this out, I explore moral realism through the *naïve* impression of evil—an untaught, innate human response against malevolence.

REPUGNANCE AS A CLUE TO THE MEANING
OF THE UNIVERSE

Elshtain was a moral realist. Like Augustine, she knew there is a *there* there: objective truths to be discovered, honored, and encoded.[23] But they also understood the present human condition includes epistemological uncertainty, for "a rupture has been effected between reality and our capacity to know that reality."[24] Yet evidence remains, among them human passions. From Augustine, Elshtain asserts that emotions are a mode of thought, *embodied* thought, and that we must remain cognizant of what the body is telling us because "the body is epistemologically significant."[25]

I remember quite clearly the first great moral shock of my life. I was four or five and had descended the steps in our old family home to find my father watching a telecast of *Les Misérables*. Depicted onscreen was a drawn and haggard prisoner, wild-eyed and chain-clad, employed with other prisoners in some harsh, backbreaking labor. He seemed a beast. Frightened, I conjectured aloud: "Bad man!" My father turned and considered me, as if sizing me up. He then told me the prisoner, prior to his arrest, was destitute, unsuccessful in his attempts to find work, and despairing over his failure to care for his starving family until finally, desperate, he broke a bakery window to snatch bread and end his family's hunger. He had been imprisoned for stealing food after no one would give him any or allow him to earn it. I was distressed, bewildered, threatened, and enraged; and I did what a child *can* do in such moments: I made a noise like a muffled howl and ran away in tears. It was the purist intellectual response of my life.

I knew, but could not then articulate, that all is not right in our world: that what-ought-not-to-be is; that I yearn for the way things ought-to-be; and that there resides within me a consequent moral indignation that strikes like tinder and determines to find remedy. Age has only confirmed the fitness of my youthful impressions. The inculpatory witness of history attests that the cultivation of hells on earth by some human beings over others is simply one aspect of the human condition made manifest; neighbor has preyed upon neighbor time out of memory. But, for most, there is another dimension to the human condition discernable in the *naïve*—because untutored or untaught—and involuntarily moral shudder in the face of evil, as if in the presence of sudden cold, and the desire to rise in fist-shaking indignation against the predators.

In Elshtain's interview earlier in this book, she notes the importance of such intuitive responses when she warns against the excision of what Leon Kass, in an essay on human cloning, called "the wisdom of repugnance." Elshtain affirmed Kass's desire to get us to pay attention to what we find "offensive," "repulsive," and "distasteful" for it might alert us to deeper realities. Like Augustine, "Kass," Elshtain writes elsewhere, "is arguing *for* the potential epistemic value of strong reactions, like horror at the sight of torture scenes, or revulsion when we see self-mutilation."[26] Elshtain knows we must not end with the emotion, of course, but neither ought we to discount it. In a culture increasingly allergic to moral judgment, she feared our capacity for repugnance is dwindling fast, a fear supported by those who criticized Kass for trying to make something theoretically substantive out of what they took to be mere aesthetic reaction. In the interview Elshtain insists, "The critique runs much deeper than that." Repugnance points to that which offends something very deep within us; "Something really . . . fundamental has been violated." Certain things simply ought-not-be. Sometimes we ought to shudder.

To the Augustinian, the fundamental thing that evil violates is nothing less than the initial goods with which God has graced the world. Evil is privation,[27] the loss of essential goodness necessary for a particular object to remain whole, in retention of its created nature. In a sense evil does not exist—much like darkness, silence, or cold, which are the absence of visible light, sound energy, or thermal movement. Evil is the break in the bones of a once-functional arm or blindness in eyes that have lost vision. Essential to this is grasping the derivative quality of evil. Evil needs something to be nothing—it cannot be nothing on its own. More to our purpose, *moral* evil is the result of the misuse of the will.[28] God created human beings to be freely rational, to not only be capable of evaluating choices between good and evil and right and wrong but to freely choose between them.

The wisdom of repugnance instructs us that we are not to be indifferent to such choices. Albert Camus, one of Elshtain's great heroes, concurred. Living in a century in which the totalitarian will swallowed tens of millions of souls in death camps and lime-pits, he paid close attention to the revulsion he felt. He could not be indifferent:

> If nothing has any meaning and if we can affirm no values whatsoever, then everything is possible and nothing has any importance. There is no pro or con: the murderer is neither right nor wrong. We are free to stoke the crematory fires or to devote ourselves to the care of lepers. Evil and virtue are mere chance or caprice.[29]

But this is not to be believed. Camus recognized that his own deep feelings of revulsion, his *repugnance*, always meant more than they were conscious of saying.[30] Elshtain insisted even childish impressions are not to be jettisoned without cause, for they may well be key ingredients of our nature. Rather we are to "form[. . .] and shape[. . .] our passions in light of certain understandings about human beings, about human willing, and about our faltering steps to act rightly."[31] For the Augustinian realist, the human compulsion to stand against injustice—whether expressed in the provision of bread to a desperate man or in the martial impulse to "stiffen the sinews and summon up the blood" against malevolence—is intended as a statement of moral fact, not a solipsistic pronouncement of personal preference. Description and evaluation are distinct but inseparable and "moral evaluation is embedded in our descriptions; how we describe is itself a moral act."[32] The distinction between right and wrong, good and evil is crucial not simply to avoid hells on earth but because we were made to know these distinctions. They help to make us happy. Shallow are the souls that have forgotten how to shudder.[33]

FREEDOM FOR EXCELLENCE

The experience of evil has helped shaped the history of moral analysis. This history can be divided into two epochs: The first ranges from Antiquity into the Middle Ages and is preoccupied with the question of happiness—or *eudemonism*.[34] This school is organized around the formation of character according to the principal virtues that refine human action without neglecting to examine opposing faults, vices, and sins.[35] Such a view acknowledges both the existence and accessibility of moral facts as well as hardwired inclination toward moral goods; therefore law is seen as a work of wisdom rather than a constraint on one's freedom. This is now all rather old school. It has largely given way to the view for which self-assertion, as a radically self-creating "self," is the means to real freedom.[36] Václav Havel, the former Czech dissident turned former Czech president, lamented the calamitous outcomes of this self-deification:

> The relativization of all moral norms, the crisis of authority, the reduction of life to the pursuit of immediate material gain without regard for its general consequences—the very things Western democracy is most criticized for—do not originate in democracy but in that which modem man has lost: his transcendental anchor, and along with it the only genuine source of his responsibility and self-respect . . . Given its fatal incorrigibility, humanity probably will have to go through many more Rwandas and Chernobyls before it understands how unbelievably shortsighted a human being can be who has forgotten that he is not God.[37]

Elshtain agreed: "One way that we have contrived to forget that we are not God is to forget we have human natures."[38] Looking at the present scene, Elshtain pointed to those who tell us we are nothing more than bundles of impulses and random combinations of DNA:

> One standard plaint goes: any talk of a specifically human nature that is not reducible to biological and genetic predicates is so much balderdash, fashioned historically in order to curb human freedom, to deny the free expression of our

polymorphously perverse sexuality, and to hand over to rigid moralists the power to control human expression.[39]

She understood, however, that none of this emerged scratch-made from the genetic revolution or, further back, the Enlightenment. As did her like-minded intellectual colleague George Weigel, Elshtain saw this identification of freedom with the will as a product of a great intellectual chasm opened up in the High Middle Ages.[40]

In the opening pages of *Sovereignty,* Elshtain interrogates William of Ockham, the chief exponent of nominalism, and the influence his view of divine freedom had on earthbound notions of political rule and individual self-sufficiency. With Ockham, the question of happiness is set aside. On issues of sovereignty, "The will . . . moves to center stage" and a new conception of "free choice applies univocally to God and to man."[41] This results in a freedom that tailors norms to the moment, "It means considering all the options before choosing a course of action, because the process of choosing is itself the overriding good. It means being faithful to who you really are, because in that fidelity lies a salutary honesty. And it means rejecting every fixed standard of right and wrong, every norm, rule, law, and belief that is external to yourself."[42] Catholic theologian Servais Pinckaers underlines what Elshtain has her sights on: With Ockham, Augustine's emphasis on a freedom of the will guided by a naturalistic morality written on the heart will be overturned and free choice will be redefined as "the power to choose *indifferently* between contraries, between yes and no, good and evil."[43]

The theory underlying the freedom of indifference emerges from the Franciscan critique of Thomas Aquinas. Thomas had already carried Augustinian thought forward, arguing that free choice proceeds from our spiritual faculties of reason and will. This power to choose is then quickened by "inclinations to truth, goodness, and happiness that animate these faculties."[44] Against this, Ockham inaugurates a revolution that "begins by breaking away from spiritual nature and its inclinations."[45] Nominalism, in denying universal concepts or principles exist in reality reduces human nature to merely a description given to common features shared among human beings. Weigel writes, "If . . . there is no 'human nature,' then there are no universal moral principles that can be 'read' from human nature."[46] The effect this has on political theory is substantial. "Morality, on a nominalist view, is simply law and obligation, and that law is always external to the human person. Law, in other words, is always coercion—divine law and human law, God's coercion of us and our coercion of each other."[47]

Elshtain was aware this leaves human beings either "stewing in a kind of permanent impotence as their agency is swamped by God's arbitrary power or, alternatively, human free willing and capacity to 'do' shrinks the realm of

divine agency as sovereign selves go to work."[48] In either case, she lamented, the moral realist's perception of an intelligible world or order in nature
discernable to human ratiocination increasingly gives way before a notion of
law derived from will and command.[49] Consequently, Pinckaers avers, "Nature . . . is henceforth subordinated to choice [and] the ideal becomes the
domination and enslavement of nature."[50] Freedom becomes nothing more
than the freedom of indifference. The human will is left unbound.

Set this against the Thomistic view of freedom with which we have already become briefly introduced. Freedom, for Thomas, "is a means to human excellence, to human happiness, to the fulfillment of human destiny."[51]
Thus, Aquinas's view is best captured in the phrase "freedom for excellence,
or perfection."[52] As "perfection" it signals teleological completion—freedom
is ordered to our created purpose. Contra Ockham, freedom is "the means by
which . . . we act on the natural longing . . . built into us as human beings."[53]
It is the power to engage in excellence, in virtuous actions that are true and
good.[54] As such, good law cannot be a heteronomous imposition but rather it
intertwines with freedom to facilitate "our achievement of the human goods
that we instinctively seek because of who we are and what we are meant to
be as human beings."[55] Freedom for excellence suggests our repugnance
toward evil and our characteristic resolve for remedy are part and parcel of
our capacity to be free. This is not, of course, instantaneous: "Freedom is the
method by which we *become* the kind of people our noblest instincts incline
us to be;"[56] freedom "engenders a moral science that directly takes up the
question...of the absolute good. . . . This science is organized according to
the principle virtues that strengthen freedom and refine human action."[57] We
are trained to "choose wisely and to act well as a matter of habit . . . as an
outgrowth of *virtue*"[58] until "the science is brought to completion in the
study of law in its educational role, a role that firmly brings together wisdom
and love, and even constraint, which is sometimes necessary in the struggle
against evil."[59]

Continuing the pedagogical image, Pinckaers writes: "From our birth we
have received moral freedom as a talent to be developed."[60] This talent is
latent, pregnant with the possibility of knowing truth and inclined toward
goodness and happiness. "At the beginning of our lives," he says, "these
capacities are weak, as is the case for a child or an apprentice. Like our
personalities, we must form our freedom through an education appropriate to
our level of development."[61] He extrapolates:

> This . . . process appears to pass through three stages analogous to the stages of
> human life. Corresponding to childhood, there is the apprenticeship of rules
> and laws of action. . . . Next there is the adolescence of the moral life, charac-
> terized by increasing independence and growing personal initiative, guided by
> one's taste for the true and the good and strengthened by experience. It is here

that virtue begins to emerge as an excellence or capacity for personal action. Then there arrives the age of maturity where virtue blossoms like a talent in the arts: It is a daring, intelligent and generous force, the capacity to bring to good completion works of long duration that bear fruit for many; it secures ease and joy in action.[62]

Freedom for excellence, then, is a process of growing in virtue, in the capacity to love and to choose what we ought—for our own happiness and for the happiness of our neighbors—both near and far off. Naturally enough, Thomistic freedom must rest in a right conception of what it means to be a human being. The Thomistic stance advances an anthropology that requires solidarity, empathy, and mutually shared responsibilities in defense of inalienable rights and human dignity. Thomas realigns freedom away from autonomy and back toward natural inclinations such as our native longing to give ourselves away in acts of other-centered self-donation—natural because we are crafted in the image a God who does just that. Individual freedom carries with it the capacity to cultivate a society in which persuasion through exhortation and counsel is preferred over coercion; in which happiness is reestablished as a "diffusion of the good";[63] and in which society is made more secure by preserving the distinction between good and evil. Thus, freedom is responsibility. Free men and women bear the responsibility to become "the kind of people who can, among other possibilities, build free and virtuous societies in which the rights of all are acknowledged, respected, and protected in law."[64]

On this last point, for our present study enough can never be said. While there is much more to the human story, evil remains a constant. Ockhamite nominalism, with the deterioration of the idea of freedom to willfulness, the detachment of freedom from moral truth, and its obsession with choice, desiccates the human capacity to make even "the most elementary moral conclusions about the imperative to resist evil"[65] or to explain "why some things that *can* be done should *not* be done."[66] The freedom of indifference cannot sustain a free society; tyranny thrives in a world in which freedom of choice is nothing but a matter of self-assertion and power and means over ends.[67] There can be no "common good" if there are only particular goods of particular men and women each acting out their own particular willfulness.[68] This suggests a necessary amendment to something I said earlier: moral evil must be something *more* than simply the misuse of the will. More exactly, if freedom is the capacity to direct our actions toward the pursuit of happiness—the union of the human person with the absolute good (who is God), then moral evil must be the privation of this essential capacity; it is the evacuation from freedom of an essential good. Evil ensues when we assert undue independence from God's dominion;[69] and assert undue independence we do.

The Augustinian realist, morally formed by the patrimony of Greek and Roman wisdom, the biblical religion, and living with eyes wide open, knows well the extent of evil to which humanity is capable. But to be a realist is not to be without hope. "Freedom for excellence," concludes Weigel, "is the freedom that will satisfy the deepest yearnings of the human heart to be free. It is more than that, though. The idea of freedom for excellence and the disciplines of self-command it implies are essential for democracy and for the defense of freedom."[70] Our efforts to more perfectly reflect the image of God, as individuals and as a society, need not be scuttled as we stand idly by and do nothing while another image of God is annihilated by the conditions of life or willful malice. Freedom is neither indifferent nor impotent. It claims that even in the midst of great darkness the virtues can be formed and humanity can develop the latent seeds within us to strive toward and achieve a measure of shared and individual good and genuine happiness. We can do this well, even excellently.

THE JUST WAR: LOVE AND JUSTICE TOGETHER AGAIN

In dark days after the planes hit, Elshtain mused to a friend: "Now we are reminded of what governments are for." September 11, 2001, she forever after insisted, made plain that "the primary responsibility of government is to provide for basic security—ordinary civic peace."[71] This responsibility is a divine mandate; the Christian tradition tells us that God institutes government. "This does not mean," she cautioned, "that every government and every public official is godly but, rather, that each is charged with a solemn responsibility for which there is divine warrant . . . a *political* ethic is an ethic of responsibility."[72] Following Augustine's hortatory temper, Elshtain insists that Christians cannot remain aloof as they await the eschaton.[73] Against the depravity, bloodshed, and injustice of the present age the security and peace necessary for human beings to enjoy human goods requires a basis upon which to reside and its preservation, because of the obduracy of human willfulness, requires force. The just war tradition guides this force toward just application.

According to Elshtain, just war finds embryonic expression in classical thinking about the rightly ordered society[74] before coming into full articulation in the Augustinian tradition as a way of reflection, driven by an account of our natures both created and fallen,[75] that "refuses to separate politics from ethics"[76] and acknowledges "the realities of coercive force and, at certain times, the ethical need to deploy it to certain ends."[77] Utilizing the fundamental categories of *jus ad bellum*—concerning the justification or obligation in resorting to force, and *jus in bello*—concerning the application of force within conflict, just war provisions ethical and analytical means to ongoingly evaluate what is and is not permissible, or incumbent, to do.[78] In all of this, the practical norm that immediately generates just war concern regarding human responsibility is the dominical command to love our neighbor.[79] This prompts the obvious questions: to *whom* are we to be responsible, and just *who* is the neighbor we are called to love?

One way Elshtain addressed this was to consider natural human sociality. On this subject, Augustine, laying the groundwork for the Thomistic portrayal of freedom, reveals just war to be fit only for a self who knows that the self is made for others. "The importance of plurality," asserts Elshtain, "of the many emerging from a unique one, cannot be underestimated in Augustine's work."[80] Having been made in the likeness of God, Augustine teaches us that "that first parent of ours . . . was created . . . as one individual with this intention: that from one . . . a multitude might be propagated, and that this fact should teach mankind to preserve a harmonious unity in plurality."[81] The affection that ought to characterize this unity is modeled in "the fact that a woman was made for the first man from his own side."[82] One need only imagine Adam's mounting frustration as he mulls through the great catalogue of new beasts but finds none worthy for partnership. Finally, mercifully, his eyes alight for the first time upon the form of his nuptial match and he exclaims, "At last! Now, *this* is bone of my bone and flesh of my flesh." Adam, made to imitate the God of his creation, finds a suitable mate only after being drawn by the laws of his nature to enter upon a fellowship with his own kind.[83]

Elshtain took this to point toward the natural human impulse toward *caritas*—our willing dependence on one another, our need for trust, and our yearning for earthly peace among friends.[84] Such friends, in Augustine's reckoning, range from kith and kin in our homes and cities to far-off strangers unknown to us.[85] Indeed, "*from one*," Elshtain writes of original human singularity, "creates a fragile but real ontology of peace, or relative peacefulness."[86] While she is careful to guard against "greeting card rostrums" about responsibility for the entire human race somehow trumping our "particular moral responsibility to those nearest and dearest to us—parents to children, friends to other friends, but also citizens to fellow citizens,"[87] Elshtain remains mindful that injustice need not be directed only against one's own before it triggers our martial obligation: "The offense of aggression may be committed against a nation or a people incapable of defending themselves against a determined adversary. If one can intervene to assist the injured party, one is justified in doing so."[88] Lauding the articulation of this sense of neighbor-love in such notions as the Responsibility to Protect (R2P), she championed the judgment "that should a nation or group of nations be the victims of systematic, egregious, and continuing violence, the international community has a responsibility to do something about it."[89]

For Elshtain, then, everyone in principle is in view in the dominical injunction of neighbor-love. But, for knowing *how* to love our neighbor, it is important to have some sense of what is *good* for him—to grasp that which leads to his flourishing. The goods about which the just war tradition can do something include the basic goods of life and health,[90] without which any effort to pursue happiness is compromised. Moreover, as Elshtain often wrote, such goods further include:

> The simple but profound good that is moms and dads raising their children, men and women going to work, citizens of a great city making their way on streets and subways, ordinary people buying airplane tickets in order to visit the grandkids in California, people en route to transact business with colleagues in other cities, the faithful attending their churches, synagogues, and mosques without fear . . .[91] Men and women, young and old, black, brown, and white—lining up to vote.[92]

Elshtain understood the quotidian quality of these descriptions but asserted they constitute superlative goods.[93] Thus, the operative principle of *caritas,* recognizing that "none of the goods that human beings cherish can flourish absent a measure of civic peace and security,"[94] animates just war commitments to make life on this earth at least a little less cruel and a little less unjust.[95]

Yet something more remains. We have already established, overruling Ockham, that law is not arbitrary; no command is its own justification.[96] So why, then, are we to love our neighbors? Here, Oxford theologian Nigel Biggar stands in agreement with Thomas's freedom as excellence in describing Christian ethics as basically eudaemonist. Writes Biggar, "Therefore, the rationale of the normative authority of Jesus's love command needs to refer to the flourishing of the one who is commanded."[97] He explains:

> We should love our neighbors because it is good for us to do so—because it profits us. The relevant profit, however, is not extrinsic but intrinsic, and its currency is not money but virtue. It is good that we should grow in the virtues of benevolence and justice; it belongs to our own good or flourishing that we should become benevolent and just. And that will remain true, even if it should cost us our very lives.[98]

The Augustinian depiction of the just war tradition, with its eudaemonist hinterland, holds that its moral obligations and duties find their fundamental rationale in the promotion of the happiness of human flourishing.[99]

Of course, the justification of the dominical command refers, additionally, to the flourishing of the one whom we are commanded to love. That protecting the life of our neighbor against evil is a means toward his flourishing seems straightforwardly obvious. But here we need to finally consider something that until now we have kept from view. When we recollect that the command to love our neighbor specifically includes our enemy-neighbor we might stop short. It is, after all, against our enemy's unjust evils that the use of coercive, possibly lethal, force in the protection of our aggressed neighbors is justified. But Augustine makes clear that the just warrior does not abandon "single-minded love" toward the enemy even when it is necessary to treat him with "unpleasant severity."[100] This, Augustine tells us, the just warrior accomplishes insofar as he shrinks from a passion for revenge, prefers to pardon wrongdoers over pursuing them, commits himself to benevolence, and so uses force to punish the enemy with a "kind harshness," in constraining him from further wrongdoing and encouraging him "to mend his ways and embrace peace."[101] Just war recognizes that "one cannot rectify injustice without punishing its perpetrator—by forcing him to stop, by deterring him from resuming, and ideally by provoking him to think again and change his aggressive ways forever."[102]

That such a view is now heavily contested Elshtain took to signal a steadily declining certainty in Western understanding—even (or especially) within Christian communities—that the taking of a human life is compatible with love. Increasingly, love is characterized by a maudlin benignity that sanitizes it of anything we find uncomfortable, including the necessity of love to stand in judgment. But if Thomas is correct that a correlation exists between happiness and our capacity for virtue, then "when we are stripping a man of the lawlessness of sin, it is good for him to be vanquished, since nothing is more hopeless than the happiness of sinners."[103] Harsh measures may yield great goods.

LAST THINGS

Emerging from Augustinian theological commitments, Elshtain took for granted that the just war tradition would take account of the dual nature of present humanity, fallen and redeemed.[104] "Just-war thinking," she wrote, "*presupposes* a 'self' of a certain kind . . . one strong enough to resist the lure of seductive, violent enthusiasms; [and] one bounded by and laced through with a sense of responsibility and accountability."[105] What does this presupposed-self look like? We return to the beginning.

Recall Mars, his martial capacity present but bound, changed and redirected by the influence of love. C. S. Lewis, smoking his pipe at his Magdalen desk and contemplating the tamed God of War, would have had called to mind the medieval ideal of chivalry. To understand the ideal, Lewis thought it best to consider the words spoken over the dead Launcelot: "Thou wert the meekest man that ever ate in hall among ladies; and thou wert the sternest knight to thy mortal foe."[106] Lewis expounds:

The important thing about this ideal is . . . the double-demand it makes on
human nature. The knight is a man of blood and iron, a man familiar with the
sight of smashed faces and the ragged stumps of lopped-off limbs; he is also a
demure, almost a maidenlike guest in hall, a gentle, modest, unobtrusive man.
He is not a compromise or happy mean between ferocity and meekness; he is
fierce to the *n*th and meek to the *n*th. [107]

Chivalry signified something more than literary artifact. Writing at the beginning of the Second World War, Lewis found the ideal to be terribly relevant:
"It may or may not be practicable—the Middle Ages notoriously failed to
obey it—but it is certainly practical; practical as the fact that men in a desert
must find water or die." [108] The key was in remembering the knight "is a
work not of nature but of art; of that art which has human beings, instead of
canvas or marble, for its medium." [109] That is to say, chivalry attempted to
bring together two things that, since the fall of humanity, have no natural
tendency to gravitate toward one another: it teaches "humility and forbear-
ance to the great warrior because everyone knew by experience how much he
usually needed the lesson" and it demands "valor of the urbane and modest
man because everyone knew that he was as likely as not to be a milksop." [110]
The danger, as Lewis saw it, was that if we cannot produce Launcelots,
humanity falls into two sections—those who can deal in blood and iron but,
like Achilles, know nothing about mercy and kill men as they cry for quar-
ter, [111] and "those who are 'meek in hall' but useless in battle." [112]

The just war tradition, too, perceives the human soul as a work to be
realized. In the face of evil, it captures our moral repugnance and strikes the
tinder of our resolve to rise against injustice and it cultivates the chivalric
capacity for meekness—not the invertebrate meekness of the milquetoast but
the Aristotelian conception of power under restraint. Elshtain understood this
to be crucial for our times. Her unease at the prospect of the loss of moral
memory helped to keep the terrorist attacks of 9/11 on her working mind.
Like her alarm over our dwindling capacity for repugnance, she feared that
with the distance of time many of us would forget what that day was really
like. "We shouldn't," she warned, "It was just as bad as we remember it. Our
emotions at the time were not extreme: They were appropriate to the horror.
Anger remains an appropriate feeling." [113] But she knew as well the human
capacity for undomesticated vengeance. She only had to recall the American
"exterminationalist rhetoric" of the 1940's endorsing a policy of annihilation
of the Japanese to know that the martial spark, once fanned, can set the whole
world alight and consume everything in its lust for retribution. [114] The just
war tradition, like the medieval ideal, is predicated on the notion that Venus
and Mars can stand together, that evil—whether external to us or that with
which are ourselves complicit—can be restrained: all so that the good can be
revealed before us.

Elshtain closes *Sovereignty* with a brief reflection of Camus's great anti-totalitarian novel *The Plague*, and so shall I. The novel ends with Dr. Rieux's realization that though the evil of the plague had been defeated, there would never be a final victory. Instead, there would be a never-ending fight against terror by those who, while not saints, were nevertheless committed to at least be healers. It was all that could be asked of them against the pestilence. Some years back in a class discussion of the novel, after Elshtain had discoursed at length on Rieux's concluding disquisition, she paused. Prior to the class she and I had spent time mapping out my dissertation project dealing with the moral experience of war. Clearly, it remained on her mind. Setting the novel aside, she smiled at the class and mused aloud, "You know, soldiers too can be healers."

NOTES

1. Rebecca Whitten Poe, *C. S. Lewis Remembered: Collected Reflections of Students, Friends and Colleagues* (Grand Rapids, MI: Zondervan, 2006), 99.

2. Peter J. Schakel, *Imagination and the Arts in C. S. Lewis: Journeying to Narnia and Other Worlds* (University of Missouri Press, 2002), 144.

3. C. S. Lewis, *All My Road Before Me: The Diary of C. S. Lewis, 1922–1927* (San Diego: Fount / Collins, 1991), 95.

4. The ancient Romans believed the peaceful dormancy of the God of War could be interrupted by ritual incantation, Mars vigala—"Mars, awaken!" See: Anthony Grafton, Glenn W. Most, and Salvatore Settis, eds., *The Classical Tradition* (Harvard University Press, 2010), 564.

5. Ibid.

6. C. S. Lewis, *Spenser's Images of Life* (Cambridge: Cambridge University Press, 1967), 104. My emphasis.

7. Grafton, Most, and Settis, *The Classical Tradition*, 564.

8. Jean Bethke Elshtain, "The Third Annual Grotius Lecture: Just War and Humanitarian Intervention," *American University International Law Review* 17, no. 1 (2001): 3.

9. Ibid., 22.

10. Jean Bethke Elshtain, *Who Are We?* (Grand Rapids, MI: Eerdmans, 2000), 25.

11. Jean Bethke Elshtain, *Augustine and the Limits of Politics*, 1st edition (Notre Dame, IN: University of Notre Dame Press, 1998), 39.

12. Jean Bethke Elshtain, *Sovereignty: God, State, and Self* (New York: Basic Books, 2008), 163.

13. Elshtain, *Augustine and the Limits of Politics*, 36.

14. Elshtain, *Sovereignty*, 161.

15. Elshtain, *Who Are We?*, 30–31.

16. Ibid., 44.

17. Elshtain, "Just War and Humanitarian Intervention," 22.

18. Elshtain, *Who Are We?*, 43.

19. Jean Bethke Elshtain, "While Europe Slept," *First Things*, no. 191 (March 2009): 33.

20. Jean Bethke Elshtain, *Just War against Terror: The Burden of American Power in a Violent World* (New York: Basic Books, 2003), 112–121; and C. S Lewis, "The Necessity of Chivalry," in *Present Concerns*, ed. Walter Hooper (San Diego: Harcourt, 2002), 15.

21. George Weigel, "A Better Concept of Freedom," *First Things*, no. 121 (March 2002): 17.

22. Jean Bethke Elshtain, *Women and War* (New York: Basic Books, 1987), 151.

23. Jean Bethke Elshtain, "The Just War Tradition and Natural Law," *Fordham International Law Journal* 28, no. 3 (2004): 743, n.8.

24. Elshtain, *Who Are We?*, 25.

25. Elshtain, *Sovereignty*, 162–64.

26. Elshtain, *Who Are We?*, 106.

27. Augustine, *The City of God*, trans. Henry Bettenson (London; New York: Penguin Books, 2003), XI.22.454. See also, Thomas Aquinas, *Summa Theologica*, I.48.3.

28. Andrew Michael Flescher, *Moral Evil* (Washington, DC: Georgetown University Press, 2013), 166.

29. Albert Camus, *The Rebel: An Essay on Man in Revolt* (New York: Vintage Books, 1956), 5.

30. Albert Camus, *The Myth of Sisyphus and Other Essays* (New York: Vintage Books, 1955), 8.

31. Elshtain, *Sovereignty*, 162–63.

32. Jean Bethke Elshtain, "What's Morality Got to Do with It? Making the Right Distinctions," *Social Philosophy and Policy* 21, no. 1 (Winter 2004): 1.

33. Leon Kass, "The Wisdom of Repugnance," *The New Republic*, June 1997, 20.

34. According to Aristotle, the fundamental role of morality is the promotion of *eudaemonia,* that is "happiness" or "flourishing."

35. Servais O. P. Pinckaers, *Morality: The Catholic View*, trans. Michael Sherwin (South Bend, IN: St. Augustines Press, 2003), 65, 70.

36. Weigel, "A Better Concept of Freedom," 17.

37. Václav Havel, "Forgetting We Are Not God," *First Things*, no. 51 (March 1995): 49, 50; quoted in: Elshtain, "The Just War Tradition and Natural Law," 744.

38. Elshtain, "The Just War Tradition and Natural Law," 744.

39. Ibid.

40. Weigel, "A Better Concept of Freedom," 15.

41. Elshtain, *Sovereignty*, 26.

42. Jean Bethke Elshtain, "The New Morality," *The Wilson Quarterly* 25, no. 3 (Summer 2001): 112.

43. Pinckaers, *Morality*, 68. My emphasis

44. Ibid.

45. Ibid., 69.

46. Weigel, "A Better Concept of Freedom," 16.

47. Ibid.

48. Elshtain, *Sovereignty*, 27.

49. Ibid., 36.

50. Pinckaers, *Morality*, 69.

51. Weigel, "A Better Concept of Freedom," 15.

52. Pinckaers, *Morality*, 68.

53. Weigel, "A Better Concept of Freedom," 15.

54. Pinckaers, *Morality*, 68.

55. Weigel, "A Better Concept of Freedom," 16.

56. Ibid. My emphasis

57. Pinckaers, *Morality*, 70.

58. Weigel, "A Better Concept of Freedom," 15.

59. Pinckaers, *Morality*, 70.

60. Ibid., 69.

61. Ibid., 69–70.

62. Ibid., 70.

63. Ibid., 75.

64. Weigel, "A Better Concept of Freedom," 16.

65. Ibid., 19.

66. Ibid., 20.

67. Ibid., 18.

68. Ibid., 16,17.

69. Flescher, *Moral Evil*, 166.

70. Weigel, "A Better Concept of Freedom," 20.

71. Elshtain, *Just War against Terror*, 46.

72. Jean Bethke Elshtain, "Luther's Lamb: When and How to Fight a Just War," *Common Knowledge* 8, no. 2 (2002): 306.

73. J. Daryl Charles nicely captures the force of Elshtain's conviction on this. He writes, "It is a fundamental assumption of just war thinking, and of Elshtain's work, that human evil must be resisted when and where we have the wherewithal to do so. To fail to act is to serve as an accomplice in the evil itself." in J. Daryl Charles, "War, Women, and Political Wisdom," *Journal of Religious Ethics* 34, no. 2 (June 2006): 363.

74. Jean Bethke Elshtain, "Just War and an Ethics of Responsibility," in *Ethics Beyond War's End*, ed. Eric Patterson (Washington, DC: Georgetown University Press, 2012), 125.

75. Elshtain, "The Just War Tradition and Natural Law," 751.

76. Elshtain, "Just War and Humanitarian Intervention," 3.

77. Alan Johnson, "Just War, Humanitarian Intervention and Equal Regard: An Interview with Jean Bethke Elshtain," *Democratiya*, no. 1 (Summer 2005): 52, http://www.dissentmagazine.org/democratiya_article/just-war-humanitarian-intervention-and-equal-regard-an-interview-with-jean-bethke-elshtain.

78. Elshtain, "Just War and Humanitarian Intervention," 5.

79. Nigel Biggar, "Natural Flourishing as the Normative Ground of Just War: A Christian View," in *Just War: Authority, Tradition, and Practice*, ed. Anthony F. Lang Jr, Cian O'Driscoll, and John Williams (Washington, DC: Georgetown University Press, 2013), 50.

80. Elshtain, "The Just War Tradition and Natural Law," 748.

81. Augustine, *The City of God*, XII.28.508.

82. Ibid.

83. Ibid., XIX.12.868.

84. Elshtain, *Augustine and the Limits of Politics*, 38.

85. Augustine, *The city of God*, XIX.3.851.

86. Elshtain, *Augustine and the Limits of Politics*, 103.

87. Elshtain, *Just War against Terror*, 108.

88. Elshtain, "Just War and Humanitarian Intervention," 8.

89. Elshtain, "Just War and an Ethics of Responsibility," 124.

90. Biggar, "Natural Flourishing as the Normative Ground of Just War," 51.

91. Elshtain, "Luther's Lamb," 306.

92. Elshtain, *Just War against Terror*, 47.

93. Elshtain, "Luther's Lamb," 306.

94. Ibid.

95. Jean Bethke Elshtain, *Public Man, Private Woman: Women in Social and Political Thought*, 2nd edition (Princeton, NJ: Princeton University Press, 1981), 66.

96. Biggar, "Natural Flourishing as the Normative Ground of Just War," 51.

97. Ibid.

98. Ibid.

99. Nigel Biggar, *In Defence of War* (Oxford: Oxford Univ. Press, 2013), 155 n.25.

100. Augustine, Letter 220: (To Boniface) in E. M. Atkins and R. J. Dodaro, eds., *Augustine: Political Writings* (Cambridge: Cambridge University Press, 2001), 222, s.8.

101. Augustine, "Letter 138 (to Marcellinus)," in *Political Writings*, ed. E. Margaret Atkins and Robert Dodaro (Cambridge: Cambridge University Press, 2001), 35 s.9, 36 s.11, 38 s.14; The neat collation is taken largely from: Biggar, *In Defence of War*, 61. What this amounts to for Biggar is the qualification of violence by forgiveness. He develops this in a profound and deeply valuable way.

102. Biggar, "Natural Flourishing as the Normative Ground of Just War," 52.

103. Aquinas, *Summa Theologiae*, 2a 2ae, q. 40, a.I, ad. 1

104. Elshtain, "The Just War Tradition and Natural Law," 747–48.

105. Elshtain, *Women and War*, 152.

106. Sir Thomas Malory, *Le Morte D'Arthur* (1485), XXI, xii.

107. Lewis, "The Necessity of Chivalry," 13.

108. Ibid.
109. Ibid., 15.
110. Ibid., 14.
111. Ibid.
112. Ibid., 15.
113. Elshtain, *Just War against Terror*, 7.
114. Elshtain, *Women and War*, 156.

Chapter Eight

Incarnational Selfhood

Dietrich Bonhoeffer as Guide to the Political Ethics of Jean Bethke Elshtain

Jens Zimmermann

INTRODUCTION

In many ways, Jean Bethke Elshtain's Gifford lectures *Sovereignty: God, State, and Self* are the crowning achievement of her career. Not only did the invitation to these talks acknowledge her as a leading political theorist of our time, but the resulting book also presents us with the summation of her efforts to provide a conceptual blueprint for a humane modern, democratic society. In all of her work, Elshtain strove to show that any aspiration for a healthy society required three things: an understanding of human nature (anthropology), a good sense of the state's role and limitations in supporting a common vision of the good life, and religion as an important resource for framing anthropology and political vision. Elshtain was thoroughly disenchanted with her discipline's lingering pretensions to scientific positivism and its fact-value split.[1] She fully recognized that a) political theory is never merely descriptive but always works with an implicit framework of values and that b) as a matter of historical record, this framework has been shaped by religious influences, even when these are secularized and merely implicit. In all her books and essays, she reminded the reader tirelessly that the philosophical analysis of politics cannot do without a framework of values and that we need to be conscious of the origin and historical genealogy of these values. She insisted on these two basic insights, because she thought them indispensible for arriving at a balanced view of society, which requires a sense of who we are and what we are capable of as human beings. We should be aware of our capabilities and also of our limitations.

Elshtain was not a theologian, but I don't think she would have objected to being called a religious thinker. She acknowledged Christianity's profound influence on Western conceptions of human dignity, which she deemed foundational to the human rights required for a healthy society. Consequently, Elshtain was much drawn to philosophical, theological and literary sources that described how human rights are not intellectual constructs but grounded in human nature itself. "Incarnational thinkers" was her favorite term for authors who believed that human existence itself furnished evidence for ethical demands. Albert Camus was such a thinker, her favorite theologian Augustine another. She also appeals frequently to Thomas Aquinas, to Catholic social teaching, particularly as expounded by John Paul II and Vatican II, and also to the writings of the Lutheran theologian and political activist Dietrich Bonhoeffer, who was easily the most politically astute theologian in her own Lutheran tradition. This essay offers a comparative analysis of Bonhoeffer's and Elshtain's social and political ethics to show why she was naturally drawn to Bonhoeffer's theology. By delineating Elshtain's convictions concerning political philosophy in comparison with Bonhoeffer's thought, I hope to demonstrate that his theology models Elshtain's own incarnational vision of humanity and politics. Elshtain, in short, was drawn to Bonhoeffer, because he both inspired and confirmed her political theory.

MAN MADE IN GOD'S IMAGE: JEAN BETHKE ELSTHAIN'S ANTHROPOLOGY

For Elshtain, any proper vision of society depends on anthropology, that is, on a fulsome understanding of human nature and personhood. In her Gifford lectures, she describes the kind of self-required for a healthy political community: "The self I have in mind seeks meaning and dignity and finds a measure of both not in liberation from nature, nor in some utopian attunement and at-oneness with nature, but, rather, in growing to become a full person according to our human natures."[2] The ideal member of a human community celebrates human potential to transcend his inherited cultural determinants but, equally important, he recognizes the limits which prescribe and thus establish our humanity. For Elshtain, transgressing our humanity by either seeking to escape this world on the basis of religious eschatology or by engineering our way out of our physical limitations through genetic enhancements are two dangerous fundamentalist tendencies of our time. Religious fundamentalists who seek to erect the kingdom of God on earth, and "genetic fundamentalists" who want to create a brave new world both denigrate true humanity.[3]

In fact, according to Elshtain, fundamentalism is itself deeply rooted in a profound misunderstanding of self and God. Fundamentalism is a logical expression of the sovereign self that willfully ignores its intrinsic social nature and its consequent civic responsibilities; the sovereign self-regards sociality and innate responsibility as obstacles to its ambitions instead of realizing that these limitations are conditions for our truly human formation in the social and political realm.

Along with other critics of modern selfhood, such as Charles Taylor, for example, Elshtain rejects this sovereign self or autonomous individual as one of the greatest dangers to modern democratic societies. The god-like independence of this self tends to view others as mere means to its own happiness. The flip side of the sovereign self is the sovereign state, for whom the citizen has to sacrifice everything. As Elshtain points out, in the revolutionary's zeal for a cause that warrants the sacrifice of human life converge the absolutizing of self and state: our fellow human beings become instruments for a higher purpose rather than persons on whom our own self-knowledge and understanding of the world depends. Nothing is more abstract, more inhumane, and more destructive of true sociality than "the will of the people," or the "good of the state" for whose absolute purity and noble cause mothers, children and dissidents have to be sacrificed. Elshtain appreciated especially Albert Camus, but also Hannah Arendt as astute critics of such totalitarian visions common to statist communism and fascism alike.[4]

Elshtain locates the origin of sovereign self and state in the departure from philosophical realism or what is commonly called the natural law tradition. She does not, of course, advocate a simplistic idea of natural law, as if the universe contained a manual for moral maxims readily discernable by human reason. Her view of natural law was more akin to that of George Grant's: "There is an order in the universe that human reason can discern and according to which the human will must act so that it can attune itself to the universal harmony. Human beings in choosing their purposes must recognize that if these purposes are to be right, they must be those that are proper to the place that mankind holds within the framework of universal law. We do not make this law, but are made to live within it."[5] Conscious of its participation in a larger intelligible cosmic order that, the self's aspirations are measured by something greater than itself. Within this worldview, both self and state are bounded by the natural order of things which they transgress at their peril. With Judaism and particularly with the Christianization of natural law that began with the church fathers and culminating in medieval theology, this cosmic moral order was personalized and found its highest expression in the divine law as presented in the Decalogue. Elshtain has never been interested, however, in constructing an explicitly Christian framework of governance.

Rather, she is interested in how philosophical and religious traditions provide the foundation for human dignity and a proper conception of human rights that allow human flourishing in a secular society, while providing natural limits for personal freedom and for the state. Within a higher, universal cosmic moral order, both self and state are accountable to that order, and within Christianized cultures that meant accountable to God. Elshtain argues that, ironically, Christian theology itself, with the advent of nominalism, undermined this natural limitation. Nominalism set in train what Elshtain, following Charles Taylor, calls "the modern phenomenon of excarnation," that is, the disembedding of self and state from natural structures of responsibility that nourish and limit them.[6] Radical nominalist theologians denied universals and also posited a God who is no longer bound to the natural order but who, in his sovereign freedom, wills arbitrarily what he wishes. This shift from "a God of love and reason to a God as command"[7] who can suspend the natural order of things if he so wills gave rise to similar conceptions of governance: "If God's sovereignty is cast voluntaristically, so too, is political authority: A command-obedience theory of secular rule takes hold."[8]

This absolutizing of governing authority went hand in hand with the creation of autonomous selfhood. In pre-modern pagan societies, the self had participated in a rational moral order. Hebrew anthropology had personalized this view by positing a self created in the image of God, and Christian theology had further enriched anthropology by construing this image in relational, Trinitarian terms. For Elshtain, it is primarily Augustine who has delineated the important features of this Trinitarian self. In terms of anthropology, the two main points she culls from his writings are the social nature of the self and its incompleteness. Complete self-sufficiency is possessed only by God himself, in whose communal image of Father, Son and Spirit we are made. The primal sin of man, with disastrous social consequences, is to arrogate to himself the self-sufficiency or "self-sameness," (*idipsum*) that belongs to God alone. According to Elshtain, assuming self-sameness, that is an autonomous self, sovereign in its reasoning and completely independent from others, is the root of modernity's problems. What has been lost in this shift from incarnate to disincarnate, self-same self? What are the positive features of Trinitarian anthropology? In epistemic terms, Trinitarian selfhood results in an inherently hermeneutic view of knowledge and thus epistemic humility. Hence, Elshtain writes,

> Augustine's ease at spelling out a hermeneutic theory of polysemy and multiple interpretations . . . omniscience is God's alone.[9] In ethical terms, Trinitarian selfhood anchors human dignity irrevocably in the human mind and body, while at the same time positing man's need for the social interaction with others (and with God) for self-completion: Being made in God's image requires, for Augustine, a brake on our own quest for self-mastery and appropriation. Absolute ownership, exploitation, and domination are forms of being

that deny what is means to be formed in the and through Trinity. Such forms diminish and amputate rather than enrich, expand, or help to make us whole. [. . .] If we presume that we are the sole and only ground of our own being, we deny our dependence on others, beginning with the Other who made us in his own image. That denial, in turn, invites a refusal of authentic companionship; it spurns the premise and promise of Trinity, of one and many, distinct yet together. [10]

For Elshtain, Augustine's Trinitarian anthropology provides both the foundational human dignity and dialogical outlook necessary for human flourishing in democratic societies. According to her, the erosion under secularism of religious resources to shape our imagination about what it means to be human is a tragic tendency. In fact, she draws a straight line from the disincarnation of self and state to the totalitarian regimes with their violations of human dignity that have marked the previous century, and continue in many ways to mark our own. [11] We need to fight this erosion by recovering the philosophical and religious traditions that have shaped western cultures as best as we can, and she clearly saw her own work as contributing to this resistance. [12] Ignorance of our own traditions, whether by intention or intellectual apathy, cuts us off from vital resources of self-understanding and possible cultural renewal. [13] She was convinced that "the drama of Democracy" is all about "permanent contestation between conservation and change, between tradition and transformation." [14]

DIETRICH BONHOEFFER'S ANTHROPOLOGY

Elshtain appreciated Bonhoeffer as an astute critic of modernity, who never forgot the crucial role of anthropology for political theology: "Bonhoeffer never forgot that it is only through foregrounding the anthropological question—What does it mean to be created in the image of God?—that theology can prevent its assimilation into some variant of an ideology external to itself, can forestall its sublimation within some political doctrine or plan or scheme, whether Bolshevism, or fascism, or even liberalism." [15] Indeed, already in his doctoral dissertation *Sanctorum Communio*, Bonhoeffer followed Augustine in positing a social self. What makes Bonhoeffer's political theology exemplary, is that like Augustine (although without explicit references to his work), his anthropology grounds human solidarity christologically. Similar to patristic theologians, such as Irenaeus, Bonhoeffer believes that with his incarnation, death and resurrection, Christ "recapitulated," or summed up in himself all of humanity. "In Jesus Christ," Bonhoeffer explains, "in the one who became human, was crucified, and rose from the dead, humanity has been renewed. What happened in Christ, happened to everyone, because he was *the* human being par excellence." [16] Since what happened in Christ pertains to humanity as a whole, Bonhoeffer sees at the very center of the Christian faith a link of solidarity between Christian and all fellow human beings. In other words, Bonhoeffer's interpretation of the incarnation fully recognizes the broader social implications of this humanist interpretation of the Gospel when he links the new humanity to the restoration of God's image in every human being through Christ. In his *Cost of Discipleship,* he affirms the general solidarity with all human beings the Christian regains through Christ's work:

> [I]n the becoming human of Christ the entire humanity regains the dignity of being made in the image of God. Whoever from now on attacks the least of the people attacks Christ, who took on human form and who in himself has restored the image of God for all who bear a human countenance. Inasmuch as we participate in Christ, the incarnate one, we also have a part in all of humanity, which is borne by him. [. . .] our new humanity now also consists in bearing the troubles and the sins of all others. The incarnate one transforms his disciples into brothers and sisters of all human beings. [17]

Elshtain and others have taken note of the existential emphasis in Bonhoeffer's Christology as the source for human solidarity. The Christian participates in the reality of Christ and thereby also shares existentially (or ontologically, if you will) in the being of all others.

Faced with the challenges posed by the Nazi regime, Bonhoeffer later extended this Christological foundation of anthropology to include natural law theory. Bonhoeffer's challenge was essentially this: how does one argue with non-Christians, and with those who deride biblical or theological sources about human dignity? For example, based on the social Darwinianism underlying their racial and biological ideologies, the Nazis extolled the strength of natural life in the healthy fit for survival and thus deemed those born with handicaps as unworthy of life. The state rounded up the handicapped for forced sterilization and euthanasia (i.e., murder) of the handicapped The state, in effect, got to decide who had the right to live. Evangelical theology at this time had either consigned the natural to sin, or regarded it as essentially good creational order. Either way, evangelical theology lacked the conceptual weapons to oppose the Nazi's theories of racial superiority.

Bonhoeffer responded to this challenge by recovering natural theology, in part with the help of Catholic social thought. When working on this topic, he admitted to his friend Eberhardt Bethke that "Catholic ethics are in many ways much more profitable and practical than ours."[18] Bonhoeffer insisted more clearly than Catholic theology, however, on the Christological unity of nature and grace. The natural has no independent meaning or significance outside of Christ's redemptive work. Otherwise, as Bonhoeffer argued in his lectures that later became the book *Creation and Fall,* one could justify just about anything pointing to natural laws, including sacrificing the weak for the survival of the strong. Creation, Bonhoeffer argued, was fallen but none-theless preserved by God for the redemption that had already redeemed it in Christ. For this work has creation been preserved and by this work has it been redeemed. Nature has its own relative value because it has been "held over" for its final redemption upon Christ's return. The ultimate reason for the value of life is its affirmation by Christ who has entered the natural in the incarnation. Only for this reason does all life have relative value and should be honored.[19] Because the natural is oriented toward God, human nature is endowed with intrinsic rights that are rooted in human existence itself and cannot be suspended by an external authority.

Bonhoeffer's basic natural right from which other rights and also human duties follow[20] is distributive justice, or the maxim "suum cuique," to each his own. This right itself, is grounded in the natural human dignity of every person that flows from their creation in God's image. For example, the natu-ral dignity and human right of each individual follows from the fact that God created individual persons for the supernatural end of eternal life. This divine origin of human dignity is a reality embedded in life, and discernible by human reason apart from its theological premise. It is not up to the state to decide what these rights are.[21] The most principal of these rights is the preservation of our bodies from harm, the flourishing of bodily life.[22] For Bonhoeffer, bodily pleasures in our natural lives are pointers that anticipate the eternal joy promised to us by God, even if people do not realize this ultimate end.[23] For the same reason, Christianity can never regard the body as prison for an immortal soul. Both life and body belong together as together they will be transformed eventually by God into new life. Clearly, from this perspective, the preservation of life is primary, and Euthanasia of supposedly "useless" life is nothing less than murder. In Bonhoeffer's words, "The right to life consist in existing and not in any values. Before God no life is worth-less, because life itself is valued by God. Since is God, the creator, sustainer, and redeemer of life, even the most impoverished life is worth living."[24]

Elshtain believed that Bonhoeffer's anthropology and natural law theolo-gy contained important insights for our own time. "Bonhoeffer," she wrote, "understood the importance of maintaining firewalls of conceptual, theologi-cal, and ethical sorts to forestall such depredations. Nor would he let us off the hook. The prevalence in our time of crude utilitarianism affords examples in abundance of the sorts of arguments and claims that Bonhoeffer repudiated as nihilism—hatred of God and creation, yielding hatred of the human it-self."[25] Bonhoeffer saw clearly that human flourishing was threatened by two excesses, by the sovereign state, and the sovereign self. A self that does not respect the other as essential for its own development but objectivizes him as means to an end, is merely the flip side of the state who does the same on a grander scale.[26]

BONHOEFFER'S POLITICAL THEOLOGY

Bonhoeffer's view of church and state is consistent with a Christian tradition that began with the New Testament church's appropriation of ancient Jewish political hopes and then was restated in Western Christianity, with varying emphases, by Augustine,[27] Gelasius,[28] Martin Luther, and subsequent Reformation theologians.[29] Already in Old Testament theology, ruling authorities are deprived of divine status because their power is granted by God, who also judges their failure to aid Israel in achieving the divine vision for a polity characterized by social justice that was ultimately to be accomplished by the Messiah. In the Christian church, this political vision remained in place; however, with Jesus revealed as the promised Messiah, Christology now shaped the theological tradition Bonhoeffer depended on. This tradition was motivated by what David Fergusson has aptly termed "the eschatological commonwealth proclaimed, expected, and enacted in Jesus' ministry" as the fulfilment of the political hopes of Israel.[30] Ferguson reminds us that the church has from early on viewed government and secular society in Christological and thus in eschatological terms. It is worth citing Ferguson at length, because it will help us to situate Bonhoeffer's political theology within the larger Christian tradition:

> "In confessing the risen Christ as Lord, therefore, the church encounters the state in two ways. On the one hand, it seeks neither to overthrow nor to replace the state. [The State] remains for the time being and can contribute in its own way by establishing the conditions for the enactment of the church's mission. Furthermore, in the limited and provisional terms outlined in Romans 13 and elsewhere, it [the State] may also contribute to the present anticipation of God's just rule. On the other hand, the church as a community already assumes some of the features of a new *polis*. . . . They have another king, Jesus, who is risen, ascended, and now present in their midst through the Holy Spirit. Their new citizenship (*politeuma*) is in heaven."[31]

In the *City of God*, Augustine provided the classical formulation of Christian political theology, arguing that citizens of the *civitas dei* comingle in civic responsibility with all other earthly citizens during the interim age between Christ's first coming and his return. This *saeculum* is the classic Christian concept of the secular, that is a time in which church and civic governance work together for human flourishing, and the Christian works side by side with the non-Christian for the common good. Bonhoeffer retrieves a similar view through Luther, seeking to restore the Reformer's original intention of the Two-Kingdom doctrine as the polemic relation of the ultimate and penultimate aspects of the one Christ reality. The incarnation demands that the one Christ reality comes only in a package of sacred and profane, conceived as "polemical unity." This, at least in Bonhoeffer's view, was how Luther intended his Two-Kingdom doctrine which was later distorted by Lutheranism into the view that the two kingdoms were completely separate.[32] According to Bonhoeffer's understanding of the doctrine, the Christian citizen experiences the relation of church and government also within this Christocentric "polemical unity." Being a responsible citizen is still service to the same Christ, albeit in another way than at church.[33] Conversely, the government too derives its authority from Christ,[34] yet it does not enact specifically Christian politics[35] but serves all citizens in conducting humane politics in accordance with the orders of creation.[36] Bonhoeffer does not argue for a political unity but for a unified purpose of the polis in the one Christ reality. Consequently, the Christian citizen can live out his faith holistically without a private public dichotomy, but his responsibility for the polis requires nonetheless great political vigilance, engagement, and, if necessary, dissent. There is, in other words, no clear cut solution on how a Christian should be political, or, put more precisely, there are neither distinctly Christian or secularist solutions to political problems but in seeking the most humane solution, the citizen is in fact pursuing "Christian" politics. Identification of Christianity with a particular political party makes no sense according to Bonhoeffer's way of thinking, nor should Christians harbour any desire for theocracy or, as he put it, for erecting God's kingdom on earth. Instead, they enter the political process by trying to bring their faith convictions to bear in a public, civic forum through the proper civic structures of governance.

Bonhoeffer's view of political society grows out of the Christian tradition and is not really reflective of modern ethnic and religious pluralism; he did, however, experience secularism, and thought about the cooperation of Christians and non-Christians in a post-Christian society after the war.[37] In *Primus Usus Legis*, he warned that one should never forget the different motivations that drive the church and the state, insisting on a shared, public, civic reason for political decisions concerning the common good. This raises the question how a secular or pagan government that is not consciously beholden to Christianity could have substantive knowledge of its duty to uphold creation mandates. Bonhoeffer's answer to this question returns us to our previous discussion of anthropology, namely his recovery of natural law in Christological terms.[38] Together with the natural law tradition of many Protestant Reformers,[39] Bonhoeffer affirms the providential congruence between the second table of God's commandments and the moral law inherent in historical life itself.[40] In *Ethics*, he provides a more detailed sketch of "the natural life" and stresses the importance of natural rights that are discernable even by sinful human reason, and our corresponding civic duties as "reflections of God's glory in the midst of a fallen world."[41] Our concern at this point is not whether Bonhoeffer's deduction of human rights is ultimately convincing,[42] but that civic law ought to recognize the priority of natural rights "over all positive law."[43] For Bonhoeffer, of course, as we have seen above, these natural rights, common to all, derive ultimately from the creator God. Bonhoeffer affirms "abiding laws of human communal life" that we violate at our peril.[44] As we might expect, the natural itself is grounded christologically and thus fits into Bonhoeffer's eschatological ultimate-penultimate schema. The natural is the fallen creation, the penultimate, which is affirmed and upheld by Christ, but only for the sake of its ultimate origin and destiny, that is, its complete renewal upon His return.[45] The basic human rights to life and justice are discernable by human reason, reason that is clouded but not totally disabled by sin.[46]

It was the blatant violation of these basic human rights by the Nazi state that prompted Bonhoeffer's political resistance, culminating in his collaboration in the plot to assassinate Hitler. Much ink has been spilled on Bonhoeffer's decision to defend the elimination of the head of state, not least because this political engagement seems to violate Bonhoeffer's clearly expressed political convictions. Recent Bonhoeffer scholarship has affirmed Bonhoeffer's pacifist convictions derive naturally from his understanding that the disciple of the prince of peace should renounce violence in the pursuit of peace. Bonhoeffer's ethics was profoundly a "peace ethics."[47] Moreover, we know that his role in the resistance under the cover of working for the department of defense was extremely minor, and that he never really was involved in any attempt to kill Hitler. At the same time, there is no reason to doubt the reports of his most intimate friend and biographer Eberhard Bethke that Bonhoeffer encouraged others in the military that such a deed was not incompatible with their Christianity, and that he even expressed his willingness to kill Hitler if necessary.[48] He accompanied this latter remark with the statement that he should have to formally and officially terminate his church membership before doing so. This remark tells us that Bonhoeffer did not, as the Niebuhrian reading goes, that Bonhoeffer came to see sense and gave up his pacifism for a more realistic Christian stance in politics. Rather, what this remark shows us, is that Bonhoeffer regarded the situation as an absolute exceptional political circumstance in which he as Christian and German citizen was required to act. His was willing, in this case, to incur for himself the guilt that ensued from taking the life of a human being, even someone like Hitler. He knew that his act was a sin, but he was willing to throw himself on God's mercy in order to act for the common good.

Jean Bethke Elshtain thought it would be helpful, in this case, to distinguish between tyrannicide and political assassination. Unlike a political assassination, Tyrannicide is motivated not by private political interests but seeks to overthrow, for the sake of the common good, a tyrannical government that no longer served this end.[49] Elshtain's distinction makes sense in light of the persons involved in the famous 1944 attempt by Stauffenberg to kill Hitler: involved were highly ranked leaders from the military, the church, the academy, and business. The goal was not to "get Hitler" but to stop the reckless destruction of Germany, to transition to a proper government, and to rescue what was left of Germany's national honor. We should not forget, that Bonhoeffer too, was a patriot (not a nationalist, but a patriot).

CONCLUSION

At the end of her Gifford lectures, Elshtain asks "where do we find modern incarnationality?"[50] It is no surprise that she cites Bonhoeffer as a crucial resource for such incarnational thinking in politics. He, perhaps more than any others, articulated the importance of theology for politics in a way that circumvents the usual fears of fundamentalism and violence we usually expect in mixing politics and religion. Elshtain appreciates Bonhoeffer because he saw that human flourishing requires more than supposed secularist neutrality and pragmatism. Sound politics and healthy democracy requires a foundation in human dignity anchored in a transcendence that limits both the sovereign self and the sovereign state. To avoid fundamentalism and the politicization of religion, this transcendence requires mediation through the material. God, as Elshtain put it, "is neither utterly transcendent—so removed that God offers not coherent analogy to our selves—nor is God so entirely immanent" that we can comprehend either him nor the mystery of human dignity. Human transcendence and freedom are always lived out concretely in concrete human communities and involving concrete political decisions.

Elshtain loved to quote Bonhoeffer on freedom: freedom is "relationship and nothing else. In truth, freedom is a relationship between two persons. Being free means 'being free for the other,' because the other has bound me to him." Bonhoeffer, in short, speaks "of incarnational realities"; even the best religious resources—and for Elshtain there was little doubt the in the history of Western cultures these were Christian—even religious resources based on divine revelation have to be recalled and lived out hermeneutically, and in the relational responsibility with all other members of the polis. Bonhoeffer's thought combines deep theological conviction with an equally deep respect for the natural freedom and rights of others who have different beliefs. This combination of faith and civic responsibility were deeply appealing to Elshtain, perhaps because this attitude resembled so closely her own.

NOTES

1. Jean Bethke Elshtain, *Sovereignty, God, State, and Self* (New York: Basic Books, 2008), x; see also similar remarks in her Bonhoeffer essay in this volume.
2. (229).
3. Elshtain, *Sovereignty*, 231.
4. Elshtain, *Democracy on Trial* (Toronto: Anansi, 1993), 122.

5. George Grant, *Philosophy in the Mass Age*, ed. William Christian (Toronto: University of Toronto Press, 1995), 27.

6. Elshtain, *Sovereignty*, 232.

7. Elshtain, *Sovereignty*, 37.

8. Elshtain, *Sovereignty*, 39.

9. Elshtain, *Augustine and the Limits of Politics* (Notre Dame: UND Press), 15.

10. Elshtain, "Augustine and Diversity," in Charles Taylor. *A Catholic Modernity?* Ed. James L. Heft, (S.M. Oxford: Oxford University Press, 1999). 95–103, 98.

11. Elshtain, *Sovereignty*, 199.

12. Ibid., 100–101.

13. Elshtain offers a vivid image of renouncing tradition. Visiting a church in France, she noticed that from many statues of saints and angels the heads were cut off. She was informed that this had been the work of 18th century revolutionaries, and it reminds her of the violence we do to ourselves when we cut off our past.

14. Elshtain, *Democracy on Trial*, 140.

15. Elshtain, "Bonhoeffer on Modernity: 'Sic et Non'" in *Journal of Religious Ethics*, vol. 29, no. 3 (Fall, 2001), 345–66, 350.

16. Dietrich Bonhoeffer, *Ethik*, Dietrich Bonhoeffer Werke, vol. 6. (Gütersloh: Gütersloher Verlag, 2010), 78.

17. Dietrich Bonhoeffer, *Nachfolge*, Dietrich Bonhoeffer Werke, vol. 4, München: Chr. Kaiser, 2002. 4, 301; cf. Dietrich Bonhoeffer, *Ethics*. Dietrich Bonhoeffer Works, vol. 6, 4. (Minneapolis: Fortress Press, 2005) 285. Translation slightly altered to emphasize the "becoming human." The English translation has "incarnation" and "incarnate one."

18. Dietrich Bonhoeffer, *Konspiration Und Haft 1940–1945*, Dietrich Bonhoeffer Werke, vol. 16, Jørgen Glenthøj, Ulrich Kabitz and Wolf Krötke. Gütersloh eds., (Kaiser Verlag, 1996, 114.

19. Bonhoeffer, *Ethik*, 166 and 171.

20. Bonhoeffer is aware that it may sound strange for Christian ethics to begin with human rights rather than duties, but it is the creator and not the creature (in contradistinction to the Enlightenment charter on human rights) that is honored here (Ibid. 6, 173–74).

21. Ibid., 175.

22. Ibid., 179.

23. Ibid., 180.

24. Ibid., 188.

25. Elshtain, "Bonhoeffer on Modernity," 353–54.

26. Ibid., 354.

27. For Augustine's referral to Christ's saying, see *Ennaratio in Psalmum* 118, 31, 1.

28. I am reading Gelasius through the eyes of Karl Rahner, who interprets him as prolongation of Augustine's church state separation: "What Augustine regarded as a lofty ideal, Gelasius made tangible: the ideal of the state as the Church's helper, of two powers in peaceful collaboration, 'ruling the world.'" (H. Rahner, *Church and State in Early Christianity*, trans. L. D. Davis, San Francisco 1992, 157). Bonhoeffer's view is even more unified than this, but at the same time more nuanced because of his Christological ultimate-penultimate scheme.

29. The similarities of these three thinkers consists in the fact that a) there are two cities, realms, kingdoms or powers (*potestas*) governing God's world, the civil and the ecclesial authorities. The state deals with civic affairs but the church alone ordains bishops and judges the conscience; b) that ideally the state serves the church and c) that granting the church freedom and fostering its well-being will benefit the state, issuing in political stability and peace. There are, of course, important differences in Bonhoeffer especially from the Roman position that increasingly defines the church's authority in terms of apostolic succession, and increasingly seeks to subjugate the emperor to the church (until theologians such as Ockham react to that). Bonhoeffer, by contrast, grounds the power of the church and its differences to the state not in papal authority as vicarious representation but in the church itself (Ibid., 176).

30. D. Fergusson, *Church, State and Civil Society* (Cambridge, U.K 2004), 15.

31. Ibid.

32. Bonhoeffer, *Ethik*, 45; Bonhoeffer, *Ethics,* 60.

33. Bonhoeffer, *Ethik*, 528.

34. Bonhoeffer, *Konspiration und Haft*, 514: "Die echte Begründung der Obrigkeit ist also Jesus Christus selbst."

35. Bonhoeffer, *Konspiration und Haft*, 519: "Nicht ein christliches Handeln, aber ein Handeln, das Jesus Christus nicht ausschliesst, ist gemeint."

36. Bonhoeffer, *Konspiration und Haft*, 523: "Die Obrigkeit hat den göttlichen Auftrag, die Welt in ihren von Gott gegebenen Ordnungen auf Christus hin zu erhalten."

37. See his essay "The Doctrine of the Primus Usus Legis" in Dietrich Bonhoeffer, *Conspiracy and Imprisonment: 1940–1945*. Translated by Lisa A. Dahill and Douglas W. Stott. Dietrich Bonhoeffer Works. Edited by Victoria J. Barnett, Jr. Wayne Whitson Floyd and Barbara Wojhoski, vol. 16, (Minneapolis: Fortress Press, 2006), 584–601 (599–60). Victoria Barnett emphasizes that Bonhoeffer's thinking was influenced by the political failure of Christianity he experienced. I do not think, however, that this positional change entails a wholesale rethinking of his ecclesiology, as Barnett seems to suggest, but that the distinction between civil society in which political solutions are found on reason rather than on the proclamation of God's word, is continuous with Bonhoeffer's two kingdom doctrine. See: V. Barnett, "Dietrich Bonhoeffer's Relevance for a Post-Holocaust Christian Theology. The Centenary of Dietrich Bonhoeffer," eds. P. Cunningham and E. Kessler, in: Council of Centers on Jewish-Christian Relations 2.1/ 2007, 53–67.

38. Bonhoeffer, *Konspiration und Haft*, 520: "Woher kennt aber die Obrigkeit diese Inhalte? . . . Für die heidnische Obrigkeit aber gilt, daß eine providentielle Übereinstimmung zwischen den Inhalten der zweiten Tafel und dem dem geschichtlichen Leben selbst innewohnenden Gesetz besteht."

39. For an overview on this topic and the treatment of natural law in the context of two kingdom theories, see David VanDrunen, *Natural Law and the Two Kingdoms: A Study in the Development of Reformed Social Thought. Emory University Studies in Law and Religion*, (Grand Rapids, MI: Eerdmans, 2010).

40. Bonhoeffer, *Konspiration und Haft* 16, 520.

41. Bonhoeffer, *Ethik*, 174. Usually, the writings of Josef Pieper are cited in this context. It is reasonable to suppose from Bonhoeffer's markings on the texts, that Pieper's *Die Wirklichkeit und Das Gute*, and *Zucht und Maaß* influenced his thinking on this topic. The first clearly influenced his theological realism, and the second his appreciation for the Aristotelian-Thomistic virtue ethics; Pieper helped him to link natural human trait to the *humanum* shared by Christians and non-Christians. See, the editors' afterword in Bonhoeffer, *Ethics*, 419, and, for the last point Dietrich Bonhoeffer, and Eberhard Bethge. *Widerstand Und Ergebung; Briefe Und Aufzeichnungen Aus Der Haft*. Dietrich Bonhoeffer Werke, vol. 8. (Gütersloh: Gütersloher Verlagshaus Mohn, 1983) 417 (Letter to Bethge 6.5.44, and n 7).

42. He deduces the uniqueness of human being (i.e., the individual is never a means to a higher purpose or within a collective; a fact which redounds to God's creation of each individual and his destination to eternal life, Ibid., 176–77); the right to bodily life (ibid., 179) and shelter (ibid., 181), and the right to life not measured according to one's usefulness in society (ibid., 188).

43. Bonhoeffer, *Ethik*, 175.

44. "After Ten Years," 37–52, Dietrich Bonhoeffer, *Ethics*, Dietrich Bonhoeffer Works, vol.8, (Minneapolis: Fortress Press, 2005), 45–46. Bonhoeffer is aware that sometimes (and obviously in his own case), extreme situations may warrant transgressing these natural principles; yet even these exceptions incur guilt, and one cannot go against the grain of the universe with impunity: "The world *is* in fact so ordered that the fundamental honoring of life's basic laws and rights at the same time best serves self-preservation, and that these laws tolerate a very brief, singular, and, in the individual case, necessary trespass against them. But those laws will sooner or later—with irresistible force—strike dead those who turn necessity into a principle and as a consequence set up a law of their own alongside them. History's immanent justice rewards and punishes the deed only, but the eternal justice of God tries and judges the hearts" (ibid., 46; the last sentence aims at the willing incurrence of guilt and surrendering that judgment to God).

45. Dietrich Bonhoeffer, *Ethics*, Dietrich Bonhoeffer Works, vol. 6. (Minneapolis: Fortress Press, 2005), 174, (Bonhoeffer, *Ethik*, 166). "Natural life may not be understood simply as a preliminary stage toward life with Christ; instead, it receives its confirmation only through Christ. Christ has entered into natural life. Only by Christ's becoming human does natural life become the penultimate that is directed toward the ultimate. Only through Christ's becoming human do we have the right to call people to natural life and live it ourselves."

46. Ibid., 167.

47. Mark Thiessen Nation, Anthony G. Siegrist, and Daniel P. Umbel, *Bonhoeffer the Assassin?* (Grand Rapids, MI: Baker Academic, 2013), 227.

48. Eberhard Bethge, *Dietrich Bonhoeffer*, *Eine Biography*, (München: Gütersloher Verlagshaus, 2004), 844.

49. See Elshtain's article "Bonhoeffer for Political Thought" in this volume, (page xx).

50. Elshtain, *Sovereignty*, 237.

Chapter Nine

Sovereignty and Chastened Liberalism

M. Christian Green

INTRODUCTION: CHASTENED LIBERALISM?

During an office appointment at the University of Chicago Divinity School one day, Professor Jean Bethke Elshtain and I discussed the relationship between religion and liberalism. The specific context was a discussion of my dissertation proposal, in which I proposed to offer a "reconstructed" liberal feminist approach to the family that would support a more participatory role for fathers in order to facilitate women's freedom to pursue public vocations beyond the largely privatized maternal and caregiving roles, still disproportionately assigned to women by religion and culture. I was proposing a "reconstructed liberal feminist" theory of justice and care that would apply to both men and women in the family. Much in the way that some of today's "third wave" feminists claim their status with the disclaimer "I'm a feminist but . . . ,"[1] I found myself insisting in connection with certain feminist critiques of the standard liberal public-private split and its implications for gender roles, "I'm a liberal but . . ."[2] Professor Elshtain sagely nodded, observing that perhaps I was a "chastened liberal."

"Chastened" was a quintessentially Elshtainian term—one that she applied widely to political and theological phenomena that failed to appreciate the circumstances and limits of the human condition. This emphasis on human finitude, both in relation to God and to others in our human communities, in many ways echoed the mid-twentieth-century critical realism of Reinhold Niebuhr, whose writings remain influential in both political and theological circles.[3] Elshtain's work was heavily informed by both Niebuhrian "critical realism" and the fallout of the fascist, communist, and other totalitarian movements that perpetrated twentieth-century horrors in service of grandiose theories of human perfection.[4] In subsequent years, as I reflected and ruminated upon the meaning of the designation that Professor Elshtain had given me,[5] further research revealed a possible origin of her "chastened liberal" reference in the political theology of the noted Methodist theologian and Christian ethicist, Georgia Harkness.

Had Elshtain read Harkness's writings? Was Harkness, either directly or indirectly, Elshtain's source for the phrase "chastened liberal"? Would Elshtain have appreciated Harkness's political theology, even though the two seem to have differed significantly over such important matters as the justness of war? Sadly, these were not questions whose answers I was able fully to explore or ascertain in Elshtain's lifetime, and review of Elshtain's writings does not reveal any citations to Harkness or specific familiarity with Harkness's writings. But the idea of "chastened liberalism"—in the form of "chastened sovereignty" of the state and "chastened autonomy" of the self— is one that runs throughout her Gifford Lectures on *Sovereignty*. In this essay, I examine the origins, nature, and implications of "chastened liberalism" in the political theologies of Georgia Harkness and Jean Bethke Elshtain in connection with states and selves. I conclude with some reflections on the implications of "chastened liberalism" for contemporary debates over religious freedom.

ORIGINS OF "CHASTENED LIBERALISM"

The roots of "chastened liberalism" in Georgia Harkness's political theology are excellently chronicled in Rebekah Miles's study, *Georgia Harkness: The Remaking of a Liberal Theologian.*[6] A noted pacifist and leader in both the ecumenical movement and in the push for women's ordination in the United Methodist Church, Harkness became the first woman theologian to earn a professorship in a United States seminary with her appointment at the Garrett Biblical Institute (later the Garrett-Evangelical Theological Seminary) in Evanston, Illinois in 1939.[7] Thus, she began her professional career just as the world was plunging into World War II, a global conflict which had a significant effect on the political and ethical reflections of a generation of theologians. The sequence of World Wars I and II in the first half of the twentieth century raised profound questions for liberal theories and theologies of the time about the possibility and pursuit of social progress and social justice. The movements of fascism, communism, and totalitarianism that emerged in this period seemed, to many, a near fatal blow to these liberal conceptions.

As Miles recounts, Harkness began this period with considerable faith in the possibilities of liberalism and liberal theology, remarking in 1938, "The centrum of American theology is liberalism. In spite of premature funeral obsequies, it is likely to remain a basic American theology for some time to come."[8] With such defenses, Harkness found herself in something of a countercultural moment. As Miles observes, "How wrongheaded Harkness must have seemed to many at the time. By the late 1930s when Harkness was offering her spirited defense of liberalism and her predictions of its continued vitality, liberal theology appeared to be *in extremis* and sinking fast."[9] *Mutatis mutandi,* liberal theologians and political theorists find themselves in much the same place today, as Mainline Protestant churches, traditionally the bastions of liberal theology, continue to hemorrhage members, and liberal legal observers in the United States lament the absence of a liberal Protestant perspective—in fact, any Protestant perspective—on the United States Supreme Court following the retirement of Justice John Paul Stevens.[10]

Against the critiques of liberalism that were building in her time, Harkness proclaimed, in an essay for the *Christian Century,* titled "A Spiritual Pilgrimage," "Ten years ago, I was a liberal in theology. I am still a *liberal, unrepentant and unashamed.*"[11] Importantly, Harkness saw no tension between liberalism and evangelicalism, even as the orthodox evangelicals of her day seemed to be going in a different direction. She proclaimed, "I have long considered myself an evangelical liberal, and still do. The kind of liberalism that has been castigated throughout the century by the fundamentalists, and since the 1930's by the neo-orthodox, I do not recognize as a true picture of the liberalism of those who did the most to mold my thought. Nor do I recognize it as the theology I have tried to teach and write."[12] As Miles observes, "When Harkness wrote of the castigation of liberal theology, she was speaking from personal experience. Harkness was widely known as a liberal and was criticized on many occasions for this affiliation. At the same time, Miles observes:

> Harkness may have been *unrepentant* in the face of criticisms of liberal theology, but she was not *unmoved.* . . . Harkness not only defended liberalism, she also repeatedly looked for ways that liberal theology could be improved upon by attending to its critics. . . . [S]he expressed gratitude to neo-orthodoxy and other theological movements for prompting a correction in the excesses of liberalism by reminding liberals of the depth of human sin, the radical need for divine grace, and the centrality of the cross.
>
> Throughout her interactions with various theologians and theological movements, Harkness was constantly looking for ways she could learn from them. This is not just a peculiarity of Harkness but is, instead, a hallmark of many liberal theologies, which are predisposed to take into account changing circumstances and changing ideas from an array of sources in order to form a new synthesis. Many liberals were confident that open reflection on various perspectives would lead one nearer to the truth. Their willingness to take into account and shift with changing ideas and circumstances is responsible in large part for the staying power of liberal theology.[13]

It was in the "Spiritual Pilgrimage" essay that Harkness would coined the phrase "chastened liberalism" to describe her perspective.

The essay begins with Harkness's enthusiastic acceptance of the editor's invitation to her to be "autobiographical"—autobiography being genre with which Elshtain also had great affinity. Reflecting on her theological evolution, Harkness maintains, in words that are as evocative for many today as they were for her many cohorts, sandwiched between the Great Depression and two World Wars, "The collapse of economic and international security, of brotherhood and mutual trust, which the world has witnessed in this decade has affected my thinking, as it must that of anyone with a shred of ethical or religious sensitivity. . . . Yet more determinative for me than what has happened in the political of theological world have been the events of my private world."[14] Of the specific impact of these events on her theology, she observes, "I have become more of a theologian, probably less of a philosopher. My religion is more Christ-centered. I have rediscovered the Bible. Mysticism and worship have taken on added richness. I seem in a small way to have become a peripatetic evangelist, speaking often on personal religious living. I was a pacifist and a socialist ten years ago and still am, but my Christian conviction in both spheres has taken on greater clarity and firmness. I am much more church-minded. Finally, I have seen a new vision of the world mission of the church."[15] On the theme of spiritual pilgrimage there is an analogy to be drawn between Harkness's shift from philosophy to theology and Elshtain's evolution from political theory to theological ethics along with a shared early commitment to socialism.[16]

Additional similarities between Harkness and Elshtain can be found in their assessments of liberalism's connection to some of the excesses of scientific modernity.[17] Having proclaimed her "unrepentant and unashamed" liberalism at an earlier point in the essay, Harkness writes, "This does not mean that I have seen nothing in liberalism that needed correction. We were in danger of selling out to science as the only approach to truth, of trusting too hopefully in man's power to remake the world, of forgetting the profound fact of sin and the redeeming power of divine grace, of finding our chief evidence of God in cosmology, art or human personality, to the clouding of the clearer light of the incarnation."[18] In Harkness's assessment, modern faith in science and technology thus threatened to obscure more fundamental truths about human nature, including both our propensity to sin and our status as beings incarnate. It also threatened to obscure truths of biblical revelations. Here, Harkness observed, "Liberalism needed to see in the Bible something more than a collection of moral adages and a compendium of great literature. It needed to see in Christ something more than a great figure living sacrificially and dying for his convictions. It needed to be called to the meaning of the cross and the power of resurrection.[19] Harkness's concerns about "technological imperatives" and "human personality" obscuring the messages of both reason and revelation are standard Elshtainian themes, as well. [20] Harkness is more sanguine than Elshtain that liberalism never "had as many utopian illusions as it is now customary in retrospect to attribute to it." [21] Elshtain never gave up the concern about "utopian illusions," but she would echo and amplify Harkness's admission that liberalism's "self-confidence has been challenged by both events and theological trends." [22]

Even with these limits and qualifications of liberalism in mind, Harkness proclaimed, in what would become the essay's signature passage:

> My liberalism is, I trust, a *chastened and deepened liberalism.* But I am more convinced than ever I was before that God reveals himself in many ways and that only through the spirit of free inquiry can Christian faith go forward. I believe in the essential greatness of man, in a social gospel which calls us to action as co-workers with God in the redemptive process, in a Kingdom which will come in this world by growth as Christians accept responsibility in the spirit of the cross. My Christian faith has its central focus, not in Paul's theology or Luther's or Calvin's, but in the incarnation of God in Jesus of the Gospels. [23]

In this statement, Harkness's theology appears more scriptural and experiential in the tradition of liberal theology than Elshtain's more theological and philosophical reflection from the more orthodox Augustinian tradition—they were working from different theological traditions and in different quadrants of the Wesleyan Quadrilateral. Harkness's statement reflects an overall attitude of liberal evangelical optimism, but the chastening effect is evident in places where Harkness approaches Elshtain's more realist perspective on the possibilities for human redemption. Thus, Harkness observes, regarding the ethics of war:

> But deeper than this is the realism that has come with the shattering of whatever illusions our liberalism had. I believe that life is inevitably a sphere of conflict and that *our choices are not often to be made between good and evil, but between alternative evils.* I believe that in all of life's dark areas the triumph which shines through tragedy comes not with the sword which our Lord rejected, but with the cross toward which he walked. I believe that only in the union of justice with suffering love is any human force redemptive and permanently curative, for only in such union is force more than human. [24]

Liberalism, in its optimism, is often more comfortable with the idea of choice than the reality of choices between evils. Harkness and Elshtain would have disagreed on the utility of war to achieve peace, but they would have agreed on the need to parse dilemmas of good and evil without illusions.

Harkness had argued, a bit earlier in the fateful decade of the 1930s—years clouded by the Great Depression, the rise of fascism and communism, and the early rumblings of Hitler's gruesomely hegemonic ambitions—for the need to forge a path between "unrealistic idealism and unidealistic realism."[25] Harkness argued that "[p]aper utopias in plenty have been established," but "[i]deals rooted in a deep sense of social justice are not mere pipe-dreams"—she was against both "pessimistic cynicism" and "over-optimistic liberalism or evangelicalism."[26] Harkness recommends a stance of humility in contrast with the sin of pride (*superbia*) the latter of which is would become prominent feature of Elshtain's discussion of sovereignty. In a similarly Elshtainian vein, Harkness cautions particularly against nationalisms derived from familial and intergroup pride, "Family pride may be a wholesome incentive to its members to live up to a great heritage; it may also be a demonic source of division . . . For national honor, which means group *superbia* on a grand scale, Christian men will fight to the death other Christians against whom personally they have not the slightest animosity."[27]

There are many similarities between Harkness and Elshtain in their situatedness between idealism and realism, but there are also profound differences—particularly when it comes to questions of pacifism and just war. Of war, Harkness argued in a way that resonates in our terror-filled times, "To seek one's own safety rather than the service of the common good is both to lose one's security and one's soul, as the experience of terror-stricken individuals and nations amply testifies, while a large measure both of inner and outer security may be found through mutual good will."[28] Harkness would later write, "I should explain why I have become a more convinced pacifist in a day when many better Christians than I have felt impelled to surrender their pacifism. The reasons are both pragmatic and theological. *War destroys every value for which Christianity stands*, and to oppose war by more war is only to deepen the morass into which humanity has fallen."[29] Harkness's pacifist commitments could not be more emphatic.

By contrast, Elshtain spoke out as a public intellectual on a national and international stage in favor of the initial incursions by the United States into Afghanistan and eventually into Iraq, as well, in the global "War on Terror," using just war arguments that some argue ended up morally underwriting an ill-founded and ill-fated war of more than a decade's duration.[30] Many have argued that U.S. counterterrorism operations have sought security at the expense of the nation's soul and squandered abundant international goodwill after the terrorist attacks of September 11, 2001. Harkness argued of the global wars of her era, "The idea of fighting 'a war to end war'—however high-minded the thought of the great Christian statesman who gave the world these words—has been discredited by the logic of events."[31] Many have argued the same of the wars of Afghanistan and Iraq, critiquing the emergence of a U.S. "imperial state" in the post-Cold War era. Elshtain's defense of the state's right to wage preemptive war against those who, arguably, threatened its sovereignty and security assigns a very high prerogative to the power of the state. Was this high view of state sovereignty chastened in her subsequent writings? Having sketched some points of comparison and contrast between Harkness and Elshtain on the concept of "chastened liberalism," it is to the view of state sovereignty in Elshtain's writings that I now turn.

THE "CHASTENED SOVEREIGNTY" OF STATES

Having located the apparent origins of the concept of "chastened liberalism" in the political theology of Georgia Harkness, where do we find evidence of chastening in Jean Bethke Elshtain's political ethics? For Elshtain, Christian political ethics has its roots in an Augustinian moral anthropology of the human person. In this vein, Elshtain argues:

> For Augustine, a creative intelligence lies behind this world and the beings that call it home. Human beings, created in God's image (*imago Dei*) participate in God's creativity. But it is pride and folly to pretend one can emulate God directly. There are limits—intrinsic, not accidental or contingent—to our capacity to understand fully, to divine (if you will) the Divine person(s). Touch sets a limit; sight sets a limit; speech sets a limit. Augustine is especially brilliant on speech and language, those imperfect ways human beings attest to what they have experienced, contemplated, or come to understand.[32]

In this light, Elshtain maintains, "It follows that human beings possess only a 'creature's knowledge' that comes in 'faded colors, compared with the knowledge that comes when it is known in the Wisdom of God.' Reason 'of itself could never directly reach the truth; it acted in the light of the faith; and was essentially an accompaniment to man in his transitory state as voyager in this world.'"[33] Compared to Harkness's liberal theological understanding, this is hard-core Augustinianism of the vintage imbibed copiously by the Lutheran and Calvinist traditions and the modern neo-orthodox movement from which Harkness distinguished herself, but which Elshtain embraced for much of her own spiritual pilgrimage. Thus, Elshtain tells us, "Augustine reminds that human beings are earthly, fallible, and unable to sustain abstract truths, especially philosophic understanding that omits grace and love."[34]

There are real-world political implications that flow from this theology. As Elshtain observes, "Tainted forever by the legacy of 'original sin,' humans must erect barriers to their worst tendencies even as they seek to realize their best. That is the only legitimate purpose of earthly dominion. Because no one can claim sovereignty in relation to another—authority is something very different—we are not denuded if we give of ourselves to others."[35] Elshtain describes justice, a hallmark concern of liberal theology, in Augustinian terms, as something that "can be a form of love" but also requires a "type of governance that builds barriers to cruel and capricious behavior on the part of earthly rulers."[36] The necessity of good governance leads to what Elshtain describes as the "*security dilemma*," in international relations theory terms, in that "People never possess a kingdom 'so securely as not to fear subjugation by their enemies . . . such is the instability of human affairs that no people has ever been allowed such a degree of tranquility as to remove all dread of hostile attacks on their life in this world.'"[37] In the Western Christian political tradition, Elshtain notes, those who possess kingdoms tyrannically live in a world of particular insecurity. In one of her frequent references to chastening, Elshtain maintains, "The ruler never enjoys sovereignty in *unchastened and willful splendor*. No earthly ruler can claim an absolute, unconditional right to power. A king gone bad is a tyrant and, perforce, ceases to be a king."[38]

This chastened sovereignty is not limited to rulers. Elshtain draws on the writings of Thomas Aquinas to argue, "Within political life, as one distinctive form of social life, no person is sufficient unto himself or herself . . . There is no such thing as sovereign self . . . No single person on his or her own can arrive at the knowledge of all [these] things through the use of his reason. Thus it is necessary for him to live in society so that one person can help another and different men can employ their reasons in different ways. Nor can groups of persons, organized as kingdoms, be solipsistically sovereign and beholden to no one or nothing outside themselves."[39] Elshtain's reading of Thomistic political ethics prompts the recommendation of another form of political chastening—this time of the law. Here, Elshtain observes:

[L]aw, too, may run amuck if it pretends that some human beings can read into the hearts of others and that law should reach in and control this interiority: a kind of moralistic omniscience. *Chastening the overreach that turns the law into a tyranny* over human beings requires that it acknowledge that it cannot eliminate or prohibit every human action, because in trying to eliminate evils, it may also do away with many good things and the interest of the common good which is necessary for human societies may be adversely affected. Tyrannical law—which does not deserve the appellation "law" at all—is characterized by pretenses that are not in accord with reason and not ordered to the common good. The tyrant uses the "law" to make war on law understood as a rational order of sentient beings directed toward a common good.[40]

In this observation, Elshtain invokes a truth familiar to lawyers and legal scholars everywhere—namely, the realization that law can not only be perverted in its ends, but also a rather blunt instrumental means in the quest for justice. And yet the inescapable reality of our distinctly non-utopian human condition is that laws and leaders are necessary, lest we lapse into antinomian anarchy.

Two tensions are often said to run throughout Christian political ethics— between love and justice and between freedom and order. Having addressed love and justice through Augustine and Aquinas, Elshtain addresses freedom and order through Luther and Calvin—arguing against antinomian anarchy. Specifically, she asks, "Why do we require temporal authority in the first instance? It is pretty simple. Human beings are sinners and tempted to do evil. Temporal authority erects barriers to the evil that they might do."[41] Luther, she argues, "fears anarchy more than he fears a tightly knit order," thus, in the end he is "compelled to rely on secular authority," which leads him to the doctrine that "temporal authority is divinely instituted."[42] The pursuit of order through temporal authority can have some rather harsh implications for freedom. Elshtain observes of the politics that flow from Luther's pessimistic view of human nature, "Given Luther's assumptions, it is more rather than less likely that force is needed to bind human beings to one another and to the law. Were we 'naturally' more good, less wicked, the hand of temporal authority could rest lighter on our heads. But we are not. So worldly authority has the power to punish and punish severely: not only power but authority. This is its legitimate task."[43] For Luther, the need for political sovereignty is prompted by the impossibility of personal sovereignty, due to our fallen human nature. Having already identified Luther with the view that we "do not live for ourselves," Elshtain differentiates Luther's understanding from that of "contemporary articulators of self-sovereignty."[44] Invoking the Augustinian notion of our dual and dueling natures, she argues, "Luther's self cannot be said to be sovereign, even in its innermost part. It may be free but this is not the same thing as being sovereign. The weakness of the human will is such that to pretend we can consistently will 'the good' is folly. We are ongoingly reminded of our creaturely status by Luther: Believers are under God, not coequal to him."[45] Luther, in Elshtain's analysis, believes that humans cannot be trusted to pursue pacific freedom and pacifist forms of love. Rather, she argues:

> Human beings—all human beings—are subjected to a form of temporal authority. That this is so is not so much from interest in a common good as the hope that the least harm might be done. Only if all persons belonged to the Kingdom of God would the need for temporal law vanish. Temporal rule restrains the unchristian and the wicked. Those believers who, naively, hold that one can rule by the gospel alone would, were they in ascendance, unleash the beasts on the world to devour, slash, and slay as they might. On this earth, if the lion lies down with the lamb, the lamb must be replaced frequently.[46]

Christian subjects are not to be wholly subsumed by the state. Nonetheless, Elshtain counsels, "Government, ordained of God is not to be despised. . . . Christ did not bear the sword, but neither did he abolish it. As to the individual Christian's own orientation: If a matter touches himself or herself alone, better to suffer evil; however, if the matter touches others, the Christian may need to act in behalf of others even unto bearing the sword."[47] This "Christianity of the sword" seems far from the pacifist views of Harkness. Neither Elshtain nor Harkness believed that the Kingdom of God was, or maybe ever could be, a realized perfection in the murky world human politics, but Harkness seemed to see more potential for perfectibility.

Both princes and perfection, or, more accurately, predestination, figure strongly into the political theology of John Calvin. As Elshtain puts it "Calvin lifts up the dignity and purpose of the temporal authority by contrast to Luther. He seeks to reintegrate what had been ripped asunder. His state aims not just to repress evil-doing but to improve man via a religio-political order."[48] This leads to a defense of political authority in an especially strong form. Elshtain argues, "Rulers are ministers of God in an important sense as a duty of office. The faithful should endure a wicked ruler with patience as his sovereign authority derives from God. It follows that no private person may resort to tyrannicide. God may, however, raise up someone to deal with the tyrant—this 'someone' cannot be a private person."[49] In this sense, Elshtain observes, "The sovereignty of God is the pivot of Calvin's theology and ethics."[50] The prince often eclipses the people in Calvin's political ethics, prompting another chastening reference in which Elshtain observes, "Calvin has a low opinion of humanity—so low that he sees human beings as innately depraved. This depravity would overwhelm humanity save for the *chastening hand of God* and his grants of authority to both Church and state."[51] Through Luther and Calvin, Elshtain traces not the elevation of the sovereignty and freedom of the individual, which she describes as a conclusion often drawn misleadingly from the Protestant Reformation, but rather the development of a "political theology that underlies the emergence of the 'Protestant' nation-state."[52]

Chastening makes its appearance a final time in Elshtain's discussion of the state when she contrasts "classical state sovereignty" and "'world order' universalism" with the alternative of a *"chastened version of sovereignty."*[53] What does chastened sovereignty look like? Elshtain tells us that the "most likely agents of such action at present are states who are constituted in and around a 'binding' of sovereignty, including the articulation and enforcement of human rights"[54] and that "sovereignty offers about as 'good a deal' as human beings can reasonably expect in a world riven by conflict and confronted daily with the specter of wars of all sorts."[55] Human rights have sometimes been described as aspirational.[56] In a similar way, Elshtain describes "chastened sovereignty" as "aspiration to sovereignty." Aspiration need not signify vain hope, but rather the crucial capacity to imagine better alternatives and seek to move toward their attainment. It is not a realized utopia, but a morally important metric of a process of perfectibility, if not perfection. Unfortunately, the most grandiose and at times narcissistic forms of aspiration have, as Elshtain describes it, "migrated, got parceled out, as it were, into those microstates proclaimed as 'sovereign selves.'"[57] Whether such self-sovereignty is irredeemably solipsistic and reductionistic is a topic that Elshtain takes up in the latter portions of the sovereignty lectures.

THE "CHASTENED AUTONOMY" OF THE SELF

Elshtain explains the transition from sovereign states to sovereign selves with the following thesis: "As sovereign state is to sovereign God, so sovereign selves are to sovereign states. Given that sovereignty in the political sense 'named' self-determination for a territorial, collective entity, it is altogether unsurprising that this logic of sovereignty came unbound and migrated, becoming attached more and more to notions of the self."[58] From Elshtain's Augustinian perspective, almost any degree of focus on self-sovereignty carries the risk of degradation into the sin of pride. As Elshtain describes it, "For Augustine, this version of freedom—power arbitrarily to choose—is a sure sign of the sin of pride, *superbia,* for the self, instead, must be pulled by love if it is to be oriented to what is genuinely good: Here the famous tug of war between *cupiditas,* which enshrines a form of self-love, and *caritas,* orientation to the good and love of the neighbor, including a recognition of one's own interdependencies."[59] Both love and limits are present in relationships of interdependency, which operates as a chastening tools in the formation of self in society.

When it comes to contemporary liberal theology, particularly liberal Protestantism, Elshtain insists that there are consequences associated with the "buoyant belief that one could in a benign way remake human nature in order that it better comport with the uplifting image of the 'Self Alone.'"[60] In Augustinian fashion Elshtain, preaches against such perfectionist projects, with their attendant risk of pride. The potential for perilous pride in attempts to transcend biological human nature is a focus of Elshtain's bioethical writings. Thus, in the sovereignty lectures Elshtain observes:

> Characteristic of all projects of self-sovereignty is a "triumph over" something, nature being one of the chosen antagonists. This triumph takes several forms of what I identify as "hard" or "soft" self-sovereignty, respectively. Each features a monistic, voluntaristic notion of the self, the self "as one" with its projects. Even as we have observed that the monistic, voluntaristic understanding of God as will, and the monistic version of state-sovereignty that triumphs all other loyalties and identities, are characteristic of strong forms of theological and political sovereignty, so the monistic self appears in dreams of radical self-sovereignty.[61]

Elshtain condemns eugenic projects, some of which she links to liberal theology, especially contemporary quests for genetic perfection, arguing, "Most of these discussions take place in a zone sanitized of any normative accounts of human nature or the human condition more generally. A quest for control has always been a feature of the quest for the sovereign self. The technocratic view of our ability to manipulate and get outcomes we desire is widespread."[62] The result of such projects, she argues, is that "Pridefulness on the individual level squeezes out space for others, hence for an appropriate self-regard consistent with our recognition of others and loving attention paid to them. Selves trapped by pride refuse to pay proper attention to the other."[63] Ultimately, she argues, "The price of self-sovereignty is high—but someone else, the most defenseless among us pays it."[64]

Chastening makes an appearance in the final chapter of Elshtain's sovereignty treatise when she suggests that just as "challenging the sovereign state leads to a *chastened patriotism* and a limited sovereignty," challenges to self-sovereignty raise a number of questions for liberal notions of the self, such as:

> If we are not fully masters in our own house, what, then, are we? If we are not perfectly autonomous, are we autonomous in any way? What sort of achievement might *chastened autonomy* be? If we lose at-oneness with our selves, if we are estranged necessarily, how, then, do we fashion a self? If radical, limitless freedom, driven by will, is a destructive dead end, what does freedom with limits offer: And what limits might those be?[65]

Ultimately, Elshtain, invoking again the idea of perfectibility, argues that "personal autonomy (rightly understood) and national sovereignty are achievements rather than presuppositions."[66] Of the promise, but also the peril of perfectibility, Elshtain writes:

> The self I have in mind seeks meaning and dignity and fines a measure of both not in total liberation from nature, nor in some utopian attunement and at-oneness with nature but, rather, in growing to become a full person according to our human natures. Because that nature is intrinsically social; because we are persons, not individuals; we must refrain from doing everything of which we are capable. If we refuse to observe a limit, we are destroyers, we become death dealers.[67]

In much the same vein, Elshtain quotes the observation of one of her favorite theologians, the Nazi-resister Dietrich Bonhoeffer, that:

> Freedom is not a quality of man, nor is it an ability. . . . it is not a possession, a presence, an object, nor is it a form of existence—but a relationship and nothing else. In truth, freedom is a relationship between two persons. Being free means "being free for the other," because the other has bound me to him. In a relationship with the other I am free. No substantial or individualistic concept of freedom can conceive of freedom.[68]

Of this Bonhoefferian notion of freedom, Elshtain observes:

> These are strong words that bespeak incarnational realities. Human life is always lived in concrete communities—not in nowhere. Even as God is dialogic and related and gives of himself, so are we called—in Christianity—to be likewise. In a society such as ours, with our history, these recollections can be ongoingly kindled, and no doubt resources from other faiths offer similar possibilities of renewal. To oversimplify, we are never in a zero-sum game in this life of ours, never in a situation where the exact sum I "give" is something taken away from me absolutely and appropriated by someone else: that is Sartre's "hell is other people," a desolate, dead, and lonely world. "Zero sum" is not the world of people who embrace the quotidian rather than despise it; who find joy in simple things; who find dignity in a decent job well done. Our bodies defined a limit, but also a possibility as we enter into community, for we can only "be" by virtue of others.[69]

In light of Elshtain's profound concern to chasten liberal understandings of state and self, it comes as no surprise to see listed at the end of the *Sovereignty* book's acknowledgements section, Elshtain's mention of gratitude for her "formation as a child in a faith that lifts up human dignity and chastens human willfulness."[70] Praise for chastening is, literally, Elshtain's last word when it comes to the sovereignty of states and selves.

CONCLUSION: SOVEREIGNTY, LIBERALISM, AND RELIGIOUS FREEDOM

In each their own way, both Georgia Harkness and Jean Bethke Elshtain had lasting significance in the development of Christian political theology. As Christian ethicists, they were both committed not only to theory, but to the practice of public scholarship and public engagement of religion with the political realm and the public square. Their writings and work demonstrated deep engagement with the great theological and political issues of their day. Both supported the engagement of religion in world affairs. Both supported the protection of human rights. Both supported promotion of religious freedom. But they supported these positions from what can be termed a position of "chastened liberalism."

The politics and ethics of religious freedom, which are alternately defended and embattled in both liberal and conservative political circles today may be an especially timely issue on which to conclude this comparison of Harkness's and Elshtain's "chastened liberalisms." Harkness described the struggle for religious freedom as one of the "great creative outpourings of the Spirit of God, which have always had ethical accompaniments, and sometimes very significant ones."[71] Nonetheless, in some circles of the academic study of religion today, the concept of religious freedom has been the subject of debate. Some religion scholars question the very possibility of religious freedom amid widely disparate understandings of religion in the postmodern world, and some particularly question the involvement of the state and the law in defining religion.[72] The complaint is that legal adjudication of religious freedom claims by the state and its courts, not only entangles the state with religion but also normalizes a particular privatized and individualistic understanding of religion linked to Enlightenment and Reformation to the detriment of religions that assume other forms.[73] In this view, state involvement in religion is an exercise in Protestant hegemony. Others question state promotion of religious freedom at home and abroad, as a matter of foreign policy.[74] In this view, state promotion of religious freedom is an exercise in religious imperialism.

What is interesting in the current moment is that many, if not most, of these critiques of religious freedom are coming from within the liberal camp. Religious freedom has often "coded" conservative in religious and political discourse, even though classic precursors of it can be found not only in Martin Luther's revolt against church authority in the Protestant Reformation, but also in the modern liberal political tradition ushered in by John Locke. The emergence of critiques from within the liberal fold arguably makes religious freedom seem even more of a conservative cause by undercutting the liberal bases of religious freedom and religious rights.[75] One scholar has argued that religious freedom is an issue that should prompt "serious self-reflection on the part of liberals" on "how they can both be in favor of religious freedom for all" while also denying protection to those they deem "uncivilized, or insufficiently liberal," particularly when the result is "religious discrimination at the hands of the majority," but not "religious freedom for those outside the mainstream."[76] According to this line of critique, liberalism, for all of its praise for toleration reduces to the idea that "religious freedom means protection only for the kind of religion they like, the private, individualized, progressive kind."[77] This critique of religious freedom coming from academic critics who in most respects occupy the liberal ends of the religious and political spectrum is friendly fire—but fire, nonetheless.

In her later years, Elshtain wrote and spoke on the significance and limits of religious freedom.[78] Elshtain was, in certain respects, more supportive of promotion of religious freedom by the state than she was of some of the religious claims of individuals. In recommending a chastened form of the liberal notion of toleration—which she called "deep toleration"—she was concerned about the tendency toward privatization and subjectivism of some religious freedom claims, as well as their tendency to get caught up in identity politics. We are in an odd moment when the language of religious freedom is being invoked by religious groups seeking state protection and sometimes special accommodation of their rights in a way that invites state entanglement—even as liberals are questioning the very ideas of religious freedom and the capacity of the law to protect it when it comes to the minority religions most in need of protection. For liberal defenders of religious freedom and religious disestablishment, it is a chastening moment, but one that through concepts like Elshtain's "deep toleration" offers possibilities for a liberal notion of religious tolerance and freedom, still unrepentant and unashamed, but maybe fruitfully chastened and reconstructed.

NOTES

1. See M. Christian Green, "From Third Wave to Third Generation: Feminism, Faith, and Human Rights," in *Feminism, Law, and Religion*, Marie A. Failinger, Elisabeth R. Schiltz, and Susan Stabile, eds. (Farnham, Surrey, England: Ashgate Publishing, 2013), 141–71.

2. For Elshtain's views on the gendered dimensions of the public and private spheres, see *Public Man, Private Woman*. See also "Antigone's Daughters," *Democracy* 2, no. 2 (April 1982), 39–45.

3. See e.g., Reinhold Niebuhr, *Moral Man and Immoral Society* (New York: Charles Scribner's Sons, 1932); *The Children of Light and Children of Darkness* (New York: Charles Scribner's Sons, 1944), and especially *The Nature and Destiny of Man*, 2 vols. (New York: Charles Scribner's Sons, 1941–1943). *The Nature and Destiny of Man* Collected Niebuhr's own Gifford Lectures.

4. In fact, Elshtain's writings on these themes, particularly the relationship of Christianity to democracy and human rights were among the first Elshtain writings that I encountered. See Jean Bethke Elshtain "In Common Together," in *Christianity and Democracy in Global Context*, ed. John Witte, Jr. (Boulder, CO: Westview Press, 1993), 65–84, and "Thinking About Women, Christianity, and Rights," in *Religion and Human Rights in Global Context: Religious Perspectives* (The Hague: Martinus Nijhoff Publishers, 1996) 143–56. See also Jean Bethke Elshtain, *Democracy on Trial* (New York: Basic Books, 1995), *Augustine and the Limits of Politics* (Notre Dame, IN: University of Notre Dame Press, 1995) and *Who Are We?: Critical Reflections and Hopeful Possibilities* (Grand Rapids, MI: W.B. Eerdmans Publishers, 2000). The last two titles, published after Elshtain's move from the Vanderbilt University Department of Political Science to the University of Chicago Divinity School, reflect her definitive "turn" toward Augustinian moral anthropology.

5. See M. Christian Green, "M. Christian Green Remembers Her Mentor Jean Bethke Elshtain," September 5, 2013, accessible at: http://cslr.law.emory.edu/news/news-story/headline/cslr-mourns-the-passing-of-scholar-jean-bethke-elshtain.

6. Rebekah Miles, ed. *Georgia Harkness: The Remaking of a Liberal Theologian* (Louisville, KY: Westminster/John Knox Press, 2010).

7. Jean Bethke Elshtain was the first woman to hold an endowed professorship at Vanderbilt University from 1988–1995 and the first woman to serve as a professor in the field of religious ethics at the University of Chicago, as Laura Spelman Rockefeller Professor of Social and Political Ethics—so Harkness and Elshtain share a similar record of "firsts" in the field of Christian ethics.

8. Miles, 1. (quoting Georgia Harkness, "The Faith of the North American Churches," lecture given to the American Delegates to the third International Mission Conference [Madras Ecumenical Conference, 1938] of the World Council of Churches, Niagara Falls, NY, June 13, 1938).

9. Ibid.

10. See Diana Butler Bass, "Elena Kagan, the Supreme Court, and a Lament for American Protestantism," beliefnet.com, May 10, 2010.

11. Ibid., 2 (quoting Georgia Harkness, "A Spiritual Pilgrimage," *Christian Century* 56 (March 15, 1939) (emphasis added).

12. Ibid. (quoting Georgia Harkness, *Our Christian Hope* (New York: Abingdon Press, 1964), 11–24.

13. Ibid., 3 (quoting Harkness . . .).

14. Miles, 20 (quoting Harkness, "A Spiritual Pilgrimage").

15. Ibid., 21.

16. On Elshtain's affinities for socialism, see Jean Bethke Elshtain, "A Personal Memoir," *Commonweal* (November 7, 1975), 526–28. The essay was one of several in a series, titled "What I Think about the Catholic Church." The article chronicles Elshtain's own spiritual pilgrimage from a Lutheran family, through the Presbyterian church that was the only option in her small-town childhood, "liberal agnosticism" in college, and eventually to the Catholic Church, into which she was received in 2011. See also Matthew Boudway, "Jean Bethke Elshtain" (obituary), *Commonweal*, August 12, 2013 (quoting Elshtain's observation in the earlier *Commonweal* essay that "A democratic socialism, erected on a foundation of respect for persons, on a belief in the dignity of each and every human person in the eyes of God and man, owes much to Christianity"). Defense of the theory of just war, however, would be one of Elshtain's more controversial legacies. Her writings on war include Jean Bethke Elshtain, *Women and War* (New York: Basic Books, 1987); *Just War on Terror The Burden of American Power in a Violent World* (New York: Basic Books, 2003).

17. Miles, 20 (quoting Harkness, "A Spiritual Pilgrimage"), 22.

18. Ibid.

19. Ibid.

20. Elshtain's writings in this area, particularly the specter of genetic determinism, were likely the basis for her appointment to the President's Council on Bioethics during the administration of President George W. Bush.

21. Miles, 22 (quoting Harkness, "A Spiritual Pilgrimage").

22. Ibid.

23. Ibid. (emphasis added).

24. Ibid., 24 (emphasis added).

25. Ibid., 47 and 56 (quoting Georgia Harkness, *The Resources of Religion* [New York: Henry Holt and Company, 1936]).

26. Ibid., 48, 49.

27. Ibid., 52–53.

28. Ibid., 56.

29. Ibid., 23 (quoting Harness, "A Spiritual Pilgrimage") (emphasis added).

30. See Jean Bethke Elshtain, *Just War Against Terror*. Elshtain was criticized by many of her colleagues following that book's publication, including a particularly bracing critique by her colleagues Stanley Hauerwas and Paul Griffiths. See Stanley Hauerwas, Paul J. Griffiths, and Jean Bethke Elshtain, "War, Peace, and Jean Bethke Elshtain," *First Things,* October 2003. *Just War on Terror* was published in paperback in 2004, with a new epilogue in which Elshtain addressed these critiques and also articulated a just war argument for the war in Iraq. On Election Day 2004, *The New York Times*, published an abbreviated version of a larger letter opposing the Iraq War that was signed by two thirds of the faculty of the University of Chicago Divinity School. See Bruce Lincoln, "Religion and War," (letter to the editor) *The New York Times,* November 2, 2004. For more on the debate underlying the letter, see Zack Werner, "Theologians Slam Bush's Use of God to Justify War in Iraq," *The Chicago Maroon,* October 31, 2004. Toward the end of her life, Elshtain was reportedly working on a book containing further reflections since 2003, tentatively titled "Torture and Terror in a Time of Troubles." See Ken Trainor, "Just War," *University of Chicago Magazine,* May-June 2010.

31. Ibid., 58.

32. Jean Bethke Elshtain, *Sovereignty: God, State, and Self* (New York: Basic Books, 2008), 4.

33. Ibid., 4–5.

34. Ibid., 5.

35. Ibid., 9.

36. Ibid., 10.

37. Ibid, 10–11.

38. Ibid., 16 (emphasis added).

39. Ibid., 17–18.

40. Ibid., 19 (emphasis added). Catholic moral theologian and law professor, Cathleen Kaveny, has recently written well of this imperative to common good at the heart of natural law. See Cathleen Kaveny, *Law's Virtues: Fostering Autonomy and Solidarity in American Society* (Washington, DC: Georgetown University Press, 2012).

41. Ibid., 82.

42. Ibid., 82–83.

43. Ibid., 83.

44. Ibid., 81. For more reflections on Luther's political ethics and understanding of the individual, see Jean Bethke Elshtain, "Does Luther Make Sense?" lecture delivered on the occasion of Reformation Day at the Candler School of Theology at Emory University on October 20, 2009. The recorded lecture, which appears to cut off just short of the end of the lecture, is accessible at: https://itunes.apple.com/us/podcast/does-luther-make-sense/id422856288?i=91636127&mt=2.

45. Ibid., 84.

46. Ibid.

47. Ibid.

48. Ibid., 87.

49. Ibid.

50. Ibid.

51. Ibid., 88 (emphasis added).

52. Ibid., 79.

53. Ibid., 157 (emphasis added).

54. Ibid., 158.

55. Ibid., 158.

56. Louis Henkin, "Human Rights: Ideology and Aspiration, Reality and Prospect" in Samantha Power and Graham Allison, eds., *Realizing Human Rights: Moving From Inspiration to Impact* (New York and Basingstoke: Palgrave Macmillan, 2006), 3–38.

57. Elshtain, *Sovereignty,* 158.

58. Ibid., 159.

59. Ibid., 163.

60. Ibid., 190.

61. Ibid., 204.

62. Ibid., 210.

63. Ibid.

64. Ibid., 216.

65. Ibid., 228 (emphases added). These questions are ones that Elshtain also takes up in the volume *Who Are We?*.

66. Ibid.

67. Ibid., 229–30.

68. Ibid., 237.

69. Ibid., 238.

70. Ibid., 250.

71. Georgia Harkness, *Christian Ethics* (New York and Nashville, TN: Abingdon, 1957), 23. This volume also contains chapters on "The Christian Conscience and the State" (ch. 10) and "War, Peace, and International Order," (ch. 11), which would have been worth further examination and comparison here, but which concerns of time and space do not permit. See also Georgia Harkness, *Understanding the Christian Faith* (New York and Nashville, TN: Abingdon Press, 1947) esp. chs. 11 (The Christian in Society) and 12 (The Church and the Present Crisis), the last of which is a specific response to implications of U.S. use of the atomic bomb in World War II for Christian understandings of war and peace. Harkness was also an early writer on the phenomena of secularism and modernity. See Georgia Harkness, *The Modern Rival of Christian Faith: An Analysis of Secularism* (New York and Nashville, TN: Abingdon-Cokesbury Press, 1952).

72. See Winnifred Fallers Sullivan, *The Impossibility of Religious Freedom* (Princeton, NJ: Princeton University Press, 2005); Winnifred Fallers Sullivan, Robert Yelle, and Matteo Taussig-Rubio, eds. *After Secular Law* (Stanford, CA: Stanford University Press, 2011); Elizabeth Shakman Hurd and Winnifred Fallers Sullivan, eds., "The Politics of Religious Freedom," *The Immanent Frame* (blog) (New York: Social Science Research Council, 2012–2013); Elizabeth Shakman Hurd, "The Specific Order of Difficulty of Religion," *The Immanent Frame* (blog) (New York: Social Science Research Council, May 30, 2014); Winnifred Fallers Sullivan, "The Impossibility of Religious Freedom," *The Immanent Frame* (blog) (New York: Social Science Research Council, July 8, 2014). See also Winnifred Fallers Sullivan and Elizabeth Shakman Hurd, guest editors "The Politics of Religious Freedom" (symposium issue) *Journal of Law and Religion* 29(3) (October 2014).

73. See Elizabeth Shakman Hurd and Winnifred Fallers Sullivan, "Symposium: Re-Thinking Religious Freedom, Editors' Introduction," *Journal of Law and Religion* 29(3) (October 2014): 4.

74. The United States and Canada have both set up government bodies for this purpose. In the United States, those agencies devoted to the promotion and protection of international religious freedom include the State Department Office of International Religious Freedom and the United States Commission on International Religious Freedom. See http://www.state.gov/j/drl/irf and http://www.uscirf.gov. In Canada, see the Office of Religious Freedom at: http://www.international.gc.ca/religious_freedom-liberte_de_religion. For critiques of promotion of international religious freedom, see Winnifred Fallers Sullivan, "The Extraterritorial Establishment of Religion," *The Immanent Frame* (blog) (New York: Social Science Research Council, March 22, 2010); Elizabeth Shakman Hurd, *The Politics of Secularism in International Relations* (Princeton, NJ: Princeton University Press, 2008). See also the following titles, unpublished at the time of this writing, but likely to be important contributions to the argument, Elizabeth Shakman Hurd, *Politics of Religious Freedom* (Chicago: University of Chicago Press, 2015) and *Beyond Religious Freedom: The New Global Politics of Religion* (Princeton, NJ: Princeton University Press, 2015).

75. Of course, Western Christianity and political liberalism are not the only sources of rights. For an account of the bases of human rights, including religious freedom rights, in range of world religions, see John Witte, Jr., "Religion," in *Oxford Handbook on International Human Rights Law*, Dinah Shelton, ed. (Oxford University Press,2013), 9–31. See also the essays in John Witte, Jr. and M. Christian Green, http://www.oup.com/us/catalog/general/subject/Politics/InternationalStudies/HumanRights/?view=usa&ci=9780199733446. *Religion and Human Rights: An Introduction* (New York: Oxford University Press, 2012).

76. Winnifred Fallers Sullivan, "The Impossibility of Religious Freedom."

77. Ibid.

78. See Jean Bethke Elshtain, "Toleration, Proselytizing, and the Politics of Recognition," in Thomas Banchoff, ed., *Religious Pluralism, Globalization, and World Politics* (New York: Oxford University Press, 2008), 89–104, and "Religious Freedom and the Politics of Proselytization," lecture delivered at the Berkley Center for Religion, Peace, and World Affairs, Georgetown University, April 29, 2011, accessible at: http://berkleycenter.georgetown.edu/events/religious-freedom-and-the-politics-of-proselytism. See also R. Scott Appleby, Richard Cizik, and Thomas Wright et al. *Engaging Religious Communities Abroad: A New Imperative for U.S. Foreign Policy* (report of the Task Force on Religion and the Making of U.S. Policy) (Chicago: Chicago Council on Global Affairs, 2010), accessible at: http://www.thechicagocouncil.org/files/Studies_Publications/TaskForcesandStudies/Religion_2010.aspx (with an appended dissent by signed by Elshtain and four other scholars recommending especially vigorous state promotion of religious freedom as a matter of foreign policy).

Chapter Ten

Sovereign Selves: 'We Have Met the Enemy and He/She is Us!'[1]

John H. A. Dyck

For one of her last public lectures, less than two months before she died, Jean Bethke Elshtain was invited to Vancouver, BC, by the Laurier Institution, the Canadian Broadcasting Corporation and the University of British Columbia to give the Milton K Wong lectures in 2013, entitled "Democracy on Trial Revisited."[2] It was the twentieth anniversary of her Massey lectures entitled *Democracy on Trial* (1993). In her 2013 manuscript Elshtain revisited the themes she had outlined in her earlier lectures, providing an update on her original tempered hope and challenge regarding the efficacy of democracy in strengthening the distinction between the private and public realms.

In 1993 she concluded her Massey Lectures with an exhortation to her audience to be vigilant in defense of democracy: "Democracy is an unpredictable enterprise. Our patience with its ups and downs, its debates and compromises, its very anti-authoritarianism, may wane as we become inured to more and more control—all in the name of freedom. We must stand on guard."[3] Noting with alarm that identity politics and the persistent blurring of the private and the public realms was eroding civil society, she urged citizens to stand on guard in defense of democracy.

Later in 2013, reflecting back on what had transpired in the course of the democratic experiment during the intervening twenty years, Elshtain added to the original call for vigilance with an urgent challenge to think and respond publicly to the continuing "tensions and conflict in public and private life and how does one determine which is which in the first instance." Elshtain wrote:

There would have been no reason to deliver lectures that turned into a book called "Democracy on Trial" if one did not believe that, indeed, democracy was challenged by political adversaries and transformations in the areas of economics, technology, communication, and neuro-biology, among others. I went on to pin-point certain quite specific concerns in cultural life, the economy, political formation, violence, race relations, tensions and conflicts in public and private life and how does one determine which is which in the first instance. Today, I hope to offer up descriptions of contemporary events that should challenge and trouble us and prompt us to think of how we, in our public capacity as citizens, can respond and in our capacity as sentient human beings, can reflect—and how the two activities can and must go together.[4]

Elshtain ended her Milton K Wong lecture manuscript on both a hopeful and a chilling note: "Perhaps we can learn to be a bit kinder, a bit more forgiving of one another and, at the same time, more demanding in what we expect from those in authority—and from ourselves—for, as the cartoon character Pogo, an opossum, said so many years ago during a different time of domestic crisis, 'we have met the enemy and he is us.'"[5]

The poignancy of Elshtain's conclusion cannot be ignored. What does it mean as democratic citizens to discover that we are our own enemies? Why is this chilling conclusion prefaced with a plea for tolerance and understanding for fellow citizens and a greater accountability from those in authority? The hope and promise is that as we recognize who we are and what we are capable of both individually and corporately, we will have the courage and the insight to exercise self-restraint and hold our public leaders accountable. This is the baton Elshtain has passed on to us.

While the full analysis of Elshtain's conclusion requires a full-length study, in this essay I will identify some of considerations, I believe, Elshtain would have us examine. Above all, Elshtain urged her audience "to think of how we, in our public capacity as citizens, can respond and in our capacity as sentient human beings, can reflect—and how the two activities can and must go together."

In this chapter, I outline J. B. Elshtain's diagnosis of the fragility of contemporary civil society in light of the modern emancipation and endorsement of the contemporary citizen who no longer recognizes its being and hope in community, instead reconstituting itself as a "sovereign self." (*Maîtres chez nous.*) If the modern individual is disengaged from an ordered world in which the parts are interdependent, where is sovereignty realized and authority located: in God? In the State? Or in the Self? In order to enrich Elshtain's discussion on the challenges facing human beings in contemporary democratic societies, I use Charles Taylor's study of the modern self, to supplement and augment her reasoning on these issues. Through exercises of historical retrieval, Taylor and Elshtain reacquaint the reader with forgotten or ignored moral sources important in recovery of the authentic expressive selfhood in its proper sphere of accountability. "I choose . . . or "the choice is mine," sums up human independence. This essay examines the complex politics involved in recognizing and affirming human diversity while at the same time founding this recognition of plurality in the mystery of *imago Dei*.

The essay has two parts. First I establish both the significance and enduring value of the thought Taylor and Elshtain have given to the human subject. In their deliberations on "the self," as both academic and public scholars, they have provided fellow academicians and ordinary citizens with compelling arguments for integrating philosophical thinking and Christian faith in understanding and explaining human action. In affirming his indebtedness to Taylor, William E. Connolly states: "Philosophy and faith are interwoven . . . so far no philosophy known to me has established itself authoritatively by argument alone."[6] In accepting the tight weave of philosophy and faith Taylor and Elshtain are sensitive to the important emancipation of the individual self through the rise of Protestantism and the Enlightenment. Individuality, individual responsibility, legal personhood, individual authenticity and moral self-reflexivity are all important markers (in the modern world) of the new worth and dignity attached to the ordinary individual person. Yet this ordinary person, created *imago dei*, is always tempted to and frequently falls into self-idolatry.

In part 2 the Cartesian disengaged self is identified as the progenitor of the modern "sovereign self" who searches for recognition. Taylor and Elshtain find this reliance on disengagement troubling since it diminishes the value of moral and ethical considerations which had held great importance in the Augustinian tradition. Taylor characterized Cartesian rationality as a shift away from substantive reasoning about the right order of being, to procedural reasoning about "standards by which we construct orders in science and life . . . The judgment now turns on properties of the activity of thinking rather than on the substantive beliefs which emerge from it."[7] This in turn has significant implications for the subsequent division of life into private and public spheres of authority and its gradual collapse under the pressure of consumerism and forces associated with the ascendance of forms of self-sovereignty. In order to give due respect and dignity to both the public and private realm, an argument is made by both Taylor and Elshtain for the necessity of a robust, tolerant civil society which mediates between individuals' private lives and the public affairs of government or state. Expressions of intimacy and bodily vulnerability need the protection and privacy of the private realm where they can be nurtured and hidden from public curiosity. Civility must attend the important exchange of ideas as citizens debate and argue about those moral and public goods which shape and guide both the individual and the spirit of the polity through participation in small voluntary associations. The affairs of government require the buffering cushion of civil society which mediates between the intimacy of the private realm where the

natural rhythmic needs—sexual relations, bodily cleansing and nourish-
ment—of humans are sheltered in privacy and the public realm where the
citizens have a right to scrutinize and hold accountable the elected representatives they have tasked with governing.

SERVING THE PUBLIC

Elshtain and Taylor recognized and accepted their roles as public intellectuals who had a responsibility to guide public action. While both Taylor and
Elshtain have always developed their arguments within a Christian frame of
reference, their engagement with public issues overlapped in certain areas
but differed in others.[8] At times Elshtain was both acerbic and feisty in her
public statements. She frequently saw her contributions to the wider public
discussion as counter-punching: "responding to the proclamations of others,
to promises that seemed to me false or feckless, to ideologies that seemed
cruel and reckless, to policies that spoke more to our resentments than to our
self-respect, to visions of the future that left too many outside the circle of
concern."[9] On occasion she accused certain feminists of proclaiming an
ideology of victimhood which identified women as passive helpless creatures
who were the prey of lustful men.[10] Her claim was that a general claim by
women of victimization diverted attention from the concrete instances of
victimization and fueled female fears, thereby disempowering women. Elshtain frequently wore her political and Christian preferences on her sleeve
when she spoke about political occurrences and addressed disputes on public
policy as she read them at the time. She supported the American invasion of
Iraq in 2003, first in arguing that humanitarian intervention in Iraq was
justified by "Just War" principles and secondly in defending the George W.
Bush administration's invasion as proper since Saddam Hussein was a tyrant
and conducted war crimes against his own people.[11] Elshtain firmly held that
the constitutional framework of rule of law and national public institutions
rest on the shared understandings and deeper sense of belonging to a common body politic than institutions and law can ever provide. There is no
substitute for the primal sense of family, of blood ties forged over genera-
tions in the context of tribe, race and shared history. This may be one reason
why Elshtain saw the terrorist attack on American values and ideals in 2001
as a defining moment in time which required a forceful response in kind. In
Just War against Terror, Elshtain made her case: "we must and will fight—
not in order to conquer any countries or to destroy peoples or religions, but to
defend who we are and what we, at our best, represent . . . we do bear an
obligation to defend the ideal of free citizens in a polity whose ordering
principles make civic freedom and the free exercise of religion available to
all."[12] This bold affirmation of American foreign policy was costly to her in

both reducing the opportunities she had to speak and write publicly and in the friendships she lost.[13]

One of the key roles Elshtain saw public intellectuals playing was reminding citizens of their past. "Our era is one of forgetting. If there is a role for the public intellectual, it is to insist that we remember, and that remembering is a moral act requiring the greatest intellectual and moral clarity."[14] Prodding, cajoling and reminding citizens of the ideals America was founded on, Elshtain spoke her mind even when it cost her friendships and excluded her from certain journals and popular magazines.[15] In 2014 Elshtain wrote: "It isn't easy in our public intellectual life, or in our church life, for that matter, to get Americans to think about anything to do with sin, the focus of much public intellectual discourse in America from Edwards to Niebuhr. We are comfortable with 'syndromes.' The word has a soothing, therapeutic sound. But the sin of pride, in the form of a triumphalist stance that recognizes no limits to human striving, is another matter."[16]

Taylor has also written and spoken frequently on public issues, yet his approach has been more reflective and tempered, less immediate to the emotional outburst of public sentiment. During the first half of his academic life, Taylor was reticent about stating his own Catholic convictions, preferring to buttress his arguments with language which was inclusive. In the last pages of *Sources of the Self*, Taylor acknowledges that a prudent strategy might be to "scale down our hopes and circumscribe our vision. But we deceive ourselves if we pretend that nothing is denied thereby of our humanity."[17] Instead, Taylor closes with a message of hope: "It is a hope that I see implicitly in Judeo-Christian theism . . . , and in its central promise of a divine affirmation of the human, more total than humans can ever attain unaided."[18] Embracing a philosophy of hope, Taylor's writings took on a more ethical and practical tone as he addressed issues related to the inclusion of others through his defense of policies promoting multiculturalism and freedom of religion.

In "A Catholic Modernity," Taylor outlines a project of Catholic Christian recovery which will meet the needs of Christians living in a secular pluralist society. He writes:

> The view I would like to defend, if I can put it in a nutshell, is that in modern secular culture there are mingled together both authentic developments of the gospel, of an incarnational mode of life, and also a closing off to God that negates the gospel. The notion is that modern culture, in breaking with the structures and beliefs of Christendom, also carried certain facets of Christian life further than they ever were taken or could have been taken within Christendom. In relation to the earlier forms of Christian culture, we have to face the humbling realization that the breakout was a necessary condition of the development.[19]

Taylor urges a much more humble application of the gospel truths by the official church letting go of its doctrine claiming hegemony of privileged truth for itself. The Christian Church needs to recognize that the huge advances in unconditional human rights founded on the dignity of man, were achieved largely because the Church's monopoly of truth and keeper of the gate had been lost. The proliferation of religious authorities even within the large Christian Church following the reformation opened the door to recognizing the importance and value of other religions addressing questions on the human condition as it pertained to their culture or civilization.

DISENGAGEMENT: COGNITIVELY AND SOCIALLY

To acknowledge the rise of the modern sovereign self as part of a larger modern emancipation from "an enchanted world" which embraced mystery is to posit a prior age when the self was not sovereign. Personhood or identity was embedded in an Order of Being which pre-existed creation and was given human form through creation. Both Taylor and Elshtain draw extensively on St. Augustine for various formulations of the self's self-understanding. Taylor paraphrases Augustine's introspective conclusions in his *Confessions* this way. "My experience of my own thinking puts me in contact with a perfection, which at one and the same time shows my own finite scope and powers to attain. There must then be a higher being on which all this depends, i.e., God."[20] Likewise, Elshtain draws attention to the embodied nature of our thinking: "For Augustine, the mind can never be transparent to itself; we are never wholly in control of our thoughts; our bodies are essential, not contingent, to who we are and how we think; and to know that we exist not because "I think therefore I am," but, rather, "I doubt, therefore I know I exist."[21] Again, emphasizing the importance of embodiment to thinking, Elshtain writes: "We must take account of what the body is telling us. The body is the mode in and through which we connect to the world and through which the world discloses itself to us. Mind is embodied; body is "thought."[22] Through our natural thinking about and longing for perfection or completion, we discover that we are part of an order of being which transcends us and sustains us. Henry Chadwick captures this natural impulse in humans to seek their creator:

> [A]t the deepest abyss of the ego ("memory" is Augustine's word for everything not at the top of the mind) the soul retains a longing for reintegration and completeness. This is realized in the love of God, and the example and expiation of Christ as the mediator, and proclaimer of that love. God has made us for himself, and the heart is ever unquiet until it rests in him.[23]

The order within which the personal self was situated transcended both in importance and in time the individual self. While the thrust of this conception exalted the individual, that exaltation was framed in terms of a created being finding its peace in glorifying its creator. This conception of a created order which transcends human mortal existence found its western apogee in the writings of the Church Fathers, particularly in St. Augustine. Yet, the universal belief in a transcendent order which subordinated the self did not withstand the questions raised by subsequent thinkers who chafed at the restrictions imposed by this order. The progression from rational detachment from the order of being to racial and gender discrimination follows a certain logic associated with self-sovereignty.

Taylor reminds us that it is Descartes who began the transformation in our thinking about the self in a quite radical manner. Descartes rejected the Platonic/Augustinian conception of an order outside of ourselves which we can discover and, when we do we understand, implicitly accept our place within the order of things. Descartes posited that the order we seek is internal and we build it. "To know reality is to have a correct representation of things—a correct picture within of outer reality, as it came to be conceived."[24] The Cartesian disengaged subject uses his or her inner mind's eye to objectively examine his or her body. This is the detached, neutral position of the observer. Self-mastery "consists in our lives being shaped by the orders that our reasoning capacity construct according to the appropriate standards."[25] But, is this all there is to knowing? As Taylor shows elsewhere, there is a significant difference between "knowing an object and coming to an understanding with an interlocutor."[26] The loyalty given to the importance of scientific objectivity (only deemed possible by a detached subject or unencumbered self) may work in fields of study where knowing an object is unilateral. However, coming to an understanding with another human agent is necessarily bilateral, party dependent and involves revising goals as the process of understanding unfolds.

In keeping with his general proclivity to see clashes of ideas in action as representing two horizons of belief systems that can be bridged through coming to an understanding that is bilateral and always subject to change, Taylor writes: ". . . social theory has to take subjects as agents of self-definition, whose practice is shaped by their understanding . . . we have to give an account of them as agents, and that we cannot do this unless we understand them, that is, grasp their self-understanding."[27] The art of understanding requires the interlocutor to enter into a real dialogue with the other position, earnestly seeking the other's perspective, wanting to hear the account from their point of view. Understanding the other involves hearing from them how they came to the position they now hold—their history is important. Indeed, Taylor argues that as such understanding of the other takes place, we also become aware of subsurface elements of our own perspective that we may not previously have been aware of. This awareness of our own biases or prejudices allows us to reframe our questions of the other's beliefs and action based on our new self-understanding. This dialogical engagement values the other's beliefs without necessarily accepting them as one's own.[28] Using this approach Taylor examines both historical and contemporary statements of belief and human action with a clear intent to valuing the good or understandable in the other's perspective, even where it conflicts with his. This fundamental approach to understand the other is exemplified in his discussion of Allan Bloom's criticism of contemporary culture in *The Closing of the American Mind* in his book *The Malaise of Modernity*.

> What I am suggesting is a position distinct from both boosters and knockers of contemporary culture. Unlike the boosters, I do not believe that everything is as it should be in this culture. Here I tend to agree with the knockers. But unlike them, I think that authenticity should be taken seriously as a moral ideal. I differ also from the various middle positions, which hold that there are some good things in this culture (like greater freedom for the individual), but that these come at the expense of certain dangers (like a weakening of the sense of citizenship), so that one's best policy is to find the ideal point of trade-off between advantages and costs . . . What we need is a work of retrieval, through which this ideal can help us restore our practice.[29]

As Taylor suggests in the quotation, playing for the middle, brokering a compromise which attempts to reach the best outcome, given the choices at hand, is not his style. Rather, Taylor, in much of his work, prepares his readers to think differently by retrieving the necessary alternations in thinking about the moral topography of the self that occurred when a major shift in modern thinking happened from Descartes forward and a new social imaginary gained popular legitimacy.[30]

In *Modern Social Imaginaries* Taylor sets this new moral topography of the self into the western social imaginary in which it is situated. "The social imaginary is not a set of ideas; rather, it is what enables, through making sense of, the practices of a society."[31] While the primary intent of the book is to establish the reasonableness of Taylor's conception, implicit in his argument is that there are other social imaginaries which enable the practices of other civilizations. It is within the social imaginary that conceptions of the self arise and give rise to the types of practices that affirm that conception of the self.

Like Taylor, who questioned the scientific achievements of the behavioural mainstream school of Political Science in the 1960s and 1970s to address adequately human action, Elshtain also regarded the reductionist aims of mainstream Political Science as inadequate to analyze and assess the complexity of humans in interaction with each other and with nature. She writes in 1979:

> The ideal subject of so-called scientific observation in political science is not (and cannot be) a self-reflexive, purposeful agent who engages the world actively and helps to shape it with thought and action, but is a narrowly calculating being who adapts, conforms, and engages in self-interested behavior, rather than in action with a social as well as a private meaning.[32]

It is clear that Taylor and Elshtain both quickly recognized that the analysis of calculating subjects who engaged in self-interested behaviour could not adequately account for intentional actions of agents in community. Elshtain quickly identified the end goal of this attenuated human agent. This "human being who is the subject of political inquiry and the object of mainstream pluralist political science is best characterized in paradigmatic form as an *abstract individual* who is said to be *sovereign*."[33] Here we have one of Elshtain's earliest statements on the modern sovereign self. She suggests that mainstream political science only provides a skeletal and emaciated conception of the human agent devoid of anything interesting. The moral topography of the self is missing.

Drawing on Tocqueville's analysis of democracy in America during the 1830s, both Elshtain and Taylor pick up his criticism of "an acquisitive commercial republic"[34] and the individualism (consumerism) that it encouraged. Paraphrasing Tocqueville, Elshtain writes; "All social webs that once held persons intact having disintegrated, the individual finds himself or herself isolated and impotent, exposed and unprotected."[35] Her fear is that a vacuum exists in the absence of social webs between citizens and this invites a highly centralized form of government. This form of egoism which Elshtain names "hard self-sovereignty," "employs the language of conquest, control over, complete self-ownership."[36] Elshtain expands her understanding of hard self-sovereignty: "In the world of hard self-sovereignty, the self stands alone, sans any mutually constitutive relationship to the world. This does not mean that hard sovereign selves refuse to marry or shun friends. No; rather, the point is that such relationships are seen as incidental to the self, not essentially definitive of one's identity. . . . The self lives in a world shorn of transcendence."[37] No longer viewing other humans as vital to our flourishing, it is easy to detach oneself from emotional entanglements which reveal our dependency and ignore the plight and tragic circumstances of others brought about directly or indirectly by our exploitive economic and social practices. The person who most exemplifies the hard version of self-sovereign is frequently found in the "jet set" cosmopolitan elite. Zygmunt Bauman describes them: Living in gated communities, their "world has no 'permanent address' except their email one and the mobile telephone number.

The new elite is not defined by any locality: it is truly and fully *exterritorial*. Exterritoriality alone is guaranteed to be a community-free zone."[38] No longer encumbered with specific obligations to others, this cosmopolitan elite regard themselves as citizens of the world rather than of any particular nation. What have been the consequences of this radical sense of self-sovereignty? Let me briefly outline one of its historical derivatives.

This sovereign self, where it resides in comfort and security, desires to retain that level of security and comfort by putting up barriers to others less fortunate who wish to come and share in the riches. Hence much effort is expended by like-minded sovereign selves to ensure that governments restrict immigration of refugees and others who have been displaced by war and civil unrest. The preference is to provide temporary shelter for displaced peoples in refugee camps in neighboring countries. But refugee camps, no matter how well they are funded, are not the answer. Being forced to flee their territorial state, these displaced refugees lose their public identity. Arendt warns: "The human being who has lost his place in a community, his political status in the struggle of his time, and the legal personality which makes his actions and part of his destiny a consistent whole, is left with those qualities which usually can become articulate only in the sphere of private life and must remain undignified, mere existence in all matters of public concern."[39] There is a danger that those no longer sovereign selves who, living an undignified mere existence in temporary refugee camps—which become permanent, will become resentful and angry at those in authority who are ignoring their plight. Suddenly the denial of basic human rights to land, citizenship, means of livelihood and becoming subjugated to external authorities for permission to travel or relocate finds voice in the concept of *dispossession*. Judith Butler and Athena Athanasiou address this systemic inhuman practice first by colonial powers and by land-hungry settlers. They set out the logic by which the "powerless" inhabitants of refugee camps become centers for radicalization.

Colonial and racist assumptions have been historically mobilized to justify and naturalize the misrecognition, appropriation, and occupation of indigenous lands in colonial and postcolonial settler contexts—such as the case of the dispossession of indigenous people and the occupation of Palestinian lands and resources by the Israeli state. In such contexts, either by means of national monoculturalism, liberal multicultural (mis)recognition, biopiracy, and reification of "cultural diversity," or apartheid, such as the separation wall in Palestine, dispossession works as an authoritative and often paternalistic apparatus of controlling and appropriating the spatiality, mobility, affectivity, potentiality, and relationality of (neo-)colonized subjects. In such contexts, "dispossession" offers language to express experiences of uprootedness, occupation, destruction of homes and social bonds, incitation to "authentic" self-identities, humanitarian victimization, unlivability, and struggles for self-determination.[40]

Butler and Athanasiou provide the logic for the demands by occupants of the "temporary turned permanent" refugee camps or reservations for restitution, compensation, and recognition. As Elshtain remarked in her 2013 reassessment of *Democracy on Trial*, in our search for and fight against the enemy of liberal democracy and best democratic practices, we have found the enemy and he/she is us.

Dispossession can take at least two forms: First there is the illegal and immoral confiscation of someone's land or means of livelihood. Butler and Athanasiou address that in their book. Secondly, dispossession also occurs on the spiritual, emotional and social level when indigenous peoples' and immigrants' religious beliefs and practices are forbidden or ridiculed because they do not "fit" into liberal democratic societies. Resentment and anger then fuel violence. Radicalization and rejection of Western liberal values occurs in spaces and specific localities in which marginalization, ghettoization and increased invasions of privacy are commonplace for minority groups who do not wish to assimilate into the dominant culture. The narrowing and suspension of rights in the name of security frightens minorities who fear the consequences of profiling. Whatever justifications have been provided in the past to condone the dispossession of indigenous lands, it is unequivocally unjust and dehumanizes the original owner. The rising cries for justice must be answered with timely changes in policy where warranted and engagement with the aggrieved party when possible in order to understand the depth of their despair and isolation.

CONCLUSION

In conclusion, the new social imaginary that has come to dominate the West (following the Cartesian revolution in rethinking how we gain knowledge to master the world we live in), reconceived the purpose of human rationality in procedural language, separating the cognition from its moral anchor. The previous enchanted Order of Being had encased human activity in light of transcendent claims on human action. While there was already a distinction drawn between the sacred and the mundane, each used the other to validate and support its space. There was a narrative which provided purpose and meaning to human existence. Individual human lives were understood to be part of a greater whole, the meaning of which was greater than the sum of all individual lives added up. In answer to the questions: "Why am I here?" "How shall I live?" there was an ascendant socio-political and a spiritual narrative which addressed these questions. Humans are created, finite beings who are born into various stations in the social order in a world created and governed by God. Humankind lives and thrives in our sufficiency insofar as we accept our *sitz im Leben*, acknowledging their dependence on their creator. Authentic human living was realized in the act of worshiping the Creator and caring for the world and its inhabitants according to his plan. Reason and faith worked together to make sense of this order. Mystery and faith augmented ordinary reasonable decisions about the practical needs of life. While fragility, disease, pain and death affected all creation, there was a plan of salvation which provided hope and joy in the midst of tears for all who believed in Jesus as Lord of their lives.

This universal narrative of hope, in its original iteration, offered salvation to all humankind. In the West, the dominance of the Catholic Church for over a millennium and its subsequent offspring created social and spiritual hierarchies that bound people into their stations for life, stultifying the human spirit. The rigid orders of feudalism enslaved the spirit of mankind and early demands for liberation from the oppressive chains associated with this order came into prominence in the Renaissance and later in the Enlightenment when the dignity and creativity of humankind was rediscovered and affirmed as truly human. Calls for social and spiritual revolution increased in intensity. The revolution began in philosophy.

The separation of reason and faith gathered momentum with Descartes and began the process of disenchantment whereby faith and mystery were repeatedly pushed aside or explained in rational scientific language which viewed knowledge as the accumulation of verifiable facts. The prioritizing of quantifiable data based on standardized methods of measurement eliminated moral claims based on love (*caritas*) and self-sacrifice. The modern social imaginary in the West was completed when the origin of purpose and meaning were allocated to humans. It was the human person who provided meaning and purpose to the world and especially to human action. The earth and its inhabitants now became subject to human will. Having discarded the all-embracing Order of Being which was governed by a Creator God, the new natural universe was governed by universal natural laws. The natural world was now measured and valued according to these immutable laws of nature which were accessible to human reasoning. Accordingly reason categorized all things into items of utility according to a measurable scale. All sentient beings, along with the natural resources of the earth, were assigned value according to a scale of utility suitable for a given epoch. This system of evaluation and appropriation also prioritized science, technology and economic capitalism over moral considerations about social, economic and political equality. Again differences in wealth, property and influence divided humankind into the rich and indigent—the powerful and the powerless. At the same time as a new social and political hierarchy became entrenched, the satisfaction of this elite was buoyed by statistical evidence which claimed that while the best off were increasing their advantage, all levels of society were better off. In other words, everyone was benefiting from a system founded on continuous natural resource extraction and refinement and the exploitation of human labour. Yet there were danger signs that the health and vitality of the polity was being compromised.

According to Elshtain, cracks in the edifice of democratic institutions portended the decline of vigorous debate among all citizens on the public good as the politics of displacement and difference divided citizens.[41] Having lost sight of the common good, citizens would be inclined to disavow politics and civic engagement. Disenchantment with politics evidenced most by falling participation in elections opens the door to the 'soft despotism' described by Taylor.[42]

The rough narrative I have provided underlies Jean Beth Elshtain's critique of liberal democratic society. For her and for Charles Taylor, the modern sovereign self needs to be chastened, humbled in its self-aggrandizement without losing its capacity for love and virtuosity shared in a community of citizens. Their contribution to this task was to identify sources of moral thought which, if adopted by citizens, can revitalize the voluntary associations of civil society, thereby strengthening the needed privacy of the personal in the private realm while requiring greater accountability in the political realm. The realization of the common good requires its citizens to be vigilant in defense of the high moral values that embody the structures and practices of liberal democratic society.

NOTES

1. The title is an adaptation of the conclusion of Pogo, a cartoon character of the 1970s that Jean Bethke Elshtain uses in her Milton K. Wong lecture, "Democracy on Trial Revisited."

2. Unfortunately Jean Bethke Elshtain became ill the week prior to the lecture and it was cancelled. She did provide a text which was subsequently published as the Milton K Wong Lecture.

3. Jean Bethke Elshtain, *Democracy on Trial*, Concord, Ontario: House of Anansi Press, 1993, 142.

4. Jean Bethke Elshtain, "Democracy on Trial Revisited," Milton K Wong Lectures, June 13, 2013. http://www.miltonkwonglecture.ca/lecture/2.

5. Ibid.

6. William E. Connolly, "Catholicism and Philosophy: A Nontheistic Appreciation," in Ruth Abby, ed., *Charles Taylor*, Cambridge: Cambridge University Press, 2004, 168–69.

7. Charles Taylor, *Sources of the Self: The Making of the Modern Identity*, Cambridge: Harvard University Press, 1989, 156.

8. Taylor and Elshtain gave the Massey Lectures in Canada in 1991 and 1993 respectively. Both Taylor and Elshtain were elected members of the *American Academy of Arts and Sciences*. In 1995 Taylor was made a Companion of the *Order of Canada*. In 2006 President George W. Bush appointed Elshtain to the Council of the *National Endowment for the Humanities*. In 2007 Taylor and Gerard Bouchard were appointed as Commissioners to a one year Quebec Royal Commission to study the reasonable accommodation of minority groups in Quebec. Both Taylor and Elshtain were invited to give the Gifford Lectures at the University of Edinburgh 1998 and 2005 respectively.

9. Jean Bethke Elshtain, *Real Politics: At the Center of Everyday Life*, Baltimore: John Hopkins University Press, 1997, vii. See also Elshtain's response to the editors' questions on public intellectuals in the "Interview" in this book.

10. *Democracy on Trial*, 50–51.

11. See Jean Bethke Elshtain, *Just War Against Terror*, New York: Basic Books, 2003. Rejecting the demands by critics of U.S. foreign policy that an American withdrawal from the Middle East would placate the hostility against Americans and stop terrorist attacks, Elshtain argued that the United States had an obligation "to defend the ideal of free citizens in a polity whose ordering principles make civic freedom and the free exercise of religion available to all." See also her response to Tom Farer in "Response to Tom Farer's 'Unjust War Against Terrorism and the Struggle to Appropriate Human Rights,'" in *Human Rights Quarterly*, 30 (2008) 758–66.

12. *Just War against Terror*, 6–7

13. See the "interview" in this book.

14. Jean Bethke Elshtain, "Why Public Intellectuals," in *Wilson Quarterly*, 38–1, 2014, online.

15. See the interview with Elshtain in this book.

16. Jean Bethke Elshtain, "Why Public Intellectuals?" in *Wilson Quarterly*, Winter, 38–1, 2014, online.

17. Charles Taylor, *Sources of the Self: The Making of the Modern Identity*, Cambridge, MA: Harvard University Press, 1989, 520.

18. Ibid. 521.

19. Charles Taylor, "A Catholic Modernity," in Charles Taylor, *Dilemmas and Connections: Selected Essays*, Cambridge, MA: Harvard University Press, 2011, 170; see also his *A Catholic Modernity?* Ed. By James L Heft, Oxford: Oxford University Press, 1999, 16.

20. Charles Taylor, *Sources of the Self: The making of the modern Identity*, Cambridge, Mass. Harvard University Press, 1989, 140.

21. Jean Bethke Elshtain, *Sovereignty: God, State, and Self*, New York: Basic Books, 2008, 162.

22. Ibid. 164.

23. Henry Chadwick, *Augustine*, Oxford: OUP, 1986, 67.

24. Charles Taylor, *Sources of the Self*, 144.

25. Ibid. 147.

26. Taylor, "Understanding the Other" 25.

27. Charles Taylor, "Understanding and Ethnicity," in *Philosophy and the Human Sciences 2*, Cambridge: CUP, 1985, 117. Taylor expands this notion of understand: "I come to understand someone when I understand his emotions, his aspirations, what he finds admirable and contemptible, in himself and others, what he yearns for, what he loathes, and so on." 119.

28. Charles Taylor, "Understanding the Other: A Gadamerian View on Conceptual Schemes," in *Dilemmas and Connections: Selected Essays*, Cambridge: Harvard University Press, 2011, 30.

29. Charles Taylor, *The Malaise of Modernity*, Concord, Ontario: Anansi Press, 1991, 22–23.

30. Charles Taylor, "The Moral Topography of the Self," in Stanley B. Messer, Louis A. Sass, and Robert L. Woolfolk, eds., *Hermeneutics and Psychological Theory: Interpretive Perspectives on Personality, Psychotherapy, and Psychopathology*, New Brunswick: Rutgers University Press, 1988, 299, 308. Arguing against incommensurability between cultures, Taylor hypothesizes that, "what we are as human agents is profoundly interpretation-dependent, that human beings in different cultures can be radically diverse, in keeping with their fundamentally different self-understandings. But I think that a constant is to be found in the shape of the questions that all cultures must address." These questions begin with "Who am I?" and "How shall I live?"

31. Charles Taylor, *Modern Social Imaginaries*, Durham, Duke University Press, 2004, 2.

32. Jean Bethke Elshtain, "Methodological Sophistication and Conceptual Confusion," in *Real Politics*, 17. In "Toleration, Proselytizing, and the Politics of Recognition," Elshtain pays tribute to Charles Taylor's pioneering early essays "Interpretation and the Sciences of Man" in

Philosophy and the Human Sciences: Philosophical Papers 2, Cambridge: Cambridge University Press, 1985 and "Self-Interpreting Animals" in *Human Agency and Language: Philosophical Papers 1*, Cambridge: Cambridge University Press, 1985 for "challenging the regime of behavioralism in the human sciences." 127.

33. Ibid. 15–16.

34. Jean Bethke Elshtain, *Democracy on Trial*, Concord, Ontario: House of Anansi Press, 1993, 11.

35. Ibid. 11

36. Jean Bethke Elshtain, *Sovereignty: God, State, and Self*, New York: Basic Books, 2008, 204.

37. Ibid.

38. Zygmunt Bauman, *Community: Seeking Safety in an Insecure World*, Oxford: Polity Press, 2001, 54.

39. Hannah Arendt, *The Origins of Totalitarianism*, New York: Meridian Books, 1958, 2nd expanded edition, 301.

40. Judith Butler and Athena Athanasiou, *Dispossession: The Performative in the Political*, Oxford: Polity Press, 2013, 10–11.

41. Elshtain, *Democracy on Trial*, 40. Elshtain writes: "If there are no distinctions between public and private, personal and political, it follows that no differentiated activity or set of institutions that are genuinely political, that are the purview of citizens and the bases of order, legitimacy, and purpose in a democratic community, exist." 43.

42. Taylor, *The Malaise of Modernity*, 112. Taylor explains: "The danger is not actual despotic control but fragmentation—that is, a people increasingly less capable of forming a common purpose and carrying it out. Fragmentation arises when people see themselves more and more atomistically, otherwise put, as less and less bound to their fellow citizens in common projects and allegiances." See also Elshtain, *Democracy on Trial*, 44.

III

Sovereignty in Context

Chapter Eleven

God and Power in the Global North and Latin America

A Comparative Analysis Based on Elshtain's
Sovereignty [1]

Andrés Pérez-Baltodano

Ideas of power in Western societies—or in any other part of the world—are the product of embodied minds that feel compelled to react to specific historical challenges within specific frameworks of material and cultural constraints and opportunities. [2] From this perspective, ideas about sovereignty should not be studied, as Jean Bethke Elshtain does, as disembodied and independent causes of history, but rather as manifestations of tensions and contradictions that emerge between the practice of power—that is inherent in the search for order—and its theological and political justifications. As this essay shows, understanding the socio-political forces and trends operating in the historical context within which these ideas emerge is crucial to appreciate their significance. [3]

Furthermore, the context within which ideas emerge needs to be taken into consideration in any attempt to explain the reasons why theological and philosophical ideas fail or succeed in shaping history and becoming dominant interpretations of reality. Elshtain simply assumes that "extreme [theoretical] formulations" tend to be more successful than "moderate" ones. These formulations, she argues, "get the lion's share of attention and even a kind of adulation" because of their extremism. [4]

As the history of the West and Latin America reveals, and as this essay shows, ideas of sovereignty become constitutive forces of history only when they enter into a relation of "elective affinity" with a dominant or potentially dominant socio-political trend or power configuration operating in the histor-

155

ical contest within which they emerge. From this perspective, a relation of elective affinity exists when ideas about sovereignty and a particular constellation of power relations gravitate to each other and facilitate their mutual legitimation.[5] The idea of the modern sovereign state, for example, could only make sense at a time when it was feasible for a secular power structure to assume the responsibility to create and reproduce social order and peace. This same idea would have not made sense—because it was clearly infeasible and even unimaginable—after the collapse of the Roman Empire in the fifth century. To be "successful," then, ideas have to "make sense" within a particular set of historical constraints and possibilities."[6]

A CONTEXTUAL INTERPRETATION OF SOVEREIGNTY IN WESTERN SOCIETIES

The basic story line behind Elshtain's *Sovereignty* goes as follows: after the collapse of the Roman Empire, the Christian God emerged in Europe as the ultimate source of power and authority. Decisions concerning life and death, good and bad, right and wrong, were God's decisions, at least as interpreted by those who claimed to represent Him.

After the sixteenth century, "claims to earthly power or *potestas* as dominion, and *autoritas*, or right authority, migrated over to politics from arguments about God's power and authority, in a word, God's sovereignty."[7] In the times of post-modernity or late modernity that we live today, sovereignty has migrated once more: from the State–as the expression of a basic social consensus about the organization of communal life–to the self. Therefore, Elshtain argues, "as sovereign state is to sovereign God, so sovereign selves are to sovereign states."[8]

THEOLOGY IN CHARGE: AUGUSTINE'S SYNTHESIS

Elshtain begins her historical narrative with Augustine, who argued that, "earthly rule and dominion and spiritual offices had different ends and were directed toward the eschaton, that which was eternal."[9] Augustine, Elshtain points out, established a relatively clear demarcation between "the City of Man," ruled by politics and necessity, and the "City of God," the society "of the faithful on earthly pilgrimage" governed by "God's rules of love and justice."[10]

The two cities, Elshtain notes, coexist in the world and this coexistence is marked by tensions and contradictions but also by possible congruencies and overlaps. From this perspective, the quality of earthly rule depends on the capacity for God's rule to permeate the City of Man.

What was Augustine trying to achieve? What were the cultural and material forces that enabled and constrained his ideas? Elshtain doesn't touch on
these issues. She doesn't explain that the Augustinian view of God's power
and of political power was an attempt to re-synchronize the Christian *wel-
tanschauung* and the new socio-political reality of the Roman Empire after
the sacking of Rome by the Visigoths in 410. Christians had learned to
perceive the Christianization of Rome after Constantine as the triumphant
outcome of a providential history.[11] Augustine himself had internalized this
"sacral" view of the Roman Empire. As R. A. Markus points out, in his
"sermons and polemical writings of the 390s and the early years of the fifth
century the extinction of paganism is frequently represented as God's work,
fulfilling the ancient prophecies."[12]

Christians, then, were naturally forced to ask: Why did not God protect
Rome against the "barbarians"? Meanwhile, non-Christian Romans interpreted the disaster as a form of punishment imposed by their Pagan gods for
the expansion of Christianity throughout the empire. To Pagans, Augustine
said: the Christian God cannot be blamed for the problems of Rome because
worse things had happened to the empire before Christianity. To Christians,
he asked not to confuse the City of Man with the City of God. The crisis of
the Roman Empire simply proved the fragility of human power. The City of
God was alive and well in the community of believers.[13]

The "two cities" thesis reconciled Christian doctrine and the particular
historical conditions in which Augustine lived. More specifically, it justified
the dominant presence of God in the world, without making God responsible
for bad and evil in human society. This rationale allowed the Church to
maintain its influence and power at a moment when it confronted the crisis of
faith and understanding produced by the declining glory of a Christianized
Rome.

Nevertheless, the reconciliation between Christian doctrine and the socio-
historical reality of Europe articulated by the Bishop of Hippo came with a
price. Despite the fact that divine providence remained central to his view of
the relationship between God and history, the Augustinian demarcation between the power of God and earthly power unintentionally legitimized the
existence of a political space separated from sacred space. As Markus points
out, "Augustine's attack on the 'sacral' conception of the Empire liberated
the Roman state, and by implication, all politics, from the direct hegemony of
the sacred. Society became intrinsically 'secular' in the sense that it is not as
such committed to any particular ultimate loyalty."[14] The same point is made
by Edward Grant who argues that Augustine and other Latin authors, "inad-
vertently emphasized the use of reason and thus began a process that would
grow increasingly more independent by the late Middle Ages."[15]

THEOLOGY IN CHARGE: AQUINAS' SYNTHESIS

Augustinianism, as Elshtain points out, was "the dominant way of thinking about God and earthly matters until the triumph of St. Thomas Aquinas and Scholasticism."[16] This "triumph," however was not, as Elshtain suggests, simply the product of "a fusion of the previous features of medieval thought–Gelasianism; Roman law; the Justinian Code . . . canon law; and so called Germanic ideas of law and kingship."[17] Aquinas's synthesis was the dialectical result of a theoretical attempt to re-synchronize the practice of power and its necessary justifications at a time when God's sovereignty was being eroded by the increasing power of reason.

The economy of Europe in the twelfth century, as David Hackett Fischer points out, had rapidly developed "from a comparatively primitive system of barter exchange toward a more complex system of market relationships."[18] Agricultural land had expanded as "better ploughs, wagons, bridle and other tools caused a more effective cultivation of the fields."[19] These new conditions contributed to the emergence of a secular faith in people's capacity to control their destiny.

This secular faith was bolstered by the discovery of Aristotle's works in the twelfth and thirteenth centuries. Aristotelian rationalism "made sense" at a time that Western Europe was experiencing a renaissance fuelled by geographical explorations, the expansion of trade and commerce, and the development of science, technology, and the arts.[20] Aquinas's revaluation of the City of Man made Christian doctrine congruent with what it meant to be human in thirteenth-century Europe. By revaluing the City of Man, Aquinas recognized the growing power of reason and revalued humanity itself.[21] In this Augustinian formula, this revaluation could only mean the devaluation of the City of God. This is because Augustine, as Edward Grant points out, "clearly subordinated secular learning to the needs of the faith.[22]

In the twelfth century, however, it was becoming more and more evident that reason had not only the capacity to illuminate and explain aspects of life that were considered part of the truth of God at the times of Augustine, but also the capacity to achieve knowledge outside the boundaries of Christianity. Greco-Arabic medicine, for example, was accepted as superior to "monastic" European medicine despite the fact that it was not based on knowledge produced within the Christian faith. Moreover, some medical procedures—such as surgery and dissection—that were prohibited by Christianity at the time of Augustine, had become legitimate practices at the time of Aquinas.[23]

Clearly, Christianity and the Church needed a new way of reconceptualizing the relationship between faith and reason. This reconceptualization would clearly involve a redefinition of the relationship between human power and the power of God. Thomas Aquinas delivered this new synthesis by proposing that there are two types of truths and two ways of reaching them. Let the Angelicus Doctor speak for himself:

> There is a twofold mode of truth in what we profess about God. Some truths about God exceed all the ability of the human reason. Such is the truth that God is triune. But there are some truths which the natural reason also is able to reach. Such are that God exists, that He is one, and the like. In fact, such truths about God have been proved demonstratively by the philosophers, guided by the light of the natural reason. [24]

Aquinas tempered the explosive nature of his argument by arguing that his revaluation of reason did not mean the devaluation of faith. After all, the natural law that guides life in the City of Man was "nothing else than the rational creature's participation in the eternal law." [25] Nevertheless, Aquinas got in trouble when in 1277, the Church declared a number of his theses heretical. [26]

The Scholastic synthesis would gradually loose its appeal throughout the fourteenth and fifteenth centuries. Ironically, by legitimizing the exercise of reason as humanity's exploration of God's mind, thinkers such as John Scotus Eriugena, Peter Abelard and especially Aquinas had paved the way for humanism, the end of scholasticism, the emergence of the modern state, and the eventual displacement of the "omnipotent God" by the "omnipotent lawgiver." [27] In this sense, Aquinas can be seen as furthering the expansion of reason beyond the limits that Augustine had imposed upon it.

PHILOSOPHY IN CHARGE: HOBBES'S SYNTHESIS

In the mid-1500s, Europe faced a great crisis produced by profound social, religious, technological, political, and economic changes that would eventually upset the medieval relationship between faith and reason articulated by Aquinas. The crisis was not only institutional but also psycho-sociological. It was a crisis of both social order and of "ontological security" [28] that required a rethinking of the most basic foundations of social and spiritual life. At the socio-political level, it centered "on the location of authority," and questions such as "What is authentic authority?" and "Where does authority come from?" At an existential level, the questions were even more fundamental: "Are there solid and stable certainties?" "What is order and how certain is it?" "What is truth and how is it achieved?" and, ultimately, "Can one rely on anything?" [29]

Scholasticism didn't have the capacity to properly answer these questions, given the limitations that religious notions of "the eternal law" imposed upon reason in this theological tradition. As Edward Grant points out, "those who applied reason to theology in the Middle Ages did not–indeed, could not–challenge the ultimate supremacy of the truths of revelation, whereas scholars in the Age of Reason began to do so."[30]

Thomas Hobbes responded to the challenges of his time announcing the arrival of a new era that would be characterized by the centrality of human being's secular faith in their capacity to control history: "This is the generation of the great Leviathan, or rather, to speak more reverently of that mortal god, to which we own under the immortal God, our peace and defense."[31] With the emergence of the great Leviathan, human security would be achieved through human and, more specifically, political intervention. Therefore, the belief expressed in the idea "no salvation outside the Church" would be replaced by "the defining maxim of modern politics: no security outside the state."[32] This new vision created the foundation for the development of society's capacity to generate "a strictly political history of chains of events," with the capacity to replace "the archaic fusion of mythical and genealogical time" that prevailed in the Middle Ages.[33]

To sum up, the old theological formulas articulated by Augustine and Aquinas had been made obsolete by the material and cultural evolution of European societies. Europe needed another dialectic integration of religion and politics. In this new synthesis, the domain of reason would have to expand at the expense of faith, or, at least, against the dogmatic faith defended by the Church. In other words, philosophy would have to displace theology as a source of answers to humanity's most fundamental questions and problems.

Hobbes succeeded in articulating an interpretation of power that was congruent with dominant socio-historical tendencies in his time. Why did he succeed? Why did he "make sense"? For Elshtain, the answer to these questions is surprisingly simple: Hobbes's ideas, like those of Machiavelli, are extremist ideas and "extremism is more fetching by far than the ordinary, the everyday, the humanly decent and moderate."[34] After having rejected "the Aristotelianized Christianity of Scholasticism," we are told, Hobbes, a "canny reductionist" went "for a nominalist construal with gusto."[35]

Less "extremist" alternative ideas about sovereignty and power articulated by Hobbes's contemporaries failed to succeed, Elshtain points out, because of their "moderation and restraint."[36] She concludes: "It is extraordinarily difficult for any thinker, no matter how deft his or her pen, to dramatize restraint and to animate moderation" (ibid.). She goes further to suggest: "It is the person who wants to denounce, trash, overthrow who gets 'the ink,' so to speak—and why?—because it is 'high drama' to our eyes and ears."[37] Ironically, she does not apply this same explanation to Augustine's and Aquinas's successful articulation of the syntheses that bridged reason and faith for a thousand years. In other words, she does not attribute their success—as she does in the case of Hobbes—to their capacity for "high drama."

Hobbes achieved what Patrick J. Deneen calls, "the great combination" between philosophy and theology and between reason and faith. He produced a "politicized theology"; that is, a political philosophy and model based on a secularized representation of Christianity.[38] This representation "made sense" because it was congruent with the historical conditions and tendencies within which it was formulated which included not only the English Civil War, but also the growing power of politics and the state.[39] In these new socio-historical circumstances, order and security would now be politically created, planned and delivered by the state in a process guided by the doctrine of *raison d'etat*, that is, by the subordination of public morality to state power.[40]

POLITICAL ECONOMY IN CHARGE: ADAM SMITH'S SYNTHESIS

With the institutionalization of the secular space of the state, the struggle for the definition of sovereignty began to take place within legal-political boundaries and, predominantly, among secular actors operating within these boundaries. The economic actors emerging from the conformation of a new set of socio-economic relations—later known as capitalism—would play a central role in this struggle and, more specifically, in the distribution of power between society, the economic system and the state.

Citizenship rights emerged in this context, as T. S. Marshall points out, as a social force that would counterbalance the tendency for capitalism to produce inequality. This struggle can be graphically illustrated as a series of concentric circles. Each circle represents the articulation of a new social consensus regarding citizenship rights, the power of the market and the state. Using Marshall's gender-blind interpretation of the development of citizenship in England as an example, the first circle can be visualized as the emergence and institutionalization of civil rights in the eighteenth century; the second represents the emergence and institutionalization of political rights in the nineteenth century; and the third, the emergence and institutionalization of social rights in the twentieth.[41]

The struggle to define and re-define relations between state, market and society shaped the intellectual context that enabled and constrained ideas about power in the work of Locke, Rousseau and other modern thinkers discussed by Elshtain. They all focused their attention on the organization of political space as "the locus wherein the tensional forces of society are related."[42] This new perspective demanded a new synthesis between faith and reason and, more specifically, between God, the power of an evolving market economy, and the state.

Adam Smith's *The Wealth of Nations* articulated the foundation of this new synthesis based on a revaluation of Christian morality. "In the Christian tradition," as Jerry Z. Muller points out, "the pursuit of self-interest was a passion and hence part of man's bodily, animal nature. For Smith, on the other hand, "it was the pursuit of self-interest through exchange that set man off from the animals and gave him his specifically human dignity."[43] Moreover, for Smith, self-interest was a human instinct implanted in humans by God.[44] Humans are "led by an invisible hand to promote an end which was no part of [their] intention." "By pursuing [their] own interest," Smith argues, "[human beings] frequently promote that of the society more effectually than when [they] really intend to promote it."[45]

Once self-interest was unchained from Christian doctrine and transformed into God's gift to humanity, the intellectual question faced by human sciences was how to deal with the pathological expressions of this human passion. Locke, Rousseau, Hegel, Kant, Descartes, Emerson, Nietzsche and Simone de Beauvoir—the authors that Elshtain reviews as precursors of the "sovereign self "—confronted the particular forms of "unsociable sociability" generated by self-interest and the market.[46]

Elshtain does not examine the context within which this confrontation took place. The authors whom she reviews and their ideas are simply presented as part of a monistic-nominalist-voluntarist tradition initiated by Ockham and solidified by Hobbes that, according to her interpretation, paved the way for the emergence of the "sovereign self " in contemporary Western societies. In these societies, she argues, will and choice have become "divinized."[47] and, as a consequence, "self pride," "nihilism," and "existential isolation" have become features of the human condition.[48]

To confront these problems, Elshtain proposes the delimitation of sovereignty within two concentric normative circles: One emerging from the "dialogic space" of a social contract articulated and reproduced through democratic engagement and deliberation; the other—containing the previous one—emerging from the revitalization of the idea of a transcendent Logos that functions as a supra-historical source of authority and meaning based on "grace and justice."[49]

To sum up, Elshtain proposes the re-articulation of a congruent relationship between "Jerusalem and Athens, belief and unbelief, skepticism and faith."[50] The new relationship would facilitate the emergence of a "responsible self," the antithesis of the hyper-individualistic "sovereign self " that she denounces in her work.

Many thinkers have explored the emergence of pathological forms of individualism in late modernity. C. B. Macpherson, for example, denounced the spread of what he called "possessive individualism" to make reference to the emergence of an instrumental view of society that is based on the assumption that "man is free and human by virtue of his sole proprietorship of his own person, and that human society is essentially a series of market-relations."[51] Carole Pateman has discussed the impact of "radical individualism" on women and its role in the development of the "sexual contract" within which Western societies operate.[52] Charles Taylor has analyzed the emergence in contemporary Western societies of what he calls an "individualism of self-fulfillment" that eclipses a society's moral horizons.[53]

Like Macpherson, Pateman and Taylor, Elshtain decries the "corruption of the social contract idea" resulting from atomistic and self-centred forms of individualism. Unlike Macpherson, Pateman, and Taylor, however, Elshtain does not contextualize the phenomenon of the "sovereign self." More specifically, she does not link the loss of "authentic relationality,"[54] and the "divinization" of "choice and will"[55] in the West, to the emergence of capitalism as "a veritable faith in man's secular salvation through a self-regulating market."[56]

Therefore, Elshtain misses the forest of the market for the trees of the "sovereign self." She fails to address the possibility that what the world faces in the twenty-first century is not simply the emergence of a philosophically constructed hyper-individualist sovereign self, but the institutionalization of a market-centered society organized within a rationale that legitimizes the existence of this asocial self and other social pathologies.

In any case, there is no doubt that the societies of the Global North that Elshtain has in mind in her discussions of sovereignty demand a new synthesis that can reconcile faith, politics and economics. However, the elements of this new synthesis will not be found in the reconstruction of the past, as Elshtain suggests, but in the future; a future that seems to belong to a post-Wesphalian international order of transnational linkages, multicultural societies, and porous states.

GOD AND THE STATE: LATIN AMERICA

The history of sovereignty in Europe is the history of a dialectical relation between ideas of power and objective power trends and configurations. This history has produced the different paradigms of relation between God and social history that are represented by Augustine, Aquinas, Hobbes, Adam Smith and others. These paradigms can be integrated into the general narrative outlined by Elshtain: the idea of sovereignty "migrated" from God to the state around the sixteenth century and we currently live a new chapter in the history of this idea.

The history of sovereignty in Europe is, then, a history of *syntheses* and *integrations*. The next section will show that, contrary to the case of Europe, the history of sovereignty in Latin America is a history of unresolved tensions and contradictions.[57] In other words, no single source of authority—God, the state or the market—has become dominant in Latin American history. Even today, it is easy to find in any country of the region the presence of patterns of inequality reproduced simultaneously by the patrimonial culture of the state, the religious culture of the Church, and the instrumental rationale of the market. To explain the specificity of Latin American history, it is necessary—once again—to pay close attention to the nature of the relations between ideas of power and objective power trends and configurations emerging throughout this history.

GOD IN CHARGE

When Hobbes published his *Leviathan* in 1651, the region of the world that we now know as Latin America was in the middle of a social experiment of unprecedented proportions. The Spanish and the Portuguese crowns were asserting their sovereignty in the continent "on behalf of the King, Don Fernando, and of Doña Juana I, his daughter, Queen of Castille and León, subduers of the barbarous nations." This rationale was based on the notion that the Spanish monarchs had received their sovereign power from God through the Pope: "God our Lord gave charge to one man, called St. Peter, that he should be Lord and Superior of all the men in the world, that all should obey him, and that he should be the head of the whole Human Race [. . .] and he commanded him to place his seat in Rome, as the spot most fitting to rule the world from [. . .] This man was called Pope, as if to say, Admirable Great Father and Governor of men." After listening to these words, Amerindians were asked "to acknowledge the Church as the Ruler and Superior of the whole world, and the high priest called Pope, and in his name the King and Queen Doña Juana our lords," or to perish (The Requirement, 1513).[58]

Spain and Portugal had escaped the religious wars that engulfed most of Europe between 1524—the year that marks the beginning of the Peasant Wars in Germany following the Reformation—and the signing of the Peace of Westphalia in 1648 that consolidated the modern sense of sovereignty in the Western world. The two countries remained Roman Catholic and became key centers of the counter-reformation efforts during the sixteenth and seventeenth centuries. They also fought against the idea of sovereignty promoted by James I of England and other European monarchs who at that time argued that God did not delegate His authority on the Pope but directly endowed kings with the power and authority to rule over people.

Francisco Suárez—the most influential theologian and philosopher in the Iberic Peninsula during the times of the Conquest and the European Religious Wars—articulated a response to the doctrine of Divine Right of Kings. For Suárez, only the Church was the direct beneficiary and recipient of God's power and authority. Rulers and Kings, on the other hand, receive their authority from the people. Therefore, people—as the recipients and beneficiaries of God's power–and the Church, as God's representative on Earth—have the right to depose Kings when they violate the principles of God-given natural law.[59]

One should not assume that in Suárez's power equation, the Church and the people were on equal footing. The modern idea of citizenship rights had not emerged at the time of Suárez. Moreover, the power of the Church was at its peak in Portugal and Spain. Clearly, Suárez's formula put the Church at the top of the power structure of sixteenth-century society.

Suárez's view of the relationship between God, the state and society was congruent with the rationale used by Spain and Portugal to conquer America and to spread God's word in the new continent. This rationale fulfilled Suárez's hierarchical vision of an omnipotent God that is legitimately represented by the Church "as the Ruler and Superior of all the men in the world."[60]

The image of an omnipotent God working through the Church and the Catholic Spanish and Portuguese monarquical states was reproduced by the theology of the conquistadores after 1492.[61] It became dominant not only because of the coercive power used by Spain and Portugal to impose it, but also because it was congruent with Amerindians' vision of life and history as processes controlled by supernatural forces that operated beyond their control, and with their condition of powerlessness after what they perceived as the catastrophic defeat of their gods at the hands of the Christian God of the conquistadores.

GOD AND THE STATE IN CHARGE

Suárez's ideas about society's right to reclaim the power endowed to them by God when kings abused their authority did not play any role in Latin America before the emergence of a colonial society. They only became relevant in the last part of the eighteenth century and the first decades of the nineteenth century, when the leaders of a well-established *Criollo* society had to justify their claims to independence from the Spanish crown. The ideas of the Enlightenment and the examples of the United States and France were also used in an eclectic and superficial way by Latin American *Criollos* to justify their desire to transform the colonial provinces of the new continent into modern sovereign states.[62]

However, the idea of the State did not find in Latin America the material conditions for its successful adaptation and institutionalization. First, the new independent countries lacked the power to operate as sovereign states within the international political and economic systems. They occupied a position of dependency in both. Second, the state bureaucracies that these countries inherited lacked the regulatory capacity that was needed to organize social relations and create national identities and "imagined communities" within their territorial boundaries. Third and finally, the social structures inherited from colonial times had been designed to exclude the masses and to protect the power of the Spanish and Portuguese crowns and their representatives in the American colonies. The *Criollo* elites that achieved power after independence used these same structures to deny citizenship to Amerindians, Afroamericans and *mestizos*.[63]

The cultural conditions of Latin America were also incongruent with the idea of the modern state. The *Leviathan* was, above all, the institutional expression of a secular faith in people's belief in their capacity to control their history. This secular faith was absent in Latin America. After all, Spain and Portugal never experienced a scientific revolution. Moreover, the Enlightenment did not make serious inroads into the Iberic peninsula. Finally, Amerindian culture, as it was indicated before, was based on the notion that supernatural forces beyond people's control regulated the world.[64]

The material and cultural context within which *Criollos* adopted the idea of the modern state explains why the transfer of authority from God to the State discussed by Elshtain and others never took place in Latin America. Throughout most of its history, Latin America has been shaped by two competing forces: providentialist visions of God as a sovereign being that regulates history; and, modern ideas of the State as an institution that is designed to express humanity's willingness and capacity to control its own collective destiny.[65] The separation of church and state that occurred in many Latin American countries during the nineteenth century did not resolve the tensions and contradictions between these two forces.

The providentialist religious culture of Mexico, for example, remained deeply providentialist after the separation of church and state introduced by the Liberals in the first half of the nineteenth century.[66] The same can be said of Colombia, whose 1863 Constitution decreed religious freedom, removed the name of God from the text and established a clear separation between church and state. However, as Rodolfo de Roux points out, after the Constitution was proclaimed, the Colombian Catholic Church continued to preserve its "hegemony over control of the symbolic goods of salvation."[67] The Mexican and Colombian cases were repeated in other Latin American countries where individual and social histories continued to be perceived as processes meticulously controlled by God.

The adoption of the idea of the modern state in a highly providentialist religious culture became a central component of the contradictory coexistence of the "legal" and the "real" countries of Latin America. In the "legal country," the "rule of law," as implemented by "secular sovereign States," defines what is right and what is wrong. In the "real country" of Latin America, however, the state lacks the capacity to articulate and enforce common legal standards of behavior.[68]

GOD, THE STATE, AND THE MARKET IN CHARGE

The incipient capitalist economy that emerged in Latin America in the nine-teenth century did not evolve—as it did in the West—into "a veritable faith."[69] Throughout Latin American history, the instrumental rationale of the market had confronted the existence of a resilient pre-modern religious and political culture that even today favors traditional-patrimonial forms of domination that are incompatible with "the spirit of capitalism." This culture responds and reproduces the collective sense of entitlement of the Latin American elites and rationalizes the exclusion of the masses in the region.

Some components of the capitalist ideology, however, have gravitated toward the historically dominant social power structures of the region, creating partial and selective relations of elective affinity between the two. The ideology of the "invisible hand" of the market, for example, works in tandem with the *digitus Dei* invoked in the most conservative doctrinal interpretations of the Catholic Church, and with states that have the capacity to ignore social aspirations and demands. Together, they determine and justify the life and death of millions of Latin Americans and, especially, of the poor.

In the late twentieth century, the neoliberal forces of globalization intensified the power of the market by encouraging the isolation of important components of the economic policy-making process from the pressures of domestic politics. These transformations had a negative effect on human security because people found themselves increasingly subjected to decisions beyond their control.[70]

Where did the vulnerable and the poor try to find a sense of security in late-twentieth-century Latin America? Not in the market or in the state or in the promise of democratic politics. The poor went to God as revealed in the rapid growth of the Pentecostal and the Charismatic movements in the region over the past four decades. These "renewalist" movements operate within an explicit providentialist theology that teaches "God is in charge and purposefully, powerfully guides nature and history."[71]

God remains powerful in twenty-first-century Latin America. In Guatemala, 80 percent of those who participated in a global survey of the *Pew Global Attitudes Project* stated that religion played a "very important role" in their lives. The same statement was made by 77 percent of participants in Brazil, 72 percent in Honduras, 69 percent in Peru, 66 percent in Bolivia, 61 percent in Venezuela, 59 percent in Mexico, and 39 percent in Argentina. Only Africans registered higher degrees of religiosity than those of Latin Americans. The corresponding percentages for some of the European countries studied by Elshtain are: 33 percent for Great Britain, 27 percent for Italy, 21 percent for Germany and 11 percent for France.[72]

Statistical data, however, do not entirely reveal the power of God in the lives of Latin Americans because the word "God" means different things for different people. The God that religious people in Europe described in this same study as playing a "very important" role in their lives is most likely a God that is not perceived as a force that regulates and controls individual and human histories. The God of most religious people in Europe is perceived as a force working in accordance with the general principles of Deism. The God of religious people in Latin America, on the other hand, is typically a powerful force that meticulously shapes and determines the course of history. It is a God that performs miracles and intervenes in the lives of individuals and societies.[73]

In synthesis, no single source of authority—God, the state or the market—has become dominant in Latin American history. Therefore, sovereignty in this region of the world is complex, multidimensional and highly contested.

CONCLUSIONS

Paraphrasing Marx, philosophers and theologians participate in the making of history. However, "they do not make it as they please; they do not make it under self-selected circumstances, but under circumstances existing already, given and transmitted from the past."[74] These circumstances need to be taken into consideration in any attempt to elucidate the role of ideas in history and, more specifically, in any attempt to explain the reasons why theological and philosophical ideas fail or succeed in shaping the very conditions that they examine.

Why did the sovereign territorial state model become more successful than the model provided by, for example, the Italian city-states in Europe? Why did this model fail to provide Latin American societies with the same sense of order and collective self-identity that it provided Western societies? Why is Hobbes more important than Richard Hooker in the history of sovereignty? Why didn't the transition from God to State take place in Latin America?

The history of power and sovereignty in the West and Latin America reviewed in this essay shows that to become dominant, ideas have to be compatible with the particular cultural and material conditions in which they are articulated and implemented. In other words, they have to develop a relation of "elective affinity" with a dominant or potentially dominant power relation, or with a predominant historical tendency operating in the context within which they emerge.

The study of relations of "elective affinity" between ideas and historical reality becomes especially important for any theorist who, like Elshtain, wants to propose solutions to the challenges of his or her time. It is impossible to make sense of Elshtain's "sovereign self" without taking into consideration how the material and cultural power of the market enables the emergence of the anomic form of individualism that she decries. Confront the market challenge, and the problem of the "sovereign self" will become a marginal case of "social deviation." Ignore it, and risk fighting (and even winning) the wrong explanatory battle.

Indeed, ignore the cultural and material forces operating in the historical context of Latin America and risk repeating the mistakes made by Latin American elites every time they have tried to transplant European ideas and institutional models into the region. As it has been shown in this essay, the *Criollos* uncritically adopted European institutional models and political ideas. Neoliberals today do the same. The result of this imitative tradition is a history of "juxtapositions;" that is, of unresolved historical contradictions.[75]

For the West and for Latin America, the intellectual challenges of the twenty-first century demand the generation of knowledge that starts from reality and returns to reality.[76] In the case of the West, the challenge is the articulation of a new cultural synthesis that can domesticate market forces and re-harmonize the spiritual needs of society, the political rationale of the state, and the instrumental rationale of the economy. For Latin America, the challenge is more complex: it demands the organization of a puzzle with no shape and with pieces that have successfully resisted harmonization in the past.

NOTES

1. Jean Bethke Elshtain, *Sovereignty: God, State and Self*. New York: Basic Books, 2008.

2. In cognitive sciences, the concept of the embodied mind expresses the notion that mental processes are not simply the product of the brain. They are "partly constituted by, partly made up of wider (i.e., extraneural) bodily structures and processes." Moreover, they are constituted "in part by the ways in which an organism acts on the world and the ways in which world, as a result, acts back on that organism" (Rowlands, 2010, 3). See also Maurice Merleau-Ponty, *The Primacy of Perception* (Evanston, IL: Northwestern University Press, 1964).

3. Elshtain is not unaware of the contextual forces that condition ideas of power. *Sovereignty* is sprinkled with socio-historical references (see also Elshtain, 2000a, 27). However, Elshtain does not present these references as representations of a context that enable and constrain the production of ideas about sovereignty and power. Rather, they are presented as marginal details in a narrative that is based on the notion that ideas are the product of theological and philosophical "contestation" (Elshtain, 2008, 6).

4. Elshtain, *Sovereignty*, 95.

5. William H. Swatos Jr., (1998), *Elective Affinity. Encyclopedia of Religion and Society*. Available from: http://hartsem.edu/ency/elective.htm [accessed 20 July 2014].

6. Bruce Wexler, *Brain and Culture* (Cambridge: MIT Press, 2006).

7. Elshtain, *Sovereignty*, 30.

8. Elshtain, *Sovereignty*, 159.

9. Elshtain, *Sovereignty*, 12.

10. Elshtain, *Sovereignty*, 10.

11. Oliver O'Donovan and Joan Lockwood O'Donovan, eds., *A Sourcebook in Christian Political Thought* (Grand Rapids, MI: William B. Eerdmans, 1999), 56–65.

12. R. A. Markus, *Saeculum: History and Society in the Theology of St. Augustine* (Cambridge: Cambridge University Press, 1988), 30.

13. Arthur Herman, *The Cave and the Light* (New York: Random House, 2014), 147–85, Alan Ryan, *On Politics* (New York: Liveright Publishing Corporation, 2012), 149–84.

14. Markus, *Saeculum*, 173.

15. Edward Grant, *God and Reason in the Middle Ages* (Cambridge: Cambridge University Press, 2001), 32. See also Genevieve Lloyd, *Providence Lost* (Cambridge, MA: Harvard University Press, 2008), 129–59.

16. Elshtain, *Sovereignty*, 7.

17. Elshtain, *Sovereignty*, 17.

18. David Hackett Fischer, *The Great Wave* (Oxford: Oxford University Press, 1996), 16, George Lakoff and Mark Johnson, *Metaphors we Live By* (Chicago: University of Chicago Press, 2003).

19. Christian Rohr, "Man and Nature in the Middle Ages," *Environment and History* 9, no. 1 (2003), 14.

20. Herman, *The Cave and the Light*, 223–42, Ryan, *On Politics*, 224–56, Rubenson, *Aristotle's Children*.

21. Walter Ullman, *The Individual and Society in the Middle Ages* (Baltimore: Johns Hopkin University Press, 1966).

22. Grant, *God and Reason in the Middle Ages*, 36.

23. Erwin H. Ackerknecht, *A Short History of Medicine* (Baltimore: Johns Hopkings University Press, 1982), 79–82.

24. Aquinas, *Summa contra Gentiles*, Book 1, Chapter 3 in Steve Wilkens, *Faith and Reason: Three Views* (Downers Grove, IL: Intervarsity Press, 2014), 154.

25. As quoted in Herman, *The Cave and the Light*, 236.

26. Rik Van Nieuwenhove, "Catholic Theology in the Thirteenth Century and the Origins of Secularism," *Irish Theology Quarterly*, vol. 75, no. 4, 339–54

27. Karl Schmitt, *Political Theology* (Chicago: University of Chicago Press, 2005), 36.

28. The concept of ontological security makes reference to people's confidence "in the continuity of their self-identity and in the constancy of their surrounding social and material environments of action" (Giddens, 1990, 92).

29. Theodore K. Rabb, *The Struggle for Stability in Early Modern Europe* (New York: Oxford University Press, 1975), 33.

30. Grant, *God and Reason in the Middle Ages*, 285.

31. Thomas Hobbes, *Leviathan*, ed. C.B. MacPherson (Harmondsworth: Middlesex: Penguin Books, 1968 [1651]), 227–28.

32. Michael Dillon, "Security, philosophy and politics," in M. Featherstone, S. Lash, and R. Robertson, eds, *Global Modernities* (London, UK: Sage, 1995), 1.

33. Niklas Luhman, *The Differentiation of Society* (New York: Columbia University Press, 1982), 333

34. Elshtain, *Sovereignty*, 200.

35. Elshtain, *Sovereignty*, 39.

36. Elshtain, *Sovereignty*, 95.

37. Elshtain, *Sovereignty*, 283.

38. Patrick J. Deneen, "The Great Combination," in Michael Jon Kessler (ed.) *Political Theology for a Plural Age* (Oxford: Oxford University Press, 2013), 4.

39. A. P. Martinich, *The Two Gods of Leviathan: Thomas Hobbes on Religion and Politics* (Cambridge: Cambridge University Press, 2002).

40. Reinhart Koselleck, *Critique and Crisis: Enlightenment and Pathogenesis of Modern Society* (Oxford, UK: Berg, 1988).

41. T. S. Marshall, *Citizenship and Social Class* (Cambridge, UK.: Cambridge University Press, 1965).

42. Sheldon Wolin, *Politics and Vision: Continuity and Innovation in Western Political Thought,* expanded edition (Princeton, NJ: Princeton University Press, 2009), 9.

43. Jerry Muller, *The Mind and the Market: Capitalism in Western Thought* (New York: Anchor Books, 2003), 61.

44. John Rogers Commons, *Institutional Economics. Vol. I: Its Place in Political Economy*)New Brunswick NJ: Transaction Publishers, 2009), 160.

45. Adam Smith, *An Inquiry Into the Nature and Causes of the Wealth of Nations* (New York: The Modern Library, 1937), 423.

46. Kant, Immanuel, "Idea for a Universal History with Cosmopolitan Interest" in Allen W. Wood, ed., *Basic Writings of Kant* (New York: The Modern Library, 2001), 122.

47. Elshtain, *Sovereignty*, 227–28.

48. Elshtain, *Sovereignty*, 181.

49. Elshtain, *Sovereignty*, 243.

50. Elshtain, *Sovereignty*, 243.

51. C. B. MacPherson, *The Political Theory of Possessive Individualism: From Hobbes to Locke* (Oxford: Oxford University Press, 1972), 270.

52. Carole Pateman, *The Problem of Political Obligation: A Critical Analysis of Liberal Theory*. London: Polity, 1985, and *The Sexual Contract* (Stanford: Stanford University Press, 1988).

53. Charles Taylor, *The Malaise of Modernity* (Toronto: Anansi, 1993), 93.

54. Elshtain, *Sovereignty*, 232.

55. Elshtain, *Sovereignty*, 227–28.

56. Karl Polanyi, *The Great Transformation* (New York: Beacon Press, 1957), 235. In her book *Democracy on Trial*, Elshtain mentions the "logic of the market" but only to criticize the left: "We now witness a morally exhausted left embracing rather than challenging the logic of the market by endorsing the "relentless translations of *wants* into *rights*." Elshtain, *Democracy on Trial* (Toronto: Anansi, 1993), 16. In *Who Are We? Critical Reflections and Hopeful Possibilities*, she offers her most explicit analysis of market economics, consumerism and commodification. Elshtain, *Who are We? Critical Reflections and Hopeful Possibilities* (Grand Rapids, MI: Eerdmans, 2000).

57. Leopoldo Zea, "Identity: A Latin American Philosophical Problem," The Philosophical Forum, no. 20 (1989), 33–42.

58. Lewis Hanke, *Latin America: A Historical Reader* (Boston: Little Brown and Company, 1974), 45–47.

59. Zenobio Saldivia, and Felipe Caro, "Francisco Suárez y el Impacto de su Teoría sobre la Potestad Divina y Monárquica en América." *Estudios Latinoamericanos*, no. 6, Año 3 (2011), 41–55, Bartomeu Forteza, "La Influencia de Francisco Suárez sobre Thomas Hobbes." *Convivum*, no. 11, vol. 2 (1998), 40–79.

60. Hanke, *Latin America*, 46.

61. Mariano Fazio Fernández, Mariano, "Interpretaciones de la Evangelización: del Providencialismo a la Utopía." Actas, *Historia de la Evangelización de América, Simposio Internacional*. Ciudad del Vaticano, 11–14 de mayo de 1992, Ciudad del Vaticano: Librería Editrice Vaticana, 1992, 609–21.

62. Bertrand Badie, *The Imported State: The Westernization of the Political Order* (Stanford: Stanford University Press, 2000).

63. Andrés Pérez-Baltodano, *Entre el Estado Conquistador y el Estado Nación: Providencialismo, Pensamiento Político y Estructuras de Poder en el Desarrollo Histórico de Nicaragua*. Managua, Nicaragua: Instituto de Historia de Nicaragua y Centroamérica (IHNCA) de la Universidad Centroamericana y Fundación Friedrich Ebert (2003; 2008).

64. Octavio Paz, *El Laberinto de la Soledad/Postdata Vuelta a El Laberinto de la Soledad*. (México: Fondo de Cultura Económica, 1998); Pablo Kraudy Medina, *Historia Social de las Ideas en Nicaragua: El Pensamiento de la Conquista* (Managua: Fondo Editorial Banco Central de Nicaragua, 2001).

65. Providentialism is a theological concept that sees the history of individuals and societies as governed by God in accordance with His plans and purposes. See Roger E. Olson, *The Mosaic of Christian Belief: Twenty Centuries of Unity and Diversity* (Downers Grove, IL: InterVarsity Press, 2002).

66. Octavio Paz, *Sor Juana Inés de la Cruz o las Trampas de la Fe* (México: Fondo de Cultura Económica, 1982), 45.

67. Rodolfo De Roux, "Las Etapas de la Laicización en Colombia," in Jean-Pierre Bastian, ed., *La Modernidad Religiosa: Europa y América Latina en Perspectiva Comparada* (México, D.F.: Fondo de Cultura Económica, 2004), 65.

68. Mónica Serrano and Paul Kenny "Colombia and the Andean Crisis." In: Simon Chesterman, Michael Ignatieff and Ramesh Thakur, eds. *Making States Work: State Failure and the Crisis of Governance.* (New York: United Nations University Press, 2005.)

69. Polanyi, *The Great Transformation*, 135.

70. Ironically, this process took place at the same time the region was undergoing processes of "democratic transition." However, in most cases these transitions were democratic only in formal terms. People were able to elect governments every few years, but did not achieve the power to domesticate the role of the state (Chalmers, et al., 1997; Goodale and Postero, 2013; Pérez-Baltodano, 2000; Weyland, 2004).

71. David A. Smilde, (1998). "Letting God Govern: Supernatural Agency in the Venezuelan Pentecostal Approach to Social Change." *Sociology of Religion* 59, no. 3 (1998), 287–303.

72. Pew Global Attitude Project, "Among Wealthy Nations . . . US Stands Alone in its Embrace of Religion," (Washington, DC: Pew Research Center, 2002). Available from: http://pewglobal.org/. (accessed 10 August, 2014).

73. Andrés Pérez-Baltodano, "Dios y el Estado: Dimensiones culturales del proceso de formación del Estado en América Latina." *Nueva Sociedad*, Buenos Aires, no. 210, Julio-Agosto 2007.

74. Karl Marx, *The Eighteenth Brumaire of Louis Bonaparte* (1852). Available at: https://www.marxists.org/archive/marx/works/1852/18th-brumaire/ch01.htm [Accessed 9 August, 2014].

75. Zea, "Identity."

76. R. G. Collingwood, *Essays in the Philosophy of History* (Austin, Texas: University of Texas Press,1965).

Chapter Twelve

No god but God? Nominalism and Political Islam

Paul S. Rowe

In June 2014, militants from the Islamic State of Iraq and al-Sham, a radical Islamist movement then fighting in Syria and Iraq, dealt a devastating blow to the Iraqi government. In the space of a few days, they took control of several important cities, including Mosul and Tikrit, from the government of Iraq. Their dramatic success in creating a putative empire stretching from Aleppo in Syria to Mosul in Iraq gave them the power to eliminate the juridical border between the two states and thereby present a challenge to the modern nation-state system. What is more, they issued a statement in late June identifying their movement as *the* Islamic State and claiming that they had restored the ancient caliphate (a term that derives from the Arabic *khila-fa*, referring to successors, or "viceregents" of the Prophet and the faith of Islam on earth) established by the successors of Muhammad.

The restoration of the caliphate was a bold move, but it reflected a common desire held by Islamist radicals throughout the past decades. After taking control of the greater part of Afghanistan in 1996, Taliban leader Mullah Muhammad Omar claimed the title *amir al-mu'minin*, a common caliphal epithet. In the wake of the 11 September 2001 attacks in the United States, al Qaeda founder Osama bin Ladin recognized Omar's claim in his public statements. For radical Sunni Islamists, the search for a means of restoring the ancient caliphate remains a high priority. While other movements do not seek the restoration of the caliphate in so dramatic a fashion, there is little doubt that the abolition of the caliphate announced by Mustafa Kemal Ataturk in 1924 ushered in a period of crisis that led to the creation of the modern Islamist movement. This epochal event came at a time of great political ferment in the Middle East, a time in which modernism arose to

173

challenge traditional notions of right and Truth. At the same time, the basic norms of sovereignty birthed in Western Europe had been embraced by a new state system emerging in the Middle East. Post-Ottoman Arab states and the modern Turkish republic alike saw their birth in the years following the 1919 Versailles settlement. For Islamists, the modern notion of sovereignty was a new battleground in an ongoing struggle over who would define the notion of state power into the future. It is a struggle that continues today.

The conflation of this struggle over sovereignty with the struggle over the role of religion in a post-caliphal age meant that Islamist scholars needed to address the same questions that European Christendom had considered during the period of the Enlightenment. In Europe, the assertion of radical forms of sovereignty linked to nominalism was a hallmark of the revolutionary movements of the nineteenth century, linked in many cases to the nationalists of the Romantic period. For Muslims, the rise of nationalism and pan-Islamism came in the late 1800s and early 1900s. Pan-Islamism, the precursor to modern Islamism, arose at the end of the nineteenth century as a response to European nationalism. Early Islamists pursued a limited political project that would restore a putative golden age of Islamic civilization. However, after the termination of the caliphate in 1924, the descent of Middle Eastern regimes into republican authoritarianism coincided with the deepening of nominalist thinking among Islamist radicals. This began with the Egyptian scholar Rashid Rida and persisted among the more radical proponents of Islamism. By the late 1960s nominalism was a common conceit of the radical Islamist fringe, with the modern jihadists taking their cue from Sayyid Qutb, the father of modern Islamist radicalism. Islamist moderates today seek to institute a limited sovereignty based on concepts such as *shura* (consultation) and *ijtihad* (independent legal reasoning). Their rivals, including powerful groups like the Islamic State, shun traditional forms of Islamic reasoning in favour of direct articulation of the Islamic law, the *shari'a*, as though their interpretation is divine guidance.

As a result, today's Islamist theoreticians continue to struggle with what Jean Bethke Elshtain would have called a self-sovereign nominalism that arose among the post-caliphal scholars. Arrogating to the Islamist movement the place of divine judgment, Islamist radicals commonly subordinate the traditional Islamic constraints on authority such as *shura, ijtihad*, and *fiqh*, even as they pay lip service to these concepts as a means of justifying their uncompromising use of authority. While many mainstream Islamic scholars work to develop the critical modes of inquiry encouraged by the early pioneers of Islam, they must frequently contend with nominalist champions of a more radical form of political Islam. In this essay, I address the way in which nominalism crept into Islamist thinking during the early years of its development and deepened in the hearts of many activists in the post-caliphal age.

NOMINALISM, SOVEREIGNTY, AND ISLAM

The notion of sovereignty developed in Western societies during the consolidation of the state system. It was already in full bloom by the time that the Peace of Westphalia enshrined state sovereignty as a principle in 1648. Mark Lilla, among others, describes how modern notions of political sovereignty evolved within Christendom as a gradual movement toward separating the rationalistic arguments about authority from their Christian moorings.[1] Hence the idea of sovereignty arose alongside secularization. According to Elshtain, this provided opportunities for other models of sovereignty—sovereignty of the state and the self—to eclipse the more limited form of sovereignty described by pre-modern theorists. Proper notions of sovereignty rest on the limitations of human understanding, on the recognition that "human finiteness" grounds all of our political actions.[2] Understanding human finiteness means that sovereign actions cannot be more than penultimate since ultimate sovereignty belongs to the divine alone (no matter how the divine is described).[3] Such a relative, voluntarist understanding of sovereignty guards human freedom by reminding the state and the self that other ties bind the individual, ties that tether the person to his or her humanity before God, to the community, or to the world as a whole.

By contrast, a nominalist notion of sovereignty is not relative: it establishes the sovereign authority as the sole source of sovereign Truth, ruling by command rather than submitting to the authority of reason as a guide to understanding. Elshtain argues that nominalism arose in the fourteenth century to become the foundation for early modern notions of divine right.[4] Nominalism later ushered in the period of extremist nationalism and individualism, creating extremist ideologies such as fascism and radical liberalism. Nominalist thinking drove the French revolutionaries, guided by the certainty of the revolutionary divine, to sacrifice humans rather than animals on the guillotines of Paris "to propitiate the revolutionary gods."[5] Likewise modern technology matched with self-sovereign hubris gives our contemporaries the divine right to "utter control over the bodies of not only ourselves but others who are not yet, or have ceased to become, self-sovereign."[6] Sovereignty in its nominalist mode uses God as a virtual object to justify the command of the sovereign, who assumes the role of God on earth, even if such a sovereign gives lip service to the existence of a God beyond this earth.

This struggle over the notion of sovereignty coincides with the long period of state-building that emerged out of the late medieval age. Sovereignty of the state and sovereignty of the self are outcomes of the nationalist and individualist responses to modernity that developed throughout the past few centuries. In Elshtain's work, these phenomena are presented as products of the Western Christian imagination. Western civilization did not arise in complete isolation, even though it was largely self-referent. The essential questions that drove Europeans to devise highly nominalist notions of state and self sovereignty may also be found in Islamic civilization. The gap in time between ancient theorists of the early caliphal age (who lived in the seventh and eighth centuries) and the modern Islamists of the present is wide, but the historical development of sovereignty as a concept proceeded from an ancient religio-political system toward the modern nation-state, affected equally by the emergence of modern nationalism and individualism in the last two centuries.

At first glance, Islamic society is clearly fertile ground for the development of nominalist forms of sovereignty. It was founded by a Prophet who is said to have presented the ultimate message of God to humanity, whose words in the Qur'an are viewed as the direct revelation of God. Indeed, the very name of Islam means submission. The God of Islam is ultimately transcendent and unknowable. The worst sin of all in Islam is *shirk*, the association of physical forms with a God that is far beyond the created sphere. Such an unknowable God demands obedience far more than understanding.

However, from earliest times Muslims have grappled with the need to articulate claims to authority and sovereignty. Debates over sovereignty have arisen based on varied interpretations of the *Shari'a*, arguments over Islamic ideals, and legal controversies at least as often as they have reflected naked struggles for power. The first ruptures within the Islamic community (the *umma*) arose over the proper claim of Muhammad's successors to sovereignty. Throughout the first century after his death, these debates centred on whether the Prophet's family through his son-in-law Ali should be recognized as his successors, or whether the most powerful of the Muslims should rule. These debates led to *fitna*, dissension in the *umma*, and to the age-old divide between the Sunni and the Shi'i.

The demands of Islam to regulate the behavior and life of the Muslim led to a complicated system of jurisprudence, or *fiqh*, in which learned scholars theorized and debated how the Islamic *Shari'a* applied to matters of public and personal life. These scholars engaged in *ijtihad* and came up with various and occasionally contradictory answers. The first centuries of the Islamic empire contributed to a wide variety of such interpretive traditions, leading to the four Sunni schools of *fiqh*, known as *madhhabs*. By the eighth to the eleventh centuries the Islamic tradition had evolved to encompass the wider study of philosophy (*falsafa*) and knowledgeable discourse (*ilm al-kalam*). Scholars known as the *ahl al-adl wal-tawhid* ("people of justice and oneness," known to their opponents as *mu'tazilah*) developed a school of thought that argued for the unity of existence, a perspective that allowed them to integrate Western philosophic thinking with their own Islamic tradition. Their particular fusion of reason and revelation was controversial among both sufi mystics and Islamic traditionalists. The former resisted the prioritization of logical reasoning over experience while the latter felt that Islamic philosophy had departed from the pure religion introduced by the Prophet. Over the next few centuries, some traditionalists argued that the "gates of ijtihad had closed." Such a declaration was a means of silencing the continued use of secular reasoning in Islamic scholarship, but in reality it did little to limit the continued passage of *fatwas* and the expansion of Muslim learning.

At the center of the relationship between Islamic *fiqh* and sovereignty was the relationship between the scholars and the caliphate, the Islamic state of the Middle Ages. Noah Feldman argues that Islamic scholars remained an important check on the nominal power of the caliph throughout the medieval period. For example, in the midst of difficult political transitions, the support of the Islamic scholars for the caliph was crucial: "the scholars' power to confer legitimacy was significant because the uncertain nature of succession demanded an affirmation of legitimacy. . . . In exchange for their conferral of legitimacy, the scholars asked just one thing of the ruler: a commitment to the rule of law."[7] Islamic philosophic and discursive practices expanded in the ninth and tenth centuries, ultimately leading to the work of medieval intellectuals such as Avicenna (c. 980–1037) and Averroes (1126–1198).

The expansion of the Islamic tradition perhaps inevitably led to a reaction among traditionalists who held that philosophy and knowledgeable discourse had brought unhealthy innovations (*bid'ah*). In hindsight, we can see the important influence of two men who argued that a purer Islam that reflected the priorities of the first Muslim community was superior to the accretions that had arisen during the Middle Ages. Taqi al-Din ibn Taymiyya (1263–1328) was a Damascene scholar who preached against the prevailing popular religion of his day, and expanded the notion of *jihad* to call on Muslims to fight in defense of the *umma*. Muhammad ibn Abd al-Wahhab (1703–1792) was an Arabian Islamic reformer who forged an alliance with the Saud family who later came to rule Saudi Arabia. His austere understanding of the Muslim religion counseled the elimination of the veneration of saints and the imposition of strict public morality in the kingdom. Both ibn Taymiyya and Abd al-Wahhab leveled devastating critiques of the combination of reason and revelation common throughout the Islamic Middle Ages.

Looking back it is common to see the roots of modern radicalism in Ibn Taymiyya's exhortation of the Muslims to *jihad* and in Abd al-Wahhab's puritanical project. It may also be that their resistance to the Islamic philosophic traditions laid the groundwork for modern Islamist nominalism. But even though they laid the foundation for modern nominalist assertions among the most radical of Islamists, they remained committed to a form of disputation—they simply asserted the superiority of original sources. If their goal was the purification of Islam, it was purification of Western sources of argumentation rather than the idea of argumentation in itself. The fundamentalism of Ibn Taymiyya and Abd al-Wahhab embraced a form of xenophobia rather than a release from all forms of rational debate.[8] This xenophobic reaction to syncretic forms of religion contributed to a condemnatory and violent response that proved to be a powerful ally of nominalist practice in the centuries to come. When later theorists denounced Western decadence and *jahiliyya* (ignorance), as did Sayyid Qutb in the 1950s, or *gharbzadegi* ("westoxication"), as did Jalal Al-e Ahmed and Ali Shari'ati in the 1960s, they were justifying deeper and deeper calls to nominalist sovereignty through xenophobia.

ISLAM AND THE ENLIGHTENMENT: THE ISLAMIC MODERNISTS

Though we may see the early influence of the medieval clerics on modern Islamism, the development of Islamist ideology did not really arise until the modern period. The political crisis that emerged out of the Enlightenment in Europe came to the Islamic world with the gradual dissolution of the Ottoman Empire and the caliphate in the nineteenth and early twentieth centuries. Though the early years of the Ottoman caliphate had seen a revival of the autocratic caliphal pattern, by the nineteenth century the caliphate was in decline, forced to accept the inevitability of governance reforms that sought to rationalize governance in the empire. The power of the caliphate was limited by legal reforms known as the *tanzimat*, undertaken in the early 1800s, and the *hatt-i sherif* undertaken in the 1830s. The latter introduced full citizenship rights for non-Muslim subjects under pressure from the empire's European allies. Over time these liberalizing reforms came to be associated with alternatives to religion in defining sovereignty. New forms of nationalism and liberalism challenged the power of Islamic tradition in the empire and set the stage for a crisis of faith amid modernity. Arab subjects of the Ottoman state were embracing European nationalism as a model of their own political organization. Anti-colonial movements began to emerge, most notably in the abortive revolt led by Egyptian Colonel Ahmed 'Orabi against the British and Khedival administration in Egypt from 1879–1882.

Nationalism was only one form of political organization available to the Arab masses, and it had its greatest appeal among Arab Christians and Westernized Arabs. Among others, the primary reference point for political organization in Muslim societies was the *umma* and the Islamic tradition. Both the nationalist and Islamist movements flowered in the late 1800s as Arab civilization enjoyed the *nahda*, the renaissance.

In the late 1800s, Sayyid Jamal al-Din al-Afghani (1838–1897) emerged as a leading critic who exposed the weakness of the caliphate even as he propounded the importance of Islamic unity. A Sunni, he supported the institution of the caliphate but only under the aegis of an enlightened ruler. Afghani promoted Islamic civilization as the equal of European civilization, and argued that the promotion of modern education would help to mobilize Muslims to their calling. Far from asserting the sovereign's nominal duty to command, Afghani stressed the limitations of divine guidance on sovereignty.

> Islamic principles are concerned with relationships among the believers, they explain the law in general and in detail, they define the executive power which administers the law, they determine sentences and limit their conditions; also they are concerned with the unique goal that the holder of power ought to be the most submissive of men to the rules regulating that power which he gains neither by heritage, nor inheritance, nor by virtue of his race, tribe material strength, or wealth. On the contrary he acquires it only if he submits to the stipulations of the sacred law, if he has the strength to apply it, and if he judges with the concurrence of the community. [9]

Afghani's vision for the sovereign was a return to an idealized caliphate that resembled the days of the Umayyads and Abbasids of the seventh to the tenth centuries—a return to the golden age of reason in Islam, not necessarily the days of the Prophet himself. Nissim Rejwan notes that Afghani combined two programs in an uneasy tandem: Islamic liberalism, "the revision of Muslim doctrine in the light of modern conditions," and an agitation for Islamic liberation from foreign influences that "made him a forerunner of modern nationalist radicalism." [10] Though Afghani was not first and foremost a nationalist, the old xenophobia of the medieval scholars was certainly close to the surface. According to Afghani, the flowering of Islamic civilization would allow the caliph to rely upon modern advances in liberal arts and sciences, all of which would enrich the life of the *umma*. As an early proponent of pan-Islamism, Afghani promoted a religious revival of sorts. But his interest was in reviving the mind of the Muslim and recovering a civilization that had been in decline for centuries rather than in renewing theological disputation over orthodoxy or orthopraxy. In order to match the technological and cultural skill of the European, the Muslim needed to marshal the full force of the intellect and thereby discover a divinely-ordained new order for the *umma*. This implied a reconstruction of the caliphate, not its destruction or replacement.

Although a skeptic and critic of the nationalists, Afghani's chief disciple Muhammad Abduh (1849–1905) was supportive of the revolutionary movement headed by Ahmad 'Orabi. Abduh's nationalism was limited: he had essentially democratic instincts and a high regard for Islam as a force far stronger and more important than national self-determination. C. C. Adams, an early interpreter of Abduh, suggested that Abduh understood Islam to teach democracy in a limited form: "representative government and legislation by representatives chosen by the people are entirely in harmony with the spirit and practice of Islam from the beginning . . . the method of realizing such representative government has not been defined by the Islamic Law (*Shari'ah*), but is to be determined by that which will best promote the ends of justice and of the common advantage."[11] Abduh was exiled for his role for several years during which he joined Afghani in Europe and promoted an Islamic alternative to Arab nationalism.

Abduh's later career as the Egyptian grand mufti and his country's leading educational reformer contributed to the rebirth of an Islamic intellectual tradition that sought to integrate Western-style learning with a traditional embrace of religion. Samira Haj argues that Abduh's philosophy formed a middle way between traditionalism and modernism in which the liberal self was "chastened" (to use Christian Green's terminology) by the "living collective" of the *umma* as a moral community.[12] She goes on to observe that

> In contrast to a "good" liberal self who seeks to be self-constitutive and sovereign, valuing a selfhood that is tradition free and detached from its social roles, 'Abduh, assuming that the essence of Islamic law resides in the self, postulated a Muslim selfhood to be formed through and within the parameters of the Muslim community.[13]

Abduh's work was carried on by his acolyte Muhammad Rashid Rida, whose monthly magazine *al-Manar* presented his vision for the application of Islamic revivalism in the Arab world. It fell to Rida to respond to the abolition of the caliphate in 1924.

COMMANDING THE FAITHFUL: THE POST-CALIPHAL AGE

The caliphate had arisen as an institution after the death of Muhammad in 632. Ensuing disputes over who should succeed the Prophet had led to the *fitna*, a civil war which led to the first Islamic empire led by Muawiya and his family, the Umayyads, after the death of Muhammad's son-in-law Ali. Supporters of Muawiya's claim to be Muhammad's successor came to be known as the Sunnis, while supporters of Ali's family came to be known as the Shi'i. For centuries, the Sunni caliphate followed the dynastic politics of one powerful dynasty to another, formally passing to the Ottoman dynasty in 1517. Though the religious and temporal authority of the caliph waxed and waned over the centuries, it remained the focal point of authority in Sunni Islam. Shi'is rejected the caliphate and followed a line of imams. Though Shi'is remain divided over the later successors to the first imams, today the largest number of Shi'is look back to the twelfth imam, who disappeared, or went into occultation, in the ninth century. Since that time, Shi'i scholars have engaged in their own pursuit of Islamic jurisprudence, or *fiqh*, as representatives of the imam on earth.

The seeds of the decline of the Sunni caliphate lay in the expansion of popular sovereignty, reason, and the limitation of arbitrary authority. When Ataturk announced its abolition on 3 March 1924 its legitimacy had been in question for several years. Calls for its replacement or restoration after 1924 became the primary motivating force behind the growth of Islamism over the next few decades. The early Islamists envisioned many different responses to the end of the caliphate. The 1920s were a time of great crisis throughout most religious communities, and liberal modernism and text criticism was having an impact among Muslims at the same time that the Scopes Trial was proceeding in the United States. For Christians, social gospel, liberal and fundamentalist movements responded to changing cultural trends. Muslims responded similarly, with the pursuit of social service and revivalist organizations, the growth of the Salafist and other traditionalist movements, and by challenging received authority through the lens of text criticism. [14]

The latter development had strong influence upon the former. In 1926, Taha Hussein, one of Muhammad Abduh's students, published *On Jahiliyya Poetry*, a text-critical analysis of his topic which made the particular assertion that the Islamic tradition of Ibrahim and Ismail was of late vintage. Hussein's work leveled a challenge to the Salafi Islamist mainstream at the time which sought retrenchment of conservative understandings of the early history of Islam rather than such liberal reinterpretations. Hussein's work set off reprisals, including an investigation by scholars at *al Azhar* University. [15] His later work, including *The Future of Culture in Egypt*, written in 1938, emphasized the way in which European culture had an influence on the development of Egyptian, and by extension, Islamic culture. The implications mooted in the work of secular liberals like Hussein, who stressed a common embrace of nationalism and European scholarship as tools for the Arab future, were matched by others who sought to find an answer to the collapse of caliphal authority in the rediscovery of the Islamic tradition. The absence of a central focal point of authority in the Muslim world was keenly felt in official and scholarly worlds. Many intellectuals felt that it merely provided an opportunity for moral authority to rightfully devolve to the individual Muslim. Others saw the need to renew the Islamic community as a means of restoring *ijma* (consensus).

Muhammad Rashid Rida was perhaps the most influential voice of the period among the traditionalists. His response to the collapse of the caliphate was to emphasize a return to the earliest traditions of Islam, a perspective that he derived from the medieval scholarship of Ibn Taymiyya and Ibn al-Kayyim al-Jawziyyah (d.1355). [16] One way of applying this was to insist upon the superiority of *Shari'a* over that of man-made law, an insistence that has since formed the foundation for constitutional articles that refer to *Shari'a* as the foundation of law in countries such as Egypt. But the definition of *Shari'a* itself is subject to the predilections of interpretation, whether voluntarist or nominalist. The expanded scope of *Shari'a* and state sovereignty in the wake of the collapse of the caliphate has created opportunities for theocrats and demagogues to rethink sovereignty in new and dangerous ways.

Rida reflected the increasing demand of the age for a return to Islamic purity, one rooted in the fundamentalist tropes of Ibn Taymiyya and Ibn Abd al Wahhab centuries earlier. The establishment of the Muslim Brotherhood in 1928 by Hassan al-Banna represented a social effort to respond to an absent caliphate. Where liberals sought to relativize Islamic culture through a modernist *nahda*, social conservatives like Banna argued that true religion would create a new society that would be a purer replacement for the caliphate. Brotherhood acolytes sought a purified social order, but one based on both the moral prescriptions and social justice demands of Islam. They shared the salafism of Taymiyya and Wahhab without their demand for the absolute elimination of certain forms of religious tradition. Banna himself had been a member of a Sufi order, a form of syncretism condemned by the early fundamentalists, but he nonetheless resonated with the Salafi call to return to the early traditions of Islam, its denunciation of mystical innovations, and its refusal to countenance scholastic forms of rational discourse that resembled Western philosophy.[17] He thus reaffirmed the cultural xenophobia of the early fundamentalists and began the firm rejection of the rationalist tradition that had been embraced by Abduh and his disciples.

THE RADICAL PATH: ALIENATION AND THE ABSENT CALIPHATE

The marginalization of the salafists of the 1920s and 1930s into the 1940s reinforced a despair that they would never attain a restoration of the caliphate through normal politics. As the Muslim Brotherhood gained political strength in the 1940s, it was repressed by a state that saw its social work as a threat rather than a contribution to civil society. Despite their original support for the Free Officers' overthrow of King Farouk in 1952, by the late 1950s the Egyptian Muslim Brotherhood had come under official persecution as an illegal opposition movement. Islamists throughout the Muslim world were similarly repressed by the secular nationalist and modernizing movements that arose in the developing world after World War II. Equally alienated from the liberal secular modernizers and Communist movements, they began to envision increasingly apocalyptic overthrow of the existing order in Muslim societies. Add to this the erosion of the powerful force of the *ulema*, the Islamic scholars, among Sunni Muslims in the wake of the collapse of the caliphate. Feldman argues that traditional Islamic scholars have been increas-

ingly marginalized by the modern Islamist movement as new social movements, defending non-rationalist approaches to Islam, have become more
influential. He writes that modern Islamism is "premised on the *replacement*
of these scholars by ordinary Muslim laymen who must be guided by their
own, nonscholarly interpretation of Islamic tradition."[18] Contemporary Islamist movements demand a place for the subaltern Muslim untrained in the
Shari'a but devout enough to want a more religious polity. At the same time,
they borrow Wahhabi demands to resist *bid'ah*, an orientation that pulls them
away from the traditions of Islamic civilization built up over the centuries.

Therefore, for a growing fundamentalist core an absent caliphate demanded a nominalism that had not been normative under most of the caliphs
themselves. Increasingly, Islamists began to look back on the caliphate as a
mythic golden age of sovereign monism that it had rarely in fact displayed.
The need for a new caliph was the need to restore a national sovereignty that
had never fully existed, one that would dutifully apply the *jizya* to non-
Muslim subjects, that would demand women's obedience to the practice of
purdah, that would police the actions of the Muslims by commending the
good and forbidding evil, or that would carry on the offensive *jihad* mandat-
ed by Ibn Taymiyya and his ideological descendants.

Writing for South Asian Muslims in the wake of the collapse of the
caliphate, Abu'l Ala Mawdudi argued that Islamic government was nothing
more than the restoration of caliphal authority to the *umma* itself. Democracy
as a Western concept, he argued, was devoid of this concept of divinely
delegated authority. "Islam has no trace of Western democracy. Islam, as
already explained, altogether repudiates the philosophy of popular sovereignty and rears its polity on the foundations of the sovereignty of God and the
vice regency (*khilafa*) of man."[19] Mawdudi's vision was the template for a
new, more radicalized understanding of Islam that emphasized the rise of
human agents in the vicregency of God. The caliphate did not need to be
reconstructed, rather it was reconstructed in the heart of the true Muslim,
who could become the representative of God on earth.

This newly exalted vice regency of man was the platform on which the
radicals of the Islamist movement built their claims to sovereignty. Seizing
upon this idea, Sayyid Qutb became one of the most influential members of
the Muslim Brotherhood.[20] He argued that true *hakimiya* (sovereignty) belonged to God and that God's viceregents on earth were only those who
obeyed a purified Islam. He therefore wrote against the ignorance of Western
and Islamic societies that had embraced values and morals that were alien to
Islam. He called such societies *jahili*, a word used by Muslims to refer to the
ignorance of pre-Islamic societies before the spread of Muhammad's religion. Qutb described the world in turmoil, split between true believers in
Islam and the world of *jahiliyya*, which had corrupted the minds and morals
of centuries of scholars and intellectuals, denying or suspending God's sove-

reignty on earth. [21] "Philosophy, the interpretation of history, psychology . . . ethics, theology and comparative religion, sociology . . . all of these sciences have a direction which in the past or the present has been influenced by *jahili* beliefs and traditions. That is why all these sciences come into conflict, explicitly or implicitly, with the fundamentals of any religion, and especially with Islam."[22] A purified Islamic society would not trade in such sciences: "If, in spite of knowing this, we rely on Western ways of thought, even in teaching the Islamic sciences, it will be an unforgiveable blindness on our part . . . A slight influence from them can pollute the clear spring of Islam."[23] The believer, uncontaminated by *jahili* traditions, is therefore "superior" to other human beings, "most superior in his law and system of life."[24] Such believers rely upon the "Qur'an [which] was creating hearts worthy of bearing the trust of the vice regency of God on earth."[25]

It is easy to overstate the influence of Sayyid Qutb on the development of the modern patterns of *jihad* and *takfir* in Islam, each of which justify violence and intolerance toward Western, non-Muslim, and *jahili* Muslim societies. But his reinvention of the notion of the caliphate to include the authority of the true Muslim provided fodder for contemporary Islamists to enshrine the divinity of their own authority. While authoritarian governments limited the power of Islamists through repression and adoption of their own Islamic credentials, many in the opposition movements deepened their condemnation of their own societies and justified violence as a means of purifying the world. The Afghan *jihad* and the spread of *Wahhabi* doctrines among radicals among the *mujahideen* fighting in the 1980s and 1990s.

Shi'i revolutionaries inspired by the Ayatollah Khomeini were latecomers to the Islamist awakening, but they were far more successful in implementing their own project to redefine the Islamic state. Part of the reason for this was that unlike Sunnis, Shi'i Muslims had no need to respond to the collapse of the caliphate. After the eleventh–twelfth centuries, the mainstream of Twelver Shi'ism had embraced political quietism in disavowal of temporal power, tainted by the *fitna* of the early years after the death of the Prophet. In the absence of a caliph (or in Shi'i theology, an imam), the ulema had interpreted the Islamic shari'a for the people. But officially Shi'i ulema eschewed the pursuit of political power which properly belonged to the imam in occultation: his authority might only be returned to a restored imam, or Mahdi. Commenting on the political implications of the absent imam, Karen Armstrong argues that his occultation "symbolized the impossibility of implementing a truly religious policy in the world."[26] Sovereignty was not to be grasped except by such a duly constituted authority, and the dispossession of the Shi'i left most of them outside the realm of power after the collapse of the Fatimid dynasty in the twelfth century. Shi'ism created a perfectionist vision of divine power without a human agent. It was not until the rise of Twelver (itna'ashari) Shi'ism as the majority religion of Iran by the nineteenth century that the foundation for a new Shi'i political theology was put in place. Article 2 of the constitution of 1906 provided a role for the ulema but the constitution was overridden by the absolute power of the Pahlavi Shahs throughout most of the twentieth century.

The constitution of 1979 enshrined *velayat-e faqih*, or guardianship of the jurist, as a constitutional principle in Iran. While it relied in part on the role provided to Islamic clerics under the 1906 constitution, *velayat-e faqih* as elaborated by the Ayatollah Khomeini created a regime in which the clergy, in particular the Supreme Guide, were virtually able to speak for God. Khomeini's vision was to establish the rule of God over men through the literal application of divine guidance. Though *fiqh* was ultimately a practice of Quranic interpretation, Khomeini paradoxically took the position that the Qur'an was clear in its essence: Mojtaba Mahdavi argues therefore that "[c]entral to Khomeinism is its anti-hermeneutic claim," a claim that provided Khomeini with the ability to establish his own office as the primary referent for what was Islamic—and what was not.[27] It was no accident that Khomeini's use of the *velayat-e faqih* referred to the Islamic cleric in the singular, not the plural. Though Article 2 of the constitution establishes that "exclusive sovereignty" belongs to the "one God," the authority of the *faqih* is ultimate under Article 5, which stated that "During the Occultation of the Wali al-Asr (may God hasten his reappearance), the wilayah and leadership of the Ummah devolve upon the just and pious faqih, who is fully aware of the circumstances of his age."

For Khomeini this authority overrode even the basics of Islamic religious practice. Behrooz Ghamari-Tabrizi argues that Khomeini's understanding of the *velayat-e faqih* went so far as to preach the primacy of the political over more mundane matters of faith.

> Khomeini's new approach took the doctrine of *velayat-e faqih* one step further toward the primacy of the *maslahat* (the political) over the authority of the *fuqaha* (the religious jurists). He marked this doctrine by placing the word *motlaqeh* (absolute) at the center of his old conception, calling it *velayat-e motlaqeh-ye faqih* (the absolute rule of the *faqih*).[28]

In Khomeini's hands, "governance" became a primary injunction of Islam for the *faqih*, even overruling the five essential pillars of Islam, like prayer, fasting, and pilgrimage. Deepening his independent authority, Khomeini affirmed the power of the Islamic State over religion in a statement regarding the passage of a new labour law in 1987. The statement was one of his final acts of defiance against his own acolytes in the Guardian Council who argued that *they* spoke for Islam. Ghamari-Tabrizi concludes that "Khomeini's open reprimand of the president and Guardian Council laid out the most radical transformation of the republic from a state conditioned, shaped, and informed by the teachings of Islam to a state that sanctioned, defined, and implemented a contingent Islam."[29]

CONCLUSIONS

The declaration of the caliphate by ISIS in June 2014 was simply the last step along a path toward the nominalist frontier of Islamism. In the declaration, the movement sought to pre-empt the objections against their authority to restore the caliphate without fulsome *shura* (consultation) among the Muslims. Their response was simple and unequivocal:

> And if they tell you, "We do not accept your authority." Then say to them, "We had the ability to establish the khilāfah [caliphate] by the grace of Allah, so it became an obligation for us to do so. Therefore, we hastened in adherence to the command of Allah (the Exalted)."[30]

The brazenness and audacity of the justification was remarkable. There is no god but Allah, but it was clear who was currently warming his throne. Their wholesale embrace of monism was on clear display over the next several months as they enforced strict interpretation of Shari'a law against the minority populations of northern Iraq. Christians were initially told to pay an extortionate *jizya* tax, then forced into exile. Yazidis, deemed *kafirun*, or heretics, were driven out and put under siege. In the end, an entire region was cleared of its non-Muslim population. Enemies were beheaded in grisly public executions. The seizure of regional power in the central regions of the earliest caliphates signaled the latest crisis in the definition of Islamic sovereignty.

As many are wont to point out, the Prophet of Islam fused the religious and political by creating the first state governed by Islam in Medina. At his death, this fusion of authority created an ongoing dilemma: should successors be excellent Muslims descended from the Prophet himself, or should they be imperialistic defenders of the faith, able to enforce religious principles with coercive authority? Over time this dispute became the foundation for *fitna* in the Islamic community and divided the Muslims on the basic idea of authority. In the modern age, *fitna* has arisen at an even more basic level: is sovereignty a matter of the arbitrary authority of the voice of God on earth, or is it something constrained by principles such as *ijtihad* (reasoning), *shura* (consultation), and the traditions of *fiqh* (jurisprudence)?

In the modern age, the collapse of the caliphate signaled a growing crisis in the Islamic community. For some, this has opened up a door for the pursuit of nominal conceptions of power that enthrone the power of the Muslim's command over the pursuit of divine truth. Among the Sunni, the crisis quickly divided between those who sought to embed Islamic thinking in the philosophic quest that resembled Western liberal discourses on democracy, legitimacy, justice, and authority and those who wanted a renewal of the caliphate in order to reinforce Islamic orthodoxy and power. Along the way, they redefined the caliphate to empower the human purveyors of Islam. Today Islamist radicals have inspired jihadism and resistance to the international order. Among the Shi'i, the early response to the occlusion of the *imam* had been the elaboration of a deeper understanding of *fiqh*. But in more recent times, even these discussions have descended into arbitrary use of power in favour of expediency, as in the Islamic Republic of the late Ayatollah Khomeini. In many cases, arbitrary authority is justified and lauded in the name of defending traditional and national forms of power. Islamism has been tainted by xenophobia. It has used *ad hominem* denunciations of Western societies as "Westoxicated," as the great or lesser Satan, rather than defending a rationalistic discourse embraced by the early modernizers such as Afghani and 'Abduh.

In response, many modern Muslims seek to return not just to the religion of their ancestors, but to the rich dialogic traditions of the early Islamic caliphates. Modern liberal and traditionalist Muslims continue to struggle to present their faith as a product of rational discourse embedded and grounded in an age-old tradition. Followers of Islam in many nations have no difficulty understanding that the Islamic faith may interact with a plurality of other traditions, comfortable with the knowledge that the faith reigns in the heart of the Muslim even if it does not dictate the rules of the society at large. The history of Muslim society has mirrored the Western struggle between nominal and constrained notions of sovereignty displayed in Western societies. Today's threats from the jihadist movement of Islam represent claims to nominalist state sovereignty that aim at monistic understandings—of the *umma*, of Islamic mores, of the right to governance, and even the legitimacy of the international system. It should come as little surprise that the nominalist claim to state and self sovereignty identified by Jean Bethke Elshtain is not unique to one civilizational tradition but a persistent concern for the world as a whole.

NOTES

1. Mark Lilla, *The Stillborn God: Religion, Politics, and the Modern West* (New York: Alfred A. Knopf, 2007).

2. Jean Bethke Elshtain, *Sovereignty: God, State, and Self* (New York: Basic Books, 2008), 5.

3. Elshtain, *Sovereignty*, 12.

4. Elshtain, *Sovereignty*, 25–68.

5. Elshtain, *Sovereignty*, 137.

6. Elshtain, *Sovereignty*, 204.

7. Noah Feldman, *The Fall and Rise of the Islamic State* (Princeton, NJ: Princeton University Press, 2008), 34–35.

8. Samira Haj, *Reconfiguring Islamic Tradition* (Stanford: Stanford University Press, 2009), 65.

9. Jamal al-Din al-Afghani, "Islamic Solidarity," in John J. Donohue and John L. Esposito, eds., *Islam in Transition*, second edition (Oxford: Oxford University Press, 2007), 17.

10. Nissim Rejwan, *Arabs Face the Modern World: Religious, Cultural, and Political Responses to the West* (Gainesville, FL: University Press of Florida, 1998), 25.

11. Charles C. Adams, *Islam and Modernism in Egypt* (New York: Russell and Russell, 1968 [1933]), 51.

12. Haj, *Reconfiguring Islamic Tradition*, 118.

13. Haj, *Reconfiguring Islamic Tradition*, 150–51.

14. The term Salafist is malleable. It refers in the first instance to those who sought a return to the putative religion of the earliest Muslims, the ancestors of the Muslim faith in the time of the rightly guided caliphs (632–61). In contemporary parlance it has a more narrow meaning that refers to Wahhabi-inspired global movements, but in earlier times it was used to refer to the broad array of traditional movements that sought a return to the "original" Islam.

15. Yunan Labib Rizk, "Taha Hussein's Ordeal," *Al Ahram Weekly*, 24–30 May 2001.

16. Adams, *Islam and Modernism*, 203.

17. Rejwan, *Arabs*, 58.

18. Feldman, *Fall and Rise*, 110.

19. Abu'l Ala Mawdudi, "Political Theory of Islam," in Donohue and Esposito, eds., *Islam in Transition*, 264.

20. It may be noteworthy in this context to mention that Sayyid Qutb famously spent time studying at the Colorado State College of Education in Greeley, Colorado, in 1948–1950 and may well have passed by the young Jean Bethke, who was raised nearby. Qutb's observations about his time in Colorado deepened his sense of the decadence of Western society. By contrast, Jean Bethke Elshtain frequently mentioned her childhood in rural Colorado as an influence on her essential trust in Western civility.

21. Sayyid Qutb, *Milestones* (Delhi: Ishaat e-Islam Trust, 1991), 174.

22. Qutb, *Milestones*, 205–6.

23. Qutb, *Milestones*, 217.

24. Qutb, *Milestones*, 270.

25. Qutb, *Milestones*, 298.

26. Karen Armstrong, *Islam: A Short History* (London: Phoenix Press, 2000), 58.

27. Mojtaba Mahdavi, "The Rise of Khomeinism" in Arshin Adib-Mughaddam, ed., *A Critical Introduction to Khomeini* (Cambridge: Cambridge University Press, 2004), 55.

28. Behrooz Ghamari-Tabrizi, "The Divine, the People, and the *Faqih*," in Mughaddam, ed., *A Critical Introduction*, 235.

29. Ghamari-Tabrizi, "Divine," 236–37.

30. "This is the Promise of Allah," Declaration of the Islamic State, Al Hayat Media Center, n.d.

Chapter Thirteen

'Revolutions' in Political Theology

Protestantism and the International State System

Robert J. Joustra

INTRODUCTION

Protestant social thought, James Gustafson has said, is just a little short of chaos. In that, Protestantism has some affinity with the international system. The organizing and ordering concept, and the bridge-concept for our intent here, between these two chaotic worlds is supposedly that all-important condition of sovereignty, the preeminent political solution of order for the chaos of the modern age.

Sovereignty, of course, is a tricky business, and nobody knew this better than Jean Bethke Elshtain in her magisterial book on the topic, *Sovereignty, God, State, and Self.* Connecting these two things—Protestant theology and the international state system—still felt to her "transgressive a bold move."[1] Yet she was led to conclude that one cannot talk about sovereignty and escape theology,[2] that—just perhaps—"theological understandings had migrated into early modern political sovereigntism."[3]

Her own question that she traced for those Gifford Lectures is not altogether different than the one I propose in this chapter, namely: Do such *theological* understandings make possible and indeed underlie the modern, ostensibly secular, concept of sovereignty, and—therefore secondly—does this not throw the whole claim of secularity and "sovereignty" into disarray, if so? If we then speak of "revolutions in sovereignty"[4] as Daniel Philpott does convincingly, doesn't that imply revolutions also in theology, or rather what I argue should be called a "revolution in political theology"?

I believe significant insight can be gained by appealing to Charles Taylor's work in *A Secular Age*, as essential connective tissue between the religious ideas and practices of the Reformation, and the transformation of sovereignty/politics. Taylor, while characteristically dour on some of the social pathologies enabled by the Reformation,[5] nonetheless yields a picture of a very broad and deep transformation of the understandings and practices of the modern self and society. To show, as Elshtain and others have, that many of those "shifts" have not only theological origins but continue to have surprisingly essential political-theological foundations, is in part to rebut Brad S. Gregory's criticisms of Taylor.[6] Gregory argues Taylor provides one of many "supersessionist" accounts of the Reformation, which he qualifies as wholesale homogenous transformation of social and political life to be "secular." *Pace* Taylor, he says, the evidence for this simply does not exist, especially in light of the global resurgence of religion,[7] and rather than asking why religion went away, the more interesting question is why we ever thought it did.[8] But, of course, Taylor is often misread precisely because of this notoriously complex term "the Secular," whose meaning Daniel Philpott counts as having at least nine common usages.[9] By secular, as in *A Secular Age*, Taylor does not mean the erasure of the religious, but rather new conditions within which the religious and the secular are given meaning, indeed that they exist as discrete entities at all, and how that shapes social and political legitimacy. He calls that "the modern social imaginary," not an irreligious age, but rather it would be more correct to call it *the religious age*, precisely because religion as discretely and social separable prior to the coming of the modern moral order was largely intelligible. Taylor's picture of the modern social imaginary is therefore what yields the core of my argument, which has explicit parallels with Elshtain: that the Reformation "prepares the way for the political theology that underlies the emergence of the 'Protestant' nation-state,"[10] that it is a necessary but not sufficient cause of the international state system, and that finally, therefore, it is not enough to talk merely about revolutions in sovereignty, but revolutions in political theology in the modern period; the installation not of a neutral/rational/secular order, but of a rival theo-political picture of human life and politics.

So we can see that contemporary problems in religion and international relations are not immune from fundamental questions about one of the major *theological* sources of sovereignty, namely the Protestant Reformation. Put basically, the Reformation was a necessary, but not sufficient cause of a *revolution in political theology*: that is, without the Reformation, we render unintelligible the meanings and practices of the religious and the secular that we have in the modern state today, and thus the meaning of sovereignty and political legitimacy. It is my final argument that a better definition for political theology, the understandings and practices that political actors have about the meaning of and relationship between the religious and the secular, and what constitutes legitimate political authority, both clarifies the impact of the Protestant Reformation on the modern state system as more than "mere" political rupture, *and* clarifies why resistance to the sovereignty of the modern state often takes (rival) religious form.

THE PROTESTANT REFORMATION AND *A SECULAR AGE*

When talking about anything as varied and diverse as Protestantism it is important not to be fatalistic, or deterministic regarding its role in major world events. But it would be equally short sighted to ignore the impact that these major revolutions in practices and understandings of the religious, and of the meaning of and limits to religious and political authority, had on the development of sovereignty. And it is indeed generally accepted that religious reformation had some effect on the modern state system and its self-understandings. But what is less generally recognized is how these religious innovations *persisted* as the basis of the modern state system, enabling concepts like sovereignty, and the Westphalian order. What is a far more striking claim is that while the Reformation may have opened up a political-theological rupture in European society, the trajectory of the nation state is neither natural, neutral, nor necessarily even enduringly Protestant. Elshtain herself, quoting Hendrik Spruyt, writes, "History has covered its tracks well. We often take the present system of sovereign states for granted and believe that its development was inevitable. But it was not."[11] She argues, "the trail of sovereignty is by no means straight and smooth."[12]

This qualification relieves us from insisting, as some do, that Protestantism somehow equals secularization (however defined), while nonetheless acknowledging the religious debt that so-called secular trajectories owed the Reformation. Those who complain about the modern state and its powers of sovereignty as a "Protestant deformation"[13] or who even call privatized religion simply the "Protestant conception of religion"[14] do a major historical disservice to a complicated theological movement, and fail to account for the fact that many of today's most ferocious critics of the "secular age" are themselves Protestant voices.[15] In fact, international theorist Scott Thomas, while unapologetically sustaining that the Reformation made possible certain self-understandings in global politics and religion, is dramatically clear in his own account of that sovereign state system calling it an "apostasy of Christendom."[16] William T. Cavanaugh likewise agrees, calling the newly sovereign state a cultic, rival theo-political power, a corruption of Christian political-theology, rather than its consummation.[17]

None of which would stand out as necessarily wrong to Charles Taylor, for whom "the secular age" is more about how human beings came to think of themselves somewhat differently than they did, than passing moral or certainly theological judgment on that change. Sovereignty and secularity may have been unintended[18] rather than intentional, but that doesn't change the essential function those theological practices played in the flattening of social and political reality. Taylor writes,

> The coming of modern secularity . . . has been coterminous with the rise of a society in which for the first time in history a purely self-sufficient humanism came to be a widely available option. I mean by this a humanism accepting no final goals beyond human flourishing, nor any allegiance to anything else beyond this flourishing. Of no previous society was this true. [19]

This is one of Taylor's most striking claims: that the modern social imaginary provides a means by which to conceive of social and political activities that are distinct from questions of transcendent or cosmic purpose, questions more often considered in the modern sense the purview of theologians or philosophers. A secular age, he argues, is "one in which the eclipse of all goals beyond human flourishing becomes conceivable; or better, it falls with the range of an imaginable life for masses of people."[20] Taylor points to several key evolutions in practice and understanding on the back of the Reformation that begin to background the "political theology" of the international system.

THE BUFFERED VERSUS THE POROUS SELF

Taylor says that secularism is often thought of as a "subtraction" story:[21] that as more naturalistic explanations of the world became available, society became disenchanted, removing prior spiritualistic reasoning, and replacing it with secular rationality. The awakened consciousness of individuals worked, over time, to remove spiritualistic and superstitious rationale from society itself. First, the subtraction story goes, human beings uncovered scientific explanations, then they began looking for alternatives to God.

But Taylor argues that scientific inquiry did not automatically invalidate transcendent images of the cosmos. Scientific inquiry may have been a problem for an enchanted universe, one of magical and spiritual power latent in material reality, but it was not necessarily a problem for God. While rebelling against certain forms of enchantment was made possible, characteristically the Church in the form of the Reformation, this did not necessarily invalidate a divine, cosmic hierarchy.[22] None of these things themselves demand either social or individual atomisation or secularity. Therefore what Taylor considers crucial for this revolution was not only the disenchantment of scientific inquiry, but also a new sense of self. He writes that this "was a new sense of the self and its place in the cosmos: not open and porous and vulnerable to a world of spirits and powers, but what I want to call 'buffered.'"[23] This was more than disenchantment. This was a new confidence in the human power of moral ordering, a recognition of the self as an incarnated moral agent, as Elshtain might have it. [24]

Taylor contrasts this to the time prior to the Reformation and the Enlightenment, what he calls pre-modern, during which human persons were imagined as porous. The porous self of pre-modern era had existential options, but they were largely between placating different kinds of powers, not of standing apart from or against them. There did exist non-theistic cosmic orders, but this is not the same thing as the modern secular. Platonism or Stoicism, for instance, have little room for magic and spirits, but they were not disenchanted orders, nor were they exclusive humanisms. A grand cosmic hierarchy still ordered the universe, which had its own *internal* meanings. Even in the Platonic and Stoic world, the line between personal agency and impersonal force was blurry at best. The pre-modern world was filled with such forces, whether the Forms or demons, relics or Satan. A complex hierarchy of invisible forces competed to bring either good or ill. Some powers, like those of the gods and goddesses of Olympia, could even conjure human love, hate, or war. The cosmos itself conspired to compromise what is now called human agency and responsibility. It was an enchanted world, which showed "a perplexing absence of certain boundaries which seem to us essential." [25]

In the pre-modern world, meanings were not exclusively created by humans; they were uncovered. Meaning already existed latent in the cosmos, and resided in things themselves. Agency was not just the privilege of human persons, but of a whole range of things. These had the power to impose meaning on humans, which was independent of their observation. Humans were not only possibly but consistently penetrated by these objects. Evil spirits, for example, were more than simply malevolent powers that could affect externalities. They were more invasive. Spirits could sap the very will to live, penetrate humans as living, willing beings, transforming purpose and intent. This is the porous self. It is radically open to the meanings and enchantment of the cosmos around it. In the enchanted world, the most powerful location of meaning is external to the self. The very idea that there is some "clear boundary, allowing us to define an inner base area, grounded in which we can disengage from the rest, has no sense." [26]

By contrast, the buffered self is external to these realities. The inner self is invulnerable, a master of meaning. It is "essentially the self which is aware of the possibility of disengagement." [27] Disengaging from what is "outside" means that ultimate purpose is only that which arises from within the self. And so the meanings of things are only defined by our response to them. These purposes may well be manipulated in a variety of ways, but in principle these can be met with counter-manipulation and resistance. The emphasis then is on keeping a rational and measured interior life, one which can avoid or dissect and respond with the appropriate meaning to externalities of distress or temptation.[28]

A pre-modern, porous self-made disbelief remarkably hard. Disbelief in, for example, God did not mean a rational retreat to the buffered self to consider what other existential options might seem practical, but a radical autonomy in the face of powerful, invisible, and penetrating forces. This was a dangerous option for the porous self. It is not to say it was never done, it's simply to argue it was unlikely to happen on a mass scale. Further, it suggests why if one brave individual did break rank with collective devotions or rituals, the response was often violent and decisive. Blasphemy and desecration activated forces well beyond the control of a porous, hierarchically bound self. Disbelief threatened not simply the person and their salvation, but the entire community. The porous self demands, "venger à toute rigueur afin de faire cesser l'ire de Dieu"[29] (exact rigorous vengeance in order to stay the anger of God).

In general, the modern self relates to the world as "more disembodied beings than our ancestors. The person stands outside, in the agent of disengaged discipline, capable of dispassionate control."[30] There are dangers implicit in this buffering of the self—Elshtain points to its role in the promotion of self sovereignty—but the secular order demanded the surrender of the porous self to a more individualistic set of values.

THE GREAT DISEMBEDDING

The second key is what Taylor calls the impersonal order, a revolution in imagination from a porous "cosmos" to a buffered "universe." Once disembedded, social order is not an imposition or a form societies enact better or worse, but a "game we play together."[31] Its order is increasingly rational and, therefore, assumed stable. Gone are the ambiguities of complementarity in the pre-modern world, between king and peasant, monk and parishioner. The new order is coherent, horizontal, and a whole. "Disenchantment brought a new uniformity of purpose and principle."[32]

The impersonal order has a buffered self as prerequisite. A porous society insists on hierarchical mediations, but a society of discrete, rational individuals might, in a providential order, build a common life for mutual flourishing. And it is this emphasis on the individual which provides an important backdrop for what comes to be called religion.

Religion, or at least the early experience of what is retrospectively call religion, was an embedded activity. Taylor means "embedded" in several important social ways. First, in pre-modern times, religious life was inseparably linked to social life. This was not particular to religious life. It would also be difficult to dissect political obligations from social obligations; these modern differentiations can often be anachronistic in history. The ways of living religion were strikingly different from the modern world. Porous experiences had profound impacts on societies; portentous dreams, for example, or divine signs, possessions, or cures. All were common experiences embedded in everyday life that might be called religious.

Second, religion was social in that the primary agency of its activity—for example praying, sacrificing, healing, protecting, and more—was the social group as a whole, or some mediator standing vicariously for the group. In early religion, writes Taylor, "we primarily relate to God as a society."[33] Powerful invocations are not idiosyncratically communal, they are necessarily so. It is a practice not of one or another individual, or even of a collection of individuals, but of a cohesive whole calling on powers of protection, of life, and of sustenance.

Third, therefore, the social order itself was sacrosanct. Functionaries, shamans, priests, chiefs, and so on, were conscripted to perform important religious actions on behalf of the community. It was not that all pre-modern cultures were theocracies, in the modern understanding, it was that they existed in an embedded hierarchy with congruent beliefs about the cosmos.

Fourth, if all important action is the doing of whole groups, then there is less conception of self apart from that society. Not only order, but meaning slips away until what is left is either barbarism or divinity.[34] Taylor likens this kind of deep social embeddedness to how the modern imaginary might think of gender. What would it be like if you, as a man, were born a woman, or as a woman, a man? To even ask this question is getting "too deep into the very formative horizon of my identity to be able to make sense of the question."[35] Not only does it not often occur to us to ask, but we have very little to offer of ourselves apart from it.

So this embeddedness makes it unlikely for a person to imagine themselves outside a certain social context. And not only, of course, in a society, but in a whole cosmos of which the society is itself hierarchically situated. Taylor writes, "Human agents are embedded in society, society in the cosmos, and the cosmos incorporates the divine."[36] So to talk about "religion" in any kind of retrospective sense may border on anachronism, as deciphering what elements exactly constitute religious versus, say, political or economic motivations begin to prove very difficult. The religious does not have an obviously discrete meaning in the pre-modern world apart from its embedded form in everyday life.

What can be said about this pre-modern picture is that the buffered identity contributes to what is essentially a great disembedding. Embeddedness is both a matter of identity (the contextual imagination of the self) and of the social imaginary (the ways we are able to think of or imagine society).[37] But a buffered self with its emphasis on personal discipline, of distance and even hostility to collective forms, rejects much of this. Society comes to be understood as an impersonal order, a mutual project of consent and exchange constituted and authorized by individuals. This is a major revolution in the way persons come to understand not only their social lives, but also the contents and practices of their sacred lives. This disembeds human beings from the social sacred, and posits a new relation to God, as designer rather than immanent sustainer, of architect, rather than incarnate. This designation, of course, may become more or less dispensable, separating God further and further from the design and sustenance of a sacred order, until His task becomes little more than setting the pieces of the great clockwork of human civilization in order. In such an order, it is probably only a matter of time until some other force may simply take God's place striking the clock.

PROVIDENTIAL DEISM

So the idea grew that human relation to God was primarily by relating to the order of things, whose moral shape can be reasonably discerned if one is not misled by superstitious or ideological notions. Following God can be done by following the patterns of things he has laid out. A rational God is the architect of a rational world, endowing His creatures with the characteristics necessary to activate the latent laws designed into its fabric. And so Deism is a kind of "natural" religion, belief that spontaneously arises when the corruptions of the superstitious mind are removed. It is available, in principle, to every human, which makes it fundamentally equal.

God's own goals settle into a kind of anthropocentrism: a single end which encompasses mostly human flourishing and mutual benefit within His designed order.[38] This is not necessarily new to the Judeo-Christian tradition, but it was always thought that in addition to this divine providence God also had greater purposes for creation, presumably love and worship of him. Therein lies a demand which supersedes human flourishing. In the modern social imaginary this demand can remain, but only if it is experienced and acted upon privately. To act on such a higher command publicly or politically would be to risk instability, and the possible repression of human flourishing.

The eclipse of any greater good than human flourishing is what Taylor calls the anthropocentric shift.[39] The first shift is the idea that people owe God nothing further than the realization of His providential plan. That is, what is owed God is essentially the achievement of our own good. Transcendence is less central to faith, but rather self-realization and mutual aid.

Second, the buffered self and the disembedded order also eclipse grace. The *original* grace, God's endowment of human creatures with rational faculties, is sufficient to achieve human good. Humans self-order, self-actualize, and self-discipline. An active, sustaining grace is, however, unnecessary.

There is only the first grace: a God who makes and endows human beings with reason with which to carry out His final plan. And in case people prove unfaithful or ungrateful, God stands at the end of history to judge with joy or punishment comparative competence with those faculties.

Third, the sense of mystery fades with the disenchantment of the world. Taylor writes, "If God's purposes for us encompasses only our own good, and this can be read from the design of our nature, then no further mystery can hide there."[40] There is discovery, certainly, but the tools and means of that discovery are already internal to people. The disciplined human heart is not mysterious, it is competent. God's providence is also emptied of mystery. His particular providences, specifically, are all but absent. Miracles do not erupt in a stable, impersonal order. Such an activity by a rational God would, in fact, seem inherently irrational and irresponsible. Indeed, the very claim that "God speaks" is seriously suspect. The idea, argues Taylor, "is scarcely conceivable that the Author of such an order would stoop to such personalized communication as a short cut, if virtuous reason alone can suffice to tell us all we need to know."[41] Such a claim has indeed become a serious clash in contemporary philosophical and theological conversations.[42]

Fourth and finally, the idea began to erode that God was planning a transformation of human beings, which would take them beyond the limitations of their present condition. The narrowing of the Christian Gospel, one which barely invokes the saving action of Christ, had little time for devotion and prayer. It turned more on God as creator and designer, producing a tandem emphasis on the things of this world and their horizontal sacredness, than on a restorative afterlife. Such an afterlife would seem to produce human beings much the same as they are now, eliminating some of the more painful and awkward externalities. For if what is human is what is internal and rational, then humans do not so much transform as simply evolve. Religion in this picture is a private discipline, a moral code of conduct which cultivates an ordered, rational interior life. It self-actualizes more than it transfigures, introspects more than contemplates, it counsels rather than repents.

Taylor's argument is that from these shifts religion emerges as distinct from society and internal to the individual, and that this condition is surprisingly widely shared. Religion is part of the bulwark of social flourishing only insofar as it can, in a utilitarian sense, contribute to that final end. But if religion is private and instrumental, it becomes confusing what legacy premodern saints like Saint Francis might have. Taylor writes,

> If God's purpose for us really is simply that we flourish, and we flourish by judicious use of industry and instrumental reason, then what possible use could he have for a Saint Francis, who in a great élan of love calls on his followers to dedicate themselves to a life of poverty? At best, this must lower GNP, by

withdrawing these mendicants from the workforce; but worse, it can lower the
morale of the productive. Better to accept the limitations of our nature as self-
loving creatures, and make the best of it.[43]

This is the emergence of a new kind of social imaginary, a revolution in more
than merely "political" sovereignty, and one in which the religious and the
secular shift to serve new political and social orders, markedly different than
those in the *Respublica Christiana*. This, in fact, is precisely what Elshtain
labours to articulate, saying that transformations in political sovereignty can
be traced to transformations in the understandings of the newly sovereign
self.[44] Political transformations are enabled by prior and concomitant social
and theological transformations

REVOLUTIONS IN POLITICAL THEOLOGY

How, then, to name this shift that Taylor describes as enabled by, but not
coterminous with, the rise of Protestantism, with the attendant dangers implied by Elshtain? Taylor simply names it as a new social imaginary, but I
think this robs some of the explanatory power of naming the distinctly, and
surprisingly, *religious* ideas which persist. Following a renewed interest in
the field of international relations,[45] I want to extend Daniel Philpott's pre-9/
11 argument just one step further and argue this was not only a revolution in
sovereignty, a case in how religious ideas changed political ones, but actually
the installation of a new theo-political order, a revolution—in other words—
of political theology. I believe this will go some way to yielding explanatory
power on the meaning of and relationship between the religious and the
secular in the post-9/11 world.

I define political theology as *the understandings and practices that political actors have about the meaning of and relationship between the religious
and the secular, and what constitutes legitimate political authority.* This
definition is explained in four parts.

First, an argument has already been implied that it is both understandings
and practices, not only ideas, that are especially important in religious and
social reformations. In *God's Century*, Toft, Philpott, and Shah labour to
demonstrate that religious convictions are not merely manifestations of other
material forces, so they argue at some length for the autonomous nature of
religious beliefs and ideas. They write, "To claim that political theology
reflects the political activities that religious actors undertake is to claim that
religious belief is powerful, autonomous, and not simply the by-product of
nonreligious factors. Ideas shape politics."[46] This is important and true as far
as it goes, since, as they argue, one of the chief complaints of religious actors
engaging with mainstream international theory is the assumption that the
religious is either irrelevant, as in positivist realism, or a manifestation of

ideologically self-interested materialism, as in Marxism and some variations of liberalism. Either way religion is rarely taken on its own terms, as though the ideas and beliefs intrinsic to it are of actual, cosmic importance. *God's Century* wants to take those claims seriously, and so it emphasizes the autonomous ideational nature of religion. However, it need not be argued that the religious is a secondary or tertiary series of beliefs or communities in order to say that its practices are also fundamental to its beliefs. Politics also shape ideas, even religious ones. As shown in the well-recognized work of Saba Mahmood, it can be the case that while understandings do enable certain practices, it is also true that certain practices carry the understandings themselves. In her Aristotelian logic, repeated habits can make certain understandings in persons. This too is Taylor's argument when he says that the modern social imaginary cannot be only summarized as a series of beliefs, but is actually embedded in important social forms. Taylor says that "such understanding is both factual and normative; that is, we have a sense of how things usually go, but this is interwoven with an idea of how they ought to go, of what missteps would invalidate the practice."[47]

So it can be suggested that religion is its own factor, has its own meaning, independent of being derivative of material, or ideological forces, while at the same time saying that the religious is as much a practice, a way of life, as it is a set of beliefs or doctrines. The question, then, becomes not whether the religious should be considered as a serious factor in international politics, but what practices, and what understandings qualify as religious, why, and what effects these have on political legitimacy. Given Philpott's own work on the meaning of the religious, and that this argument parallels in many respects this work,[48] this amendment to the definition of political theology can probably be considered friendly.

Secondly, a major intervention in this definition is in talking about the political theology of political actors, not just religious actors. To say that, for example, political actors generally, not just religious ones, have certain political theological assumptions that merit, even require, study is a significant claim. It is a claim that *God's Century* does not necessarily agree with, but it is a necessary one if we are to usefully explain the shift in the meaning of the religious and the secular following the Reformation. That shift affects more than religious people, it affects the whole constitution, and indeed the shape of legitimacy, of political orders. What is essential to recognize is that these shifts in the definition of the religious and the secular, defined oppositionally, one as the inverse of the other, is not only a political decision, it is also a theological one. The prohibition against religious actors promoting religious ideas with political consequences not only creates a specific kind of meaning for the secular, but also creates a special kind of religion. It changes persons and communities' religious experience and powers, and it does so in a highly specific way.

This is not the preamble for theocracy. Indeed scholars may be satisfied enough, as many are, with the boundaries that exist between the religious and the secular in the modern social imaginary, but by ordering these boundaries in this way, specific things are said about both the religious and the secular and what constitutes political legitimacy. The very assumption that a theocracy is totally illegitimate in the modern international relations deserves explanation, an explanation that cannot be given without appealing to the modern meanings of the religious and the secular, and why those meanings are preferable. Not only theocracy, but even rival versions of the religious and the secular in modern democracy are hard to adjudicate without deliberately engaging the understandings and practices that political actors, not just religious ones, have about their meanings. Therefore for political theology to serve as an approach that is in fact capable of disclosing these often untested assumptions about political authority it must include the understandings and practices that also non-religious actors carry about the meanings of the religious and the secular.

Third, this definition differs by asking after the meanings of the concepts themselves, not only the effects that one of them, the religious, has on political legitimacy. This is an extension, not a disagreement with what Toft, Philpott, and Shah are arguing. It is true that religious actors have ideas that help constitute what is and is not politically legitimate, but it is also true that who qualifies as a religious actor, and what qualifies as a religious idea, have shifted over time. Carl Schmitt, for his part, argues at great length that the modern state is made possible by a variety of once theological ideas. [49] Early Christian Realists, like Martin Wight, Herbert Butterfield, Reinhold Niebuhr, and others argued in a similarly plain fashion, debating the nature of the state and of the person theologically, not just in secular terms. Taylor's summative social forms of the modern social imaginary are all understandings and practices that depend on revolutions in not only secular thought, but also in theological thought. These forms depend on a specific separation of the religious and the secular, on the optionality of religion, and the horizontal neutrality of the secular. The meaning of the religious and the secular is therefore not incidental to, but fundamental for the concept of political legitimacy.

Finally, the legitimacy of political authority depends not only on the meaning of the religious and the secular, but also on the interrelationship of secular and religious authority. This is consistent with Toft, Philpott, and Shah's definition, but by adding in the meanings of the religious and the secular, what can be studied is not only how legitimacy is shaped by the religious and secular actors, but also how the meanings of the concepts themselves shape legitimacy. What is at stake, therefore, is not simply how these concepts are defined, but also how the secular and the religious are imagined to be able to interrelate on that basis. Is, for example, public religion a productive democratic force, or not? Can it serve as a "force multiplier" for social goods, as Toft, Philpott, and Shah argue, or is any public intervention by religious actors necessarily divisive and potentially disastrous? These are major questions which depend not only on empirical evidence for resolution, but also on justifying why those categories should be arranged as they are, and how that will prefigure our answers.

Talking about revolutions in political theology, and using this definition of political theology specifically, enables us to make better sense of the theo-political choices that followed from the Reformation, to intelligibly contest the Protestant legacy in sovereign state system, and recognize the trajectories and influences that these theological practices and understandings have had. We see, in short, how basic doctrines like Sola Fide or Sola Scriptura may contribute to a flattening of social and political reality, how disembedded persons could reimagine themselves and their political communities, and how shifts in the meaning of the religious and the secular are necessary, if not necessarily sufficient, causes.

CONCLUSION—POLITICAL THEOLOGY APPLIED

If we accept the foregoing argument, there are several troubling conclusions, fore among them: Is it the case that the Westphalian construction of the nation-state itself sustains what Schmitt calls formerly theological concepts, and is therefore not only a rival political order, but also a rival religious one? If political theology, so defined, means political actors—not just religious ones—practice often contestable assumptions about the religious and the secular, could this partly explain why "the global resurgence of religion" is most powerfully manifest in areas with weak states, and strong religion? Is this, in fact, as Thomas says, a "clash of rival apostasies"?

At least two authors have begun to explore this question in detail, and have found their way into conversation with international theorists, Elshtain included: William T. Cavanaugh, a political theologian, and Paul Kahn, a legal-philosopher. Cavanaugh's recent books, *The Myth of Religious Violence* and *Migrations of the Holy*, and one earlier book, *Theopolitical Imagination*, all touch on this question.[50] In that work he has engaged with international theorists, including Scott Thomas. Paul Kahn was recently featured on the Canadian CBC *Ideas* series, "The Myth of the Secular" in which he discussed his controversial book, *Political Theology: Four New Chapters on the Concept of Sovereignty*.[51] His engagements with Schmitt, and his work on American and international law, yield parallel insights to Cavanaugh's own.

William Cavanaugh's arguments expand on the idea that the boundary between the secular and the religious has shifted in modernity, to argue that this shift was not just a renegotiation, but a fundamentally new sacred, political order. He likens the establishment of the nation-state and its Wars of Religion to a hostile takeover, saying that the evolution of the state has been a slow, often violent, migration of the holy. In *Theopolitical Imagination*, he writes,

> We are often fooled by the seeming solidity of the materials of politics, its armies and offices, into forgetting that these materials are marshaled by acts of the imagination. How does a provincial farm boy become persuaded that he must travel as a solider to another part of the world and kill people he knows nothing about? He must be convinced of the reality of borders, and imagine himself deeply, mystically, united to a wider national community that stops abruptly at those borders.[52]

Cavanaugh's point is one with which scholars of nationalism, following Benedict Anderson, are familiar. But he is arguing something more fundamental than simply that the nation-state has a hold on human imagination and what it values. He is saying that nation-states have a hold on a sacred imagination, one so powerful that persons and communities will willingly sacrifice, kill, and die for it. This is political theorist David T. Koyzis's argument in *Political Visions and Illusions* where he identifies nationalism as one of the ideologies of modernity, which he describes as "incurably religious."[53] Koyzis makes a long argument that the nation-state, and especially its totalitarian manifestations, is profoundly inscribed with a religious narrative about genesis, deification, evil, and salvation

So when Cavanaugh writes that the "transfer of power from the church to the state appears not so much as a solution to the wars in question, but as a *cause* of those wars," he is not only talking about a powerful polity, he is talking about a sacred politics, one whose powers of sacralization have been borrowed, and enlisted from an earlier Christian era. "The so-called wars of religion appear as wars fought by state-building elites for the purpose of consolidating their power over the church and other rivals."[54] It was this transfer of power from the church to the state that was actually the root cause of the wars.

The problem, argues Cavanaugh, is not that these definitions "condemn certain kinds of violence, but that it diverts moral scrutiny from other kinds of violence. Violence labelled religious is always reprehensible; violence labelled secular is often necessary and sometimes praiseworthy."[55] He concludes,

> Among those who identify themselves as Christians in the United States, there are very few who would be willing to kill in the name of the Christian God, whereas the willingness under certain circumstances, to kill and die for the nation in war is generally taken for granted. The religious-secular distinction

thus helps to maintain the public and lethal loyalty of Christians to the nation-state, while avoiding direct confrontation with Christian beliefs about the supremacy of the Christian God over all other gods.[56]

Eric Hobsbawm argues that ours is an unliturgical age in most respects, with the striking exception of the public life of the citizen in the nation-state.[57] Citizenship is tied to the kinds of rituals and symbols that are comprehensible in every way to the history of human society, with the one difference that ours claims to be neutral, secular, and rational. Cavanaugh argues that it should be no surprise that the transition into a secular state by nonmodern societies around the globe is anything but painless. The growth of secular Westphalian state-hood across the planet is, in his argument, a political-theological conversion project on a scale as never before witnessed.

Yet, Cavanaugh is also singularly pessimistic about this new arrangement, essentially arguing that the sacred forms embedded in the nation-state have now become bankrupt. His theological criticisms come into focus in his later works, especially *Migrations of the Holy*, where he argues not only that the nation-state has installed these sacred, liturgical elements in its background, but that these elements are essentially destructive idolatries to which Christian people owe no allegiance. The nation-state, he says, has so stripped the earlier moral and theological content of the secularized Christian social forms it now inhabits, that being asked to kill and die for it is a bit like being asked to kill for the telephone company.[58] This coincides with the arguments of those like Oliver O'Donovan, that cut loose from its deep moral reasoning the state is nothing but abstract formalism, "a house swept and garnished waiting for seven worse devils."[59] Cavanaugh's arguments may sound radical, but they have already received a serious reception by several noted scholars in international relations. Scott Thomas served as a reader and conversation partner for Cavanaugh's *Myth of Religious Violence*,[60] Mariano Barbato, Chiara de Franco, and Brigitte le Normand cite Cavanaugh's argument at length as a foil in critiquing R. Scott Abbleby's argument in *The Ambivalence of the Sacred*, and Cavanaugh himself served as appreciative critic of *God's Century*, in a series of published responses in *Politics, Religion and Ideology*.[61] His strong political-theological criticisms provide an intelligible context within which charges of an "apostasy" of western order can be understood, and if only for that reason his work continues to receive modest attention in international relations.

Paul Kahn is also not an international theorist, but in his reading of Schmitt's original *Political Theology* he attempts, as a legal and political scholar, to make sense of how contemporary secular theory sees secular moral order. He is particularly keen to understand acts of political violence as an expression of liberal political theory, not as the exception, but as an integral part of a sacred, sacrificial order of the state. He writes, "This is not hidden but celebrated in our ordinary political rhetoric: to serve and die for the nation is commonly referred to as the ultimate sacrifice."[62] The sovereign, he writes, "is no more imaginable from without than is a god to those outside of the faith."[63]

Kahn's project, like Cavanaugh's, takes for granted some of the basic arguments in this book, namely "that the break between the secular and the theological is not what we might have thought,"[64] but he goes further to say that "there is continuity, not discontinuity, between the theological and the political."[65] He clarifies,

> The claim here is not that such a break [between the theological and the secular] should not have occurred and that politics must be put back on a religious foundation. . . . Political theology does not just challenge a particular configuration of legal institutions, as if the question were one of scaling down the wall of separation between church and state. It challenges the basic assumptions of our understandings of the meaning of modernity, the nature of individual identity, and the character of the relationship of the individual to the state. . . . Political theology must be . . . not the subordination of the political to religious doctrine and church authority, but recognition that the state creates and maintains its own sacred space and history.[66]

In this, Kahn is consistent with Cavanaugh: freeing the state from the church did not banish the sacred from the political, it merely reconfigured it. Seen against this backdrop it might indeed be said that Europe's religious wars were religious, and that the sacred order of the secular state won; not the secular versus the religious, but two (or many) religious orders pitted in violent confrontation. The Wars of Religion were not a contest resolved by peaceable secularity, but a conquest of a new political theology masquerading as neutrality. Writes Kahn, "It is an accident of history that the struggle of the state to free itself of the church was framed not as a conflict of faiths but as a conflict over the place of faith in the organization of political power."[67]

This counter-narrative of political theology is as unsettling as it is uncommon, but it has the major advantage of providing a theoretical account of sacred experiences in the nation-state and taking seriously religious resistors to its forms. He writes,

> Political theology argues that secularization, as the displacement of the sacred from the world of experience, never won, even though the church may have lost. The politics of the modern nation-state indeed rejected the church but simultaneously offered a new site of sacred experience.[68]

There are domestic as well as international aspects to this. Kahn writes that political theology must "not only help us to understand ourselves but also to understand how and why our political imagination makes our [America's] relationship to the rest of the world so exceptional."[69] It is a poor theory, he argues, "that fails to express a community's experience of the sacred, even if it is good at explaining why theological speculation takes the form that it does."[70] This is his indictment of dominantly liberal theory when it comes to explaining the state.

None of which necessarily means we need to accept the fatalism of critics like Cavanaugh, though applying the lens of political theology to global affairs, as defined here, does render a picture of previously incomplete rivalries. What, for example, is religiously at stake in the manifestation of liberal democratic institutions? Several things, as it turns out, including the meaning of the religious and the secular, and the self-understandings of persons and societies that fund those things. This may go some way to help explain why strong religions and weak states still make up so much of the world, as communities struggle to make—or not to make—these revolutions in political theology.

This, then, is the critical application of political theology: political theology informs us not only that certain contestable theo-political forms persist in the international order, but also that resistance to those forms may often take a religious character, most especially in areas where "religious" and "secular" meanings are not as typically (modernly) defined.

Policy makers should then admit to the contestability, historicity, and even political theology, implied in doing foreign affairs and advocating the values and forms funded by those things. They then have the choice, not unlike other human choices about our deepest values and beliefs: to openly sustain those choices as, perhaps not perfect, but proximately better, and engage actors, religious and otherwise, on that basis of disclosure; or to ignore those basic choices, pretend to their neutrality, and foreclose dialogue and engagement with actors on those levels. Political theology certainly does not demand retreat or relativism in foreign affairs, but it does demand disclosure, sustained answers for *why* we think imagining political, religious, and social communities the way that we do is better than it was, and better than it is, in many regions of the world. That, certainly, does not lack for controversy, but it does make for authenticity, one which names our revolutions and our reformations truthfully, and encourages others toward the same.

NOTES

1. *Parts of this chapter were published in Robert Joustra, "Always reforming: Protestantism and international security" in *The Routledge Handbook of Religion and Security* (London and New York: Routledge, 2013). It was originally presented at the International Studies Association in Toronto (Canada), and I would like to thank Jodok Troy especially for his comments. Jean Bethke Elshtain, *Sovereignty* (New York: Basic Books, 2008), xii.

2. Ibid., xiii.

3. Ibid., xiv.

4. Daniel Philpott, *Revolutions in Sovereignty: How Ideas Shaped Modern International Relations* (Princeton, NJ: Princeton University Press, 2001). See also Philpott, "The Religious Roots of Modern International Relations" in *World Politics* 52, no. 2 (2000): 206–45 and Philpott, "The Challenge of September 11 to Secularism in International Relations" in *World Politics* 55 (October 2002): 66–95.

5. See, for example Taylor, *The Malaise of Modernity.*

6. Brad S. Gregory, *The Unintended Reformation: How a Religious Revolution Secularized Society* (Harvard: Belknap University Press, 2012).

7. See, for example, Scott Thomas, *The Global Resurgence of Religion and the Transformation of International Relations* (New York: Palgrave Macmillan, 2005).

8. Gregory, 13.

9. Daniel Philpott, "Has the Study of Global Politics Found Religion?" *Annual Review of Political Science* 12 (2009): 183–202.

10. Elshtain, 79.

11. Elshtain, 92.

12. Ibid., 92–93.

13. James Kurth, "Religion and Globalization" in Dennis Hoover and Douglas Johnston, *Religion and Foreign Affairs* (Waco, TX: Baylor University Press, 2012).

14. See, for example, Saba Mahmood, "Religious Freedom, the Minority Question, and Geopolitics in the Middle East" in *Contemporary Studies in Society and History* (2012 52:2), 418–46 and Mahmood, *The Politics of Piety: The Islamic Revival and the Feminist Subject* (Princeton, NJ: Princeton University Press, 2004).

15. Here consider major American protestant theologians and cultural critics like Stanley Hauerwas, William T. Cavanaugh, or John Milbank. For more on this debate see Brad S. Gregory, *The Unintended Reformation: How a Religious Revolution Secularized Society* (Cambridge: Belknap Press, 2012).

16. Scott Thomas, "Reading Religion Rightly: The Clash of 'Rival Apostasies' amidst the global resurgence of religion" in Jonathan Chaplin and Robert Joustra (eds), *God and Global Order* (Baylor University Press, 2010), 187.

17. See for example William T. Cavanaugh, *Migrations of the Holy* (Grand Rapids, MI: Eerdmans, 2011).

18. See for example Brad S. Gregory, *The Unintended Reformation: How A Religious Revolution Secularized Society* (Harvard: Belknap Press of Harvard University Press, 2012).

19. Charles Taylor, *A Secular Age*, 18.

20. Taylor, *A Secular Age*, 19–20.

21. Taylor, *A Secular Age*, 26–27.

22. Jim Payton, *Getting the Reformation Wrong: Correcting some Misunderstandings* (Downers Grove, IL: InterVarsity Press, 2010). Payton argues in fact that the Reformation was understood by its leaders—including Luther and Calvin—to be an internal correction of abusive and heretical teachings of the Church and the Papacy, not a revolution, and certainly not a political or secularizing effort.

23. Taylor, *A Secular Age*, 27.

24. Elshtain, *Sovereignty*, 231–38.

25. Taylor, *A Secular Age*, 33.

26. Charles Taylor, *A Secular Age*, 38.

27. Charles Taylor, *A Secular Age*, 42.

28. Charles Taylor, *A Secular Age*, 37–38.

29. As quoted in Charles Taylor, *A Secular Age*, 43.

30. Charles Taylor, *A Secular Age*, 141.

31. Charles Taylor, *A Secular Age*, 142.

32. Charles Taylor, *A Secular Age*, 146.

33. Charles Taylor, *A Secular Age*, 148.

34. Recall Aristotle's famous phrasing in the *Politics* that "outside the polis man is either beast or god."

35. Charles Taylor, *A Secular Age*, 149.

36. Charles Taylor, *A Secular Age*, 152.

37. Charles Taylor, *A Secular Age*, 156.

38. Charles Taylor, *A Secular Age*, 221.

39. See "Providential Deism" in *A Secular Age*, 221–69.

40. Charles Taylor, *A Secular Age*, 223.

41. Charles Taylor, *A Secular Age*, 292.

42. For further reflection on this, Nicholas Wolterstorff writes at length on this problem in *Divine Discourse: Philosophical Reflections on the Claim that God Speaks* (Cambridge: Cambridge University Press, 1995).

43. Charles Taylor, *A Secular Age*, 230.

44. See especially the final chapters of Elshtain on *Sovereignty*, "The Creation of the Sovereign Self," "Self-Sovereignty: Moralism, Nihilism, and Existential Isolation," and "The Sovereign Self: Dreams of Radical Transcendence."

45. Much of the interaction that follows is with Philpott, Shah, and Toft's book *God's Century* in which they explicitly enlist political theology as an organizing category. They define political theology as "the set of ideas that a religious actor holds about what is legitimate political authority" (*God's Century*, 27).

46. Toft, Philpott, and Shah, 29.

47. Charles Taylor, *Modern Social Imaginaries*, 24.

48. See especially Daniel Philpott, "The Challenge of September 11 to Secularism in International Relations," *World Politics* 55 (October 2002), 66–95.

49. Carl Schmitt, *Political Theology: Four Chapters on the Concept of Sovereignty*. Translated by George Schwab. Foreword by Tracey B. Strong (Chicago: University of Chicago Press, 2006), 36.

50. William T. Cavanaugh, *Theopolitical Imagination* (London: T&T Clark, 2002)—*The Myth of Religious Violence* (Oxford: Oxford University Press, 2009)—*Migrations of the Holy: God, State, and the Political Meaning of the Church* (Grand Rapids, MI: Eerdmans, 2011).

51. Paul W. Khan, *Political Theology: Four New Chapters on the Concept of Sovereignty* (New York: Columbia University Press, 2011).

52. William Cavanaugh, *Theopolitical Imagination* (T&T Clark, London and New York, 2002), 1.

53. David T. Koyzis, *Political Visions and Illusions*, 27.

54. Cavanaugh, *The Myth of Religious Violence*, 162.

55. Ibid., 121.

56. Ibid., 122.

57. Eric Hobsbawm, "Introduction: Inventing Traditions," in *The Invention of Tradition*, ed. Eric Hobsbawm and Terence Ranger (Cambridge: Cambridge University Press, 1983), 12.

58. William T. Cavanaugh, "Killing for the Telephone Company: Why the Nation-State is Not the Keeper of the Common Good," in *Migrations of the Holy*, 7–45.

59. O'Donovan, "Response to Jonathan Chaplin," in *A Royal Priesthood*, 313.

60. See Cavanaugh, "Acknowledgements," *The Myth of Religious Violence*.

61. William T. Cavanaugh, "God's Century: Resurgent Religion and Global Politics," *Politics, Religion and Ideology*, 13:3, 398–99.

62. Paul Kahn, 7.

63. Ibid., 12.

64. Ibid., 17.

65. Ibid., 18.

66. Ibid., 18.

67. Ibid., 23.

68. Ibid., 26.

69. Ibid., 10.

70. Ibid., 119.

Bibliography

Ackerknecht, Erwin H., *A Short History of Medicine*, Baltimore: The Johns Hopkins University Press, 1982.

Adams, Charles C., *Islam and Modernism in Egypt*, New York: Russell and Russell, 1968 [1933].

Adib-Mughaddam, Arshin, ed., *A Critical Introduction to Khomeini*, Cambridge: Cambridge University Press, 2004.

Anderson, Benedict, *Imagined Communities: Reflections on the Origin and Spread of Nationalism*, London: Verso, 1983.

Arendt, Hannah, *The Human Condition*, Chicago: The University of Chicago Press, 1958.

———, *The Origins of Totalitarianism*, 2nd expanded edition, New York: Meridian Books, 1958.

Armstrong, Karen, *Islam: A Short History*, London: Phoenix Press, 2000.

Atkins, E. M., and R. J. Dodaro, eds, *Augustine: Political Writings*, Cambridge: Cambridge University Press, 2001.

Augustine, *Anti-Pelagian Writings: Nicene Fathers of the Christian Church, Part 5,* edited by Philip Schaff. trans. by Peter Holmes and Robert Wallis, Whitefish, MT: Kessinger, 2004.

———, *The City of God.* trans. by Henry Bettenson, London; New York: Penguin Books, 2003.

———, *Confessions*, edited by Michael P. Foley, trans. by F. J. Sheed, Indianapolis: Hackett Publishing, 2006.

———. *The Confessions of S. Augustine.* translated by E.B. Pusey, Oxford: John Henry Parker, 1840.

———, "Letter 138 (to Marcellinus)," In *Political Writings*, edited by E. Margaret Atkins and Robert Dodaro, Cambridge: Cambridge University Press, 2001.

Badie, Bertrand, *The Imported State: The Westernization of the Political Order*, Stanford: Stanford University Press, 2000.

Barbato, Mariano, Chiara de Franco and Brigitte Le Normand, "Is There a Specific Ambivalence of the Sacred? Illustrations from the Apparition of Medjugorje and the Movement of Sant'Egidio," *Politics, Religon & Ideology*, 13, no. 1 (2012), 53–73.

Bartelson, Jens, *A Genealogy of Sovereignty*, Cambridge: Cambridge University Press, 1993.

Bartholomew, Craig, Jonathan Chaplin, Robert Song, and Al Wolters, *A Royal Priesthood? The Use of the Bible Ethically and Politically: A Dialogue with Oliver O'Donovan.* Scripture and Hermeneutics Series, V. 3. Grand Rapids, MI: Zondervan, 2002.

Bethge, Eberhard, *Dietrich Bonhoeffer. Eine Biography*, München: Gütersloher Verlagshaus, 2004.

Biggar, Nigel, *In Defence of War,* Oxford: Oxford Univ. Press, 2013.

————, "Natural Flourishing as the Normative Ground of Just War: A Christian View," in *Just War: Authority, Tradition, and Practice*, edited by Anthony F. Lang Jr., Cian O'Driscoll, and John Williams, Washington, DC: Georgetown University Press, 2013.

Bonhoeffer, Dietrich, *Conspiracy and Imprisonment: 1940–1945*, trans. Lisa A. Dahill and Douglas W. Stott, edited by Victoria J. Barnett, Jr. Wayne Whitson Floyd and Barbara Wojhoski Dietrich Bonhoeffer Works, vol. 16, Minneapolis: Fortress Press, 2006.

————, *Ethics*. New York: Touchstone, 1995.

————, *Ethics: Dietrich Bonhoeffer Works, Volume 6*, trans. Reinhard Krauss, Charles C. West, and Douglas W. Scott, ed. Clifford J. Green, Minneapolis: Fortress Press, 2005.

————, *Ethik*. Dietrich Bonhoeffer Werke, vol. 6. Gütersloh: Gütersloher Verlag, 2010.

————, *Konspiration Und Haft 1940-1945*, Dietrich Bonhoeffer Werke, vol. 16, Jørgen Glenthøj, Ulrich Kabitz and Wolf Krötke, eds., Gütersloh: Chr. Kaiser Verlag, 1996.

————, *Nachfolge*. Dietrich Bonhoeffer Werke, vol. 4, München: Chr. Kaiser, 2002.

————, *Witness to Jesus Christ: Making of Modern Theology*, Ed. by John de Gruchy. Minneapolis: Augsburg Fortress, 1991.

Bonhoeffer, Dietrich, and Eberhard Bethge, *Widerstand Und Ergebung; Briefe Und Aufzeichnungen Aus Der Haft*, Dietrich Bonhoeffer Werke, vol. 8, Gütersloh: Gütersloher Verlagshaus Mohn, 1983.

Boyte, Harry C., Review of *Democracy on Trial*, in *Journal of Politics*, 58, no. 1 (February 1996), 262–64.

Bridges, Thomas, *The Culture of Citizenship: Inventing Postmodern Civic Culture*, New York: State University of New York Press, 1994.

Butler, Judith, *Frames of War: When is Life Grievable?* London: Verso, 2010.

————, *Giving an Account of Oneself*, New York: Fordham University Press, 2005.

Butler, Judith, and Athena Athanasiou. *Dispossession: The Performative in the Political*, Cambridge, UK: Polity Press, 2013.

Butler, Judith, and Gayatri Chakravorty Spivak, *Who Sings the Nation-State?* New York: Seagull Books, 2007.

Camus, Albert, *The First Man*, New York: Alfred A. Knopf, 1995.

————, *The Myth of Sisyphus and Other Essays*, New York: Vintage Books, 1955.

————, *The Plague*, New York: Vintage, 1991.

————, *The Rebel*, New York: Vintage Books, 1958.

Cavanaugh, William, *Theopolitical Imagination*, Continuum International Publishing, 2002.

————, "Killing for the Telephone Company: Why the Nation-State is Not the Keeper of the Common Good," *Modern Theology* 20, no. 2 (2004): 243–74.

————, *Being Consumed: Economics and Christian Desire*, Grand Rapids: Eerdmans, 2008.

————, *The Myth of Religious Violence*, Oxford: Oxford University Press, 2009.

————, *Migrations of the Holy: God, State, and the Political Meaning of the Church*, Grand Rapids, MI: Eerdmans, 2011.

Chalmers, A. Douglas, et al., *The New Politics of Inequality in Latin America: Rethinking Participation and Representation*, Oxford: Oxford University Press, 1997.

Chaplin, Jonathan with Robert Joustra, eds., *God and Global Order: The Power of Religion in American Foreign Policy*, Baylor University Press, 2010.

Charles, J. Daryl, "War, Women, and Political Wisdom," *Journal of Religious Ethics* 34, no. 2 (June 2006): 341–69.

Collingwood, R. G., *Essays in the Philosophy of History*, Austin, TX: University of Texas Press, 1965.

Commons, John Rogers, *Institutional Economics. Vol. I: Its Place in Political Economy*, New Brunswick, NJ: Transaction Publishers, 2009.

Coward, Harold, and Gordon S. Smith, eds., *Religion and Peacebuilding*, Albany: State University of New York Press, 2004.

Daly, Markate, ed., *Communitarianism: A New Public Ethics*, Belmont, CA: Wadsworth Inc., 1994, 335–44.

Deneen, Patrick J., "The Great Combination" in Michael Jon Kessler, ed., *Political Theology for a Plural Age*, Oxford: Oxford University Press, 2013, 43–61.

De Roux, Rodolfo, "Las Etapas de la Laicización en Colombia," in Jean-Pierre Bastian, ed., *La Modernidad Religiosa: Europa y América Latina en Perspectiva Comparada*. México, D.F.: Fondo de Cultura Económica, 2004, 61–73.

Dillon, Michael, "Security, philosophy and politics," M. Featherstone, S. Lash, and R. Robertson, eds., *Global Modernities*. London, UK: Sage, 1995.

Donohue, John J., and John L. Esposito, eds., *Islam in Transition*, second edition, Oxford: Oxford University Press, 2007.

Dreyfus, Hubert L. and Paul Rabinow, *Michel Foucault: Beyond Structuralism and Hermeneutics*. second edition, Chicago: University of Chicago Press, 1983.

Dyck, John H. A., Paul S. Rowe and Jens Zimmerman, eds. *Politics and the Religious Imagination*, Abingdon, Oxon: Routledge, 2010.

Ehrenberg, John, *Civil Society: The Critical History of an Idea*, New York: New York University Press, 1999.

Elshtain, Jean Bethke. "Against Liberal Monism." *Daedalus* 132, no. 3 (2003): 78–79.

———, "Antigone's Daughters," *Democracy* 2, no.2 (April 1982), 39–45.

———, *Augustine and the Limits of Politics*, Notre Dame, Ind.: University of Notre Dame Press, 1998.

———, "Between Heaven and Hell: Politics Before the End-Time," *Process Politics* 40, no. 2 (2011), 215–26.

———, "Bonhoeffer on Modernity: 'Sic et Non,'" *Journal of Religious Ethics*, vol. 29, no. 3 (Fall, 2001), 345–66.

———, "In Common Together," in John Witte, Jr., ed., *Christianity and Democracy in Global Context*, Boulder, CO: Westview Press, 1993.

———, *Democracy on Trial*, Toronto: Anansi, 1993.

———, "Democracy on Trial Revisited," Milton K. Wong Lecture, June 13, 2013. http://www.miltonkwonglecture.ca/lecture/2 (accessed 6 March 2015).

———, "Democratic Authority at Century's End," *The Hedgehog Review* (Spring 2000), 24–39.

———, "Elegy and Eulogy," *Common Knowledge* 14, no. 2 (2008), 291-95.

———, "The Ethics of Fleeing: What America Still Owes Iraq," *World Affairs* Spring 2008, 91–98.

———, "How Does—or Should?—Theology Influence Politics?" *Political Theology* 5, no. 3 (2004), 265–74.

———, "Intellectuals and Their America," *Dissent* 57, no. 2 (2010), 44–45.

———, "International Justice as Equal Regard and the Use of Force," unpublished manuscript, circa 2003.

———, "Is There Such a Thing as the Female Conscience?" *Virginia Quarterly* 88, no. 4 (2012), 16–25.

———, *Jane Addams and the Dream of American Democracy*, New York: Basic Books, 2002.

———, *Just War against Terror*, New York: Basic Books, 2003.

———, "Just War and an Ethics of Responsibility," In *Ethics Beyond War's End*, ed. by Eric Patterson, Washington, DC: Georgetown University Press, 2012.

———, "Just War and Humanitarian Intervention," *Ideas* from the National Humanities Center, 8, no. 2 (2001), 1–21.

———, "Just War, Humanitarian Intervention and Equal Regard," in Alan Johnson, ed., *Global Politics After 9/11: The Democratiya Interviews*. London: Foreign Policy Centre, 2008, 26-60.

———,"The Just War Tradition and Natural Law," *Fordham International Law Journal* 28, no. 3 (2004), 742.

———, "Just War Tradition and the New War on Terrorism: A discussion of the origins and precepts of just war principles and their application to a war on terrorism," panel discussion between Jean Bethke Elshtain, Stanley Hauerwas, and James Turner Johnson. Sponsored by the Pew Forum on Religion and Public Life. Available http://www.pewforum.org/2001/10/05/just-war-tradition-and-the-new-war-on-terrorism/ (accessed 6 March 2015).

———, "Luther's Lamb: When and How to Fight a Just War," *Common Knowledge* 8, no. 2 (2002): 304–9.

————, *Meditations on Modern Political Thought: Masculine/Feminine Themes from Luther to Arendt*, University Park: Penn State University Press, 1986.

————,"The New Morality," *The Wilson Quarterly* 25, no. 3 (Summer 2001): 112–13.

————, "On Loyalty: the 2012 Erasmus Lecture," *First Things* Aug/Sept, 2013, 27–31.

————, "A Performer of Political Thought," in Ian Shapiro and Judith Wagner DeCew, eds., *Theory and Practice: Nomos XXXVII*, New York: New York University Press, 1995, 464–82.

————, "A Personal Memoir," *Commonweal*, November 7, 1975, 526–28.

————, "Persons, Politics, and a Catholic Understanding of Human Rights," in Douglas Farrow, ed., *Recognizing Religion in a Secular Society: Essays in Pluralism, Religion and Public Policy*, McGill-Queen's University Press, 2004, 69–82.

————, *Public Man, Private Woman: Women in Social and Political Thought*, second edition. Princeton, NJ: Princeton University Press, 1981.

————, *Real Politics: At the Centre of Everyday Life*, Baltimore: The John Hopkins University Press, 1997.

————, "Reflections on War and Political Discourse: Realism, Just War, and Feminism in a Nuclear Age," in Jean Bethke Elshtain, ed., *Just War Theory*, New York: New York University, 1992, 260–79.

————," "Reinhold Niebuhr and Richard John Neuhaus on Religion and Democracy in the United States," *Political Theology* 14, no. 3 (2013), 375–385.

————, "The Risks and Responsibilities of Affirming Ordinary Life," in James Tully, ed., *Philosophy I an Age of Pluralism: The philosophy of Charles Taylor in Question*, Cambridge: Cambridge University Press, 1994, 67–80.

————, "Should the U.S. stay Militarily involved in Afghanistan?" *Christianity Today*, September 8, 2010, 72.

————, *Sovereignty: God, State, and Self*, New York: Basic Books, 2008.

————, "Terrorism, Regime Change, and Just War: Reflections on Michael Walzer," *Journal of Military Ethics* 6, no. 1 (2007), 131–137.

————, "Three Meditations on Human Flourishing," unpublished manuscript, circa 2002.

————, "Toleration, Proselytizing, and the Politics of Recognition," in Thomas Banchoff, ed., *Religious Pluralism, Globalization, and World Politics*, New York: Oxford University Press, 2008, 89–104.

————, "When Faith Meets Politics," In *Faith, Freedom, and the Future: Religion in American Political Culture*, edited by Charles W. Dunn, 67–76. Lanham, MD: Rowman & Littlefield, 2003.

————, *Who Are We? Critical Reflections and Hopeful Possibilities*, Grand Rapids, MI: Wm. B. Eerdmans, 2000.

————, "The Theory of Civil Religion," *Chronicle of Higher Education* 53, no. 15 (2006), 12–13.

————,"The Third Annual Grotius Lecture: Just War and Humanitarian Intervention," *American University International Law Review* 17, no. 1 (2001).

————, "Thinking About Women, Christianity, and Rights," in *Religion and Human Rights in Global Context: Religious Perspectives*, The Hague: Martinus Nijhoff Publishers, 1996.

————, "What's Morality Got to Do with It? Making the Right Distinctions," *Social Philosophy and Policy* 21, no. 1 (Winter 2004), 1–13.

————, "While Europe Slept," *First Things*, no. 191 (March 2009).

————, "Why Public Intellectuals?" *Wilson Quarterly* 38, no. 1 (Winter 2014), 76–88.

————, *Women and War*, New York: Basic Books, 1987.

————, "The World as We Know it," *Political Theology* 12, no. 5 (2011), 691–695.

Fazio Fernández, Mariano,"Interpretaciones de la Evangelización: del Providencialismo a la Utopía." in *Actas, Historia de la Evangelización de América, Simposio Internacional*. Ciudad del Vaticano, 11–14 de mayo de 1992, Ciudad del Vaticano: Librería Editrice Vaticana, 609-621.

Feldman, Noah, *The Fall and Rise of the Islamic State*, Princeton, NJ: Princeton University Press, 2008.

Fergusson, David, *Church, State and Civil Society*, Cambridge: Cambridge University Press, 2004.

Fischer, David Hackett, *The Great Wave: Price Revolutions and the Rhythm of History*, Oxford: Oxford University Press, 1996.

Flescher, Andrew Michael, *Moral Evil*, Washington, DC: Georgetown University Press, 2013.

Forteza, Bartomeu, "La Influencia de Francisco Suárez sobre Thomas Hobbes," *Convivum* 2, no. 11 (1998), 40–79.

Foucault, Michel, "The Juridical Apparatus," in William Connolly, ed., *Legitimacy and the State*, Oxford: Blackwell, 1984, 201–22.

———, *"Society Must be Defended": Lectures at the Collège De France 1975–1976*, New York: Picador, 1997.

———, *Security, Territory, Population: Lectures at the Collège De France 1977–1988*, New York: Palgrave Macmillan, 2007.

Giddens, Anthony, *The Consequences of Modernity*, Stanford: Stanford University Press, 1990.

Goodale, Mark and Nancy Postero, *Neoliberalism Interrupted: Social Change and Contested Governance in Contemporary Latin America*, Stanford: Stanford University Press, 2013.

Grafton, Anthony, Glenn W. Most, and Salvatore Settis, eds. *The Classical Tradition*, Harvard University Press, 2010.

Grant, Edward, *God and Reason in the Middle Ages*, Cambridge: Cambridge University Press, 2001.

Grant, George, *Philosophy in the Mass Age*, ed. William Christian, Toronto: University of Toronto Press, 1995.

Green, M. Christian, "From Third Wave to Third Generation: Feminism, Faith, and Human Rights," in *Feminism, Law, and Religion*, Marie A. Failinger, Elisabeth R. Schiltz, and Susan Stabile, eds., Farnham, Surrey, England: Ashgate Publishing, 2013.

Gregory, Brad S., *The Unintended Reformation: How a Religious Revolution Secularized Society*, Harvard: Belknap Press, 2012.

Habermas, Jürgen, "What does the Legitimation Crisis Mean Today? Legitimation Problems in Advanced Capitalism," in William Connolly, ed., *Legitimacy and the State*. Oxford: Basil Blackwell, 1984, 134–55.

Habermas, Jürgen, *Zwischen Naturalismus und Religion*, Philosophische Aufsätze, Frankfurt am Main: Suhrkamp, 2005.

Haj, Samira, *Reconfiguring Islamic Tradition*, Stanford: Stanford University Press, 2009.

Hanke, Lewis, *Latin America: A Historical Reader*, Boston: Little Brown and Company, 1974.

Harkness, Georgia, *Christian Ethics,* New York and Nashville, TN: Abingdon, 1957.

———, *The Modern Rival of Christian Faith: An Analysis of Secularism*, New York and Nashville, TN: Abingdon-Cokesbury Press, 1952.

———, *Understanding the Christian Faith*, New York and Nashville, TN: Abingdon Press, 1947.

Hartman, Mary S., *The Household and the Making of History: A Subversive View of the Western Past*, Cambridge: Cambridge University Press, 2004.

Hauerwas, Stanley, Paul J. Griffiths, and Jean Bethke Elshtain, "War, Peace, and Jean Bethke Elshtain," *First Things* 136, October 2003, 41–47.

Harris, Sam, *The End of Faith*, New York: W. W. Norton, 2004.

Havel, Václav, "Forgetting We Are Not God." *First Things*, no. 51 (March 1995), 47–50.

Heft, James L., ed., *A Catholic Modernity?* Oxford: Oxford University Press, 1999.

Heller, Thomas C., Morton Sosna, and David E. Wellbery, eds., *Reconstructing Individualism: Autonomy, Individuality, and the Self in Western Thought*, Stanford: Stanford University Press, 1986.

Henkin, Louis, "Human Rights: Ideology and Aspiration, Reality and Prospect" in Samantha Power and Graham Allison, eds., *Realizing Human Rights: Moving From Inspiration to Impact*, New York and Basingstoke: Palgrave Macmillan, 2006, 3–38.

Herman, Arthur, *The Cave and the Light: Plato Versus Aristotle, and the Struggle for the Soul of Western Civilization*, New York: Random House, 2014.

Hitchens, Christopher, *God is not Great*, New York: Twelve, 2007.

Hobbes, Thomas, *Leviathan*. C. B. MacPherson, ed. Harmondsworth: Middlesex: Penguin Books, 1968 [1651].

Hobbes, Thomas. *Leviathan: With Selected Variants from the Latin Edition of 1668*. Indianapolis: Hackett Publishing, 1994.

Hoover, Dennis and Douglas M. Johnston, eds., *Religion and Foreign Affairs: Essential Readings*, Waco, TX: Baylor University Press, 2011.

Hurd, Elizabeth Shakman, *The Politics of Secularism in International Relations*, Princeton, NJ: Princeton University Press, 2008.

Hurd, Elizabeth Shakman and Winnifred Fallers Sullivan, "Symposium: Re-Thinking Religious Freedom, Editors' Introduction," *Journal of Law and Religion* 29, no. 3 (October 2014), 358–62.

Huxley, Julian, "The Coming New Religion of Humanism," *The Humanist* 22 (January–February 1962).

John Paul II, "Centesimus Annus," in *The Encyclicals of John Paul II*, ed. by C.S.C. and J. Michael Miller, 511–62. Huntington, IN: Our Sunday Visitor, 2001.

———, Encyclical Redemptor Hominis, London: Catholic Truth Society, 1978.

———, Encyclical Letter: The Gospel of Life, Evangelium Vita, trans. by the Vatican. Boston, MA: Pauline Books & Media, 1995.

———, On Human Work: Encyclical Laborem Exercens. Washington, DC: United States Catholic Conference, 1982.

———, "Veritatis Splendor." In The Encyclicals of John Paul II, ed. by C.S.C. and J. Michael Miller, 583–662. Huntington, IN: Our Sunday Visitor, 2001.

Johnson, Alan, "Just War, Humanitarian Intervention and Equal Regard: An Interview with Jean Bethke Elshtain." *Democratiya*, no. 1 (Summer 2005). Available at http://www.dissentmagazine.org/democratiya_article/just-war-humanitarian-intervention-and-equal-regard-an-interview-with-jean-bethke-elshtain.

Kahn, Paul, *Political Theology: Four New Chapters on the Concept of Sovereignty*, New York: Columbia University Press, 2012.

Kant, Immanuel, "Idea for a Universal History with Cosmopolitan Interest." In: Alan W. Wood, ed., *Basic Writings of Kant*. New York: The Modern Library, 2001.

Kass, Leon, "The Wisdom of Repugnance" *The New Republic* 216, no. 22 (June 1997), 17–26.

Kaveny, Cathleen, *Law's Virtues: Fostering Autonomy and Solidarity in American Society*, Washington, DC: Georgetown University Press, 2012.

Kolb, David, *The Critique of Pure Modernity: Hegel, Heidegger, and After*, Chicago: University of Chicago Press, 1986.

Koselleck, Reinhart, *Critique and Crisis: Enlightenment and Pathogenesis of Modern Society*, Oxford, UK: Berg, 1988.

Koyzis, David T., *Political Visions and Illusions: A Survey and Christian Critique of Contemporary Ideologies*, Downers Grove, IL: InterVarsity, 2003.

Kraudy Medina, Pablo, *Historia Social de las Ideas en Nicaragua: El Pensamiento de la Conquista*, Managua: Fondo Editorial Banco Central de Nicaragua, 2001.

Kurth, James, "The Protestant Deformation and American Foreign Policy," *Orbis* 42 (Spring 1998), 221–38.

Lakoff, George and Mark Johnson, *Metaphors we Live By*, Chicago: The University of Chicago Press, 2003.

Levi, Primo, *Survival in Auschwitz*, New York: Touchstone, 1996.

Lewis, C. S., "The Necessity of Chivalry." In *Present Concerns*, ed. by Walter Hooper. San Diego: Harcourt, 2002.

———, *All My Road Before Me: The Diary of C. S. Lewis, 1922–1927*. San Diego: Fount / Collins, 1991.

———, *Spenser's Images of Life*, Cambridge: Cambridge University Press, 1967.

Lilla, Mark, *The Stillborn God: Religion, Politics, and the Modern West*, New York: Alfred A. Knopf, 2007.

Lloyd, Genevieve, *Providence Lost*, Cambridge Massachusetts: Harvard University Press, 2008.

Locke, John, "A Letter Concerning Toleration," In *Two Treatises of Government and A Letter Concerning Toleration*, edited by Ian Shapiro, 211–54. Binghamton, NY: Yale University, 2003.

Luhmann, Niklas, *The Differentiation of Society*, New York: Columbia University Press, 1982.

Maclure, Jocelyn and Charles Taylor, *Secularism and Freedom of Conscience*, trans. Jane Marie Todd, Cambridge, MA: Harvard University Press, 2011.

MacPherson, C. B., *The Political Theory of Possessive Individualism: From Hobbes to Locke*, Oxford: Oxford University Press, 1972.

Mahmood, Saba, *Politics of Piety: The Islamic Revival and the Feminist Subject*, Princeton: Princeton University Press, 2005.

Markus, R. A., *Saeculum: History and Society in the Theology of St. Augustine*, Cambridge: Cambridge University Press, 1988.

Marshall, T. S., *Citizenship and Social Class*, Cambridge, UK.: Cambridge University Press, 1965.

Martinich, A. P., *The Two Gods of Leviathan: Thomas Hobbes on Religion and Politics*, Cambridge: Cambridge University Press, 2002.

Marx, Karl, *The Eighteenth Brumaire of Louis Bonaparte* (1852), Available at: https://www.marxists.org/archive/marx/works/1852/18th-brumaire/ch01.htm (accessed 9 August, 2014).

May, Collin, Review of *Sovereignty: God, State, and Self*, in *Society* 46, no. 4 (2009), 383–86.

McFayden, Alistair, *Bound to Sin: Abuse, Holocaust and the Christian Doctrine of Sin*, Cambridge, UK: Cambridge University Press, 2000.

Mendieta, Eduardo and Jonathan VanAntwerpen, eds., *The Power of Religion in the Public Sphere*, New York: Columbia University Press, 2011.

Merleau-Ponty, Maurice, *The Primacy of Perception: And Other Essays on Phenomenological Psychology, the Philosophy of Art, History and Politics*, Evanston, IL: Northwestern University Press, 1964.

Miles, Rebekah, ed. *Georgia Harkness: The Remaking of a Liberal Theologian*, Louisville, KY: Westminster/John Knox Press, 2010.

Muller, Jerry Z., *The Mind and the Market: Capitalism in Western Thought*, New York: Anchor Books, 2003.

Murray, John Courtney, "The Governmental Repression of Heresy." Catholic Theological Society of America (1948): 26–98.

———, "Leo XII and Pius XII: Government and the Order of Religion," In *Religious Liberty: Catholic Struggles with Pluralism*, edited by J. Leon Hooper, 49–125. Louisville, KY: Westminster/John Knox, 1955.

———, *We Hold These Truths: Catholic Reflections on the American Proposition*, New York: Sheed & Ward, 1960.

Nation, Mark Thiessen, Anthony G. Siegrist, and Daniel P. Umbel, *Bonhoeffer the Assassin?* Grand Rapids: Baker Academic, 2013.

Niebuhr, Reinhold, *The Children of Light and Children of Darkness*, New York: Charles Scribner's Sons, 1944.

———, *Moral Man and Immoral Society*, New York: Charles Scribner's Sons, 1932.

———, *The Nature and Destiny of Man*, volumes 1–2, New York: Charles Scribner's Sons, 1941, 1943.

O'Donovan, Oliver, *The Desire of the Nations: Rediscovering the Roots of Political Theology*, Cambridge: Cambridge University Press, 1996.

O'Donovan Oliver and Joan Lockwood O'Donovan, *A Sourcebook in Christian Political Thought*, Grand Rapids, MI/Cambridge U.K.: William B. Eerdmans Publishing Company, 1999.

Olson, Roger E., *The Mosaic of Christian Belief: Twenty Centuries of Unity and Diversity*, Downers Grove, IL: InterVarsity Press/ Leicester: England: Apollos, 2002.

Pateman, Carole, *The Problem of Political Obligation: A Critical Analysis of Liberal Theory*, London: Polity, 1985.

———, *The Sexual Contract*, Stanford: Stanford University Press., 1988.

Payton, James, *Getting the Reformation Wrong: Correcting Some Misunderstandings*, Downers Grove, IL: InterVarsity Press, 2010.

Paz, Octavio, *Sor Juana Inés de la Cruz o las Trampas de la Fe*, México: Fondo de Cultura Económica, 1982.
————, *El Laberinto de la Soledad/Postdata Vuelta a El Laberinto de la Soledad*, México: Fondo de Cultura Económica, 1998.
Pérez-Baltodano, Andrés, "La Transnacionalización del Estado y la Reconstrucción de Identidades Políticas en América Latina," In Sergio Rodríguez G. in ed., *La Posibilidad de Seguir Soñando: Las Ciencias Sociales de Iberoamérica en el Umbral del Siglo XXI*, Guijón, Spain, 2000, 159–78.
————, "Dios y el Estado: Dimensiones culturales del proceso de formación del Estado en América Latina," *Nueva Sociedad*, Buenos Aires, no. 210, Julio-Agosto, 2007.
————, *Entre el Estado Conquistador y el Estado Nación: Providencialismo, Pensamiento Político y Estructuras de Poder en el Desarrollo Histórico de Nicaragua* , Managua, Nicaragua: Instituto de Historia de Nicaragua y Centroamérica (IHNCA) de la Universidad Centroamericana y Fundación Friedrich Ebert, 2003, 2008.
Pew Global Attitude Project, "Among Wealthy Nations . . . US Stands Alone in its Embrace of Religion," (2002), Available from: http://pewglobal.org/ (accessed 10 August, 2014).
Philpott, Daniel, *Just and Unjust Peace: An Ethic of Political Reconciliation*. Oxford: Oxford University Press, 2012.
————, "The Challenge of September 11 to Secularism in International Relations," *World Politics* 55 (October 2002), 66–95.
————, "Explaining the Political Ambivalence of Religion," *American Political Science Review* 101, no. 3 (2007), 505–25.
————, "Has the Study of Global Politics Found Religion?" *Annual Review of Political Science* 12 (2009), 183–202.
————, "One Professor's Guide to Studying International Relations and Peace Studies from a Catholic Perspective," *University of Notre Dame Magazine*, Summer 2009. http://magazine.nd.edu/news/11933.
————, ed., *The Politics of Past Evil: Religion, Reconciliation and the Dilemmas of Transitional Justice*, Notre Dame, IN: University of Notre Dame Press, 2006.
————, "The Religious Roots of Modern International Relations," *World Politics* 52, no. 2 (2000), 206–45.
————, *Revolutions in Sovereignty: How Ideas Shaped Modern International Relations*, Princeton, NJ: Princeton University Press, 2001.
————, "Westphalia and Sovereignty in International Society," *Political Studies* 47, no. 3 (1999), 566–89.
Pinckaers, Servais O. P., *Morality: The Catholic View*, trans. by Michael Sherwin, South Bend, IN: St. Augustines Press, 2003.
Poe, Rebecca Whitten, *C. S. Lewis Remembered: Collected Reflections of Students, Friends and Colleagues*, Grand Rapids, MI: Zondervan, 2006.
Polanyi, Karl, *The Great Transformation: The Political and Economic Origins of Our Time*, New York: Beacon Press, 1957.
Power, Samantha. *A Problem from Hell*. New York: Harper Collins, 2002.
Qutb, Sayyid, *Milestones*, Delhi: Ishaat e-Islam Trust, 1991.
Rabb, Theodore K, *The Struggle for Stability in Early Modern Europe*, New York: Oxford University Press, 1975.
Rahner, Hugo, *Church and State in Early Christianity,* trans. L. D. Davis, San Francisco: Ignatius Press, 1992.
Rejwan, Nissim, *Arabs Face the Modern World: religious, cultural, and political responses to the West*, Gainesville, FL: University Press of Florida, 1998.
Robinson, Marilynne, *Gilead*, New York: Picador, 2004.
Rohr, Christian, "Man and Nature in the Middle Ages," *Environment and History* 9, no. 2 (2003), 127–49.
Rosenblum, Nancy Lipton, "Review of *Public Man, Private Woman*", in *Journal of Politics* 45, no. 1 (February 1983), 243–44.
Rousseau, Jean-Jacques, *On the Social Contract*, Edited by Paul Negri and Drew Silver. trans. by G. D. H. Cole, Mineota, NY: Dover Publishing, 2003.

Rowlands, Mark, *The New Science of the Mind: From Extended Mind to Embodied Phenome-nology*, Cambridge, MA: Massachusetts Institute of Technology, 2010.

Roy, Oliver, *Holy Ignorance: When Religion and Culture Part Ways*, trans. by Ros Schwartz, New York: Columbia University Press, 2010.

Rubenstein, Richard E., *Aristotle's Children: How Christians, Muslims, and Jews Rediscov-ered Ancient Wisdom and Illuminated the Middle Ages*, New York: Harcourt, 2003.

Ryan, Alan, *On Politics, Book One*, New York: Liveright Publishing Corporation, 2012.

Saldivia, Zenobio and Felipe Caro, "Francisco Suárez y el Impacto de su Teoría sobre la Potestad Divina y Monárquica en América," *Estudios Latinoamericanos*, no. 6, Año 3 (2011), 41–55.

Sartre, Jean-Paul, *No Exit and Three Other Plays*, New York: Vintage, 1989.

Schakel, Peter J., *Imagination and the Arts in C. S. Lewis: Journeying to Narnia and Other Worlds*, University of Missouri Press, 2002.

Schmitt, Carl. *Political Theology: Four Chapters on the Concept of Sovereignty*, translated by George Schwab, Chicago: University of Chicago Press, 2006.

———, *Political Theology II: The Myth of the Closure of any Political Theology*, translated by Michael Hoelzl, Cambridge: Polity Press, 2008.

Serrano, Mónica and Paul Kenny, "Colombia and the Andean Crisis," in Simon Chesterman, Michael Ignatieff and Ramesh Thakur (eds.) *Making States Work: State Failure and the Crisis of Governance*. New York: United Nations University Press, 2005.

Schmitt, Carl, *Political Theology: Four Chapters on the Concept of Sovereignty*, trans. George Schwab. Chicago: University of Chicago Press, 1985 [1922].

Shattuck, Roger. *Forbidden Knowledge*. Orlando, FL: Harcourt Brace, 1997.

Smilde, David A., "Letting God Govern: Supernatural Agency in the Venezuelan Pentecostal Approach to Social Change," *Sociology of Religion*, 59, no. 3 (1998) 287–303.

Smith, Adam, *An Inquiry Into the Nature and Causes of the Wealth of Nations*, New York: The Modern Library, 1937.

Sullivan, Winnifred Fallers, *The Impossibility of Religious Freedom*, Princeton, NJ: Princeton University Press, 2005.

Sullivan, Winnifred Fallers, Robert Yelle, and Matteo Taussig-Rubio, eds., *After Secular Law*, Stanford, CA: Stanford University Press, 2011.

Taylor, Charles M., "Charles Taylor Replies," in James Tully, ed., *Philosophy in an Age of Pluralism: The Philosophy of Charles Taylor in Question*, Cambridge: Cambridge Univer-sity Press, 1994, 213–257.

———, *Dilemmas and Connections: Selected Essays*. Cambridge: Harvard University Press, 2011.

———, *The Explanation of Behaviour*, London: Routledge & Kegan Paul, 1964.

———, *Hegel and Modern Society*, Cambridge: Cambridge University Press, 1979.

———, "Hegel's *Sittlichkeit* and the Crisis of Representative Institutions," in Yirmiahu Yovel, ed., *Philosophy of History and Action*, Dordrecht: Reidel Publishing Company, 1978, 133–54.

———, "The Hermeneutics of Conflict" in James Tully, ed., *Meaning and Context: Quentin Skinner and his Critics*, Princeton, NJ: Princeton University Press, 1988, 218-28.

———, *Human Agency and Language: Philosophical Papers I*, Cambridge: Cambridge Uni-versity Press, 1985.

———, "The Immanent Counter-Enlightenment," in Ronald Beiner and Wayne Norman eds. *Canadian Political Philosophy: Contemporary Reflections*. Oxford: Oxford University Press, 2001, 386-400.

———, "The Immanent Counter-Enlightenment: Christianity and Morality," trans. Ian Jen-nings, *South African Journal of Philosophy* 24, no. 3 (2005), 224–39.

———, "Interview with Professor Charles Taylor," Marcos Ancelovici and Francis Dupuis-Déri *Citizenship Studies* 2, no. 2, 247–55.

———, *The Malaise of Modernity*, Toronto: Anansi, 1991.

———, *Modern Social Imaginaries*, Durham and London: Duke University Press, 2004.

———, "The Moral Topography of the Self" in Stanley B. Messer, Louis A. Sass, Robert L. Woolfolk, eds., *Hermeneutics and Psychological Theory: Interpretive perspectives on Per-*

sonality, Psychotherapy, and Psychopathology, New Brunswick: Rutgers University Press, 1988, 298–320.

————, *Multiculturalism: Examining the Politics of Recognition*, Amy Gutmann, ed., Princeton, NJ: Princeton University Press, 1994.

————, *Philosophical Arguments*. Cambridge, Harvard University Press, 1995.

————, "Philosophy and its History" in Richard Rorty, J. B. Schneewind, and Quentin Skinner eds., *Philosophy in History*, Cambridge: Cambridge University Press, 1984, 17–30.

————, *Philosophy and the Human Sciences: Philosophical Papers 2*, Cambridge: Cambridge University Press, 1985.

————, "Political Theory and Practice," in Christopher Lloyd, ed., *Social Theory and Practice*, Oxford: Clarendon Press, 1983, 61–85.

————, *Reconciling the Solitudes: Essays on Canadian Federalism and Nationalism*, Guy Laforest, ed., Montreal: McGill-Queen's University Press, 1993.

————, "Religious Mobilizations," *Public Culture* 18, no. 2 (2006), 281–300.

————, *A Secular Age*, Cambridge, MA: Harvard University Press, 2007.

————, *Sources of the Self: The Making of the Modern Identity*, Harvard: Belknap University Press, 1992.

————, "The 'Twice-Born,'" *Crosscurrents* Fall 2003, 339–52.

————, "Two Theories of Modernity," *Hastings Center Report* 25, no. 2 (1995), 24–33.

————, *Varieties of Religion Today*, Cambridge, MA: Harvard University Press, 2002.

————, "Why Democracy Needs Patriotism," *Boston Review* 19, no. 5 (Oct/Nov 1994), 72.

Thomas, Scott M., "Faith, History, and Martin Wight: The Role of Religion in the Historical Sociology of the English School of International Relations," *International Affairs* 77, no. 4 (2001), 905–29.

————, *The Global Resurgence of Religion and the Transformation of International Relations: The Struggle for the Soul of the Twenty-First Century*, New York: Palgrave Macmillan, 2005.

————, "Isaiah's Vision of Human Security: Virtue-Ethics and International Politics," *The Review of Faith and International Affairs* 4, no. 3, Winter 2006.

————, "A Globalized God," *Foreign Affairs*, November/December 2010, 93–101.

Toft, Monica Duffy, Daniel Philpott, and Timothy Shah, *God's Century: Resurgent Religion and Global Politics*, New York: W.W. Norton & Company, 2011.

Ullmann, Walter, *The Individual and Society in the Middle Ages*, Baltimore: Johns Hopkins University Press, 1966.

Van Drunen, David, *Natural Law and the Two Kingdoms: A Study in the Development of Reformed Social Thought*, *Emory University Studies in Law and Religion*, Grand Rapids, MI: Eerdmans, 2010.

Van Nieuwenhove, Rik, "Catholic Theology in the Thirteenth Century and the Origins of Secularism," *Irish Theology Quarterly*, 75, no. 4 (2010), 339–54.

Weigel, George. "A Better Concept of Freedom" *First Things*, no. 121 (March 2002), 14–21.

West, Cornell, "Prophetic Religion and the Future of Capitalist Civilization," in Judith Butler, Jurgen Habermas, Charles Taylor, and Cornel West, eds., *The Power of Religion and the Public Sphere*, New York: Columbia University Press, 2011, 92–100.

Wexler, Bruce E., *Brain and Culture: Neurobiology, Ideology, and Social Change*, Cambridge, MA: MIT Press, 2006.

Weyland, Kurt, "Neoliberalism and Democracy in Latin America: A Mixed Record." *Latin American Politics and Society*, 46, no. 1 (2004), 135–57.

Wilkens, Steve, *Faith and Reason: Three Views*, Downers Grove, IL, InterVarsity Press, 2014.

Williams, Christine L., "Review of *Women and War* and *Gender and the Two World Wars*," in *Gender and Society* 3, no. 1 (March 1989), 127–31.

Witte, John Jr., and M. Christian Green, *Religion and Human Rights: An Introduction* , New York: Oxford University Press, 2012.

Wolfe, Alan, "Why Me? The case against the sovereign self," *Slate* 9 June 2008.

Wolin, Sheldon, *Politics and Vision: Continuity and Innovation in Western Political Thought*, expanded edition, Princeton, NJ: Princeton University Press, 2009.

Zea, Leopoldo "Identity: A Latin American Philosophical Problem," *The Philosophical Forum*, no. 20 (1989), 33–42.

NEWS AND ONLINE SOURCES

Al Ahram Weekly
The Immanent Frame
The New York Times

Index

About the Contributors

John H. A. Dyck is assistant professor of political studies at Trinity Western University and senior research fellow in the Religion, Culture, and Conflict Research Group.

Jean Bethke Elshtain was Laura Spelman Rockefeller Professor of Social and Political Ethics at the University of Chicago. She passed away in 2013.

M. Christian Green is senior fellow at the Center for the Study of Religion at Emory University and book review editor and general co-editor of the *Journal of Law and Religion.*

Robert Joustra is assistant professor of international studies at Redeemer University College.

Marc Livecche is a PhD candidate at the University of Chicago Divinity School.

Andrés Pérez-Baltodano is professor of political science at Western University.

Paul S. Rowe is associate professor of political and international studies at Trinity Western University and senior research fellow in the Religion, Culture, and Conflict Research Group.

Jens Zimmermann is Canada Research Chair in Interpretation, Religion, and Culture and professor of English and philosophy at Trinity Western

University as well as senior research fellow in the Religion, Culture, and Conflict Research Group.